Moon Books Duets

Rhiannon
&
Blodeuwedd

This edition is a bind up of two books:

Pagan Portals – Rhiannon
First published by Moon Books 2018
Text copyright: Jhenah Telyndru 2017
ISBN: 978 1 78535 468 7 (Paperback)
ISBN: 978 1 78535 469 4 (e-book)

Pagan Portals – Blodeuwedd
First published by Moon Books, 2021
Text copyright: Jhenah Telyndru 2020
ISBN: 978 1 78535 212 6 (Paperback)
ISBN: 978 1 78535 922 4 (e-book)
Cover image copyright: Dan Goodfellow

Moon Books Duets

Rhiannon
&
Blodeuwedd

Jhenah Telyndru

**MOON
BOOKS**

London, UK
Washington, DC, USA

CollectiveInk

First published by Moon Books, 2025
Moon Books is an imprint of Collective Ink Ltd.,
Unit 11, Shepperton House, 89 Shepperton Road, London, N1 3DF
office@collectiveinkbooks.com
www.collectiveinkbooks.com
www.moon-books.net

For distributor details and how to order please visit the 'Ordering' section on our website.

Text copyright: Jhenah Telyndru 2024

ISBN: 978 1 80341 755 4
978 1 80341 983 1 (ebook)
Library of Congress Control Number: 2024948947

A CIP catalogue record for this book is available from the British Library.

Design: Lapiz Digital Services

UK: Printed and bound by CPI Group (UK) Ltd, Croydon, CR0 4YY

We operate a distinctive and ethical publishing philosophy in all areas of our business, from our global network of authors to production and worldwide distribution.

INTRODUCTION

I am deeply honored to introduce this special edition collection, which brings together my explorations into the mythic legacies of the Welsh Goddesses Rhiannon and Blodeuwedd. These remarkable figures have not only shaped the landscape of Welsh culture and tradition but have also profoundly influenced my own journey into sovereignty and personal transformation.

Modern Pagans and polytheists who feel called to honor the deities of Wales are faced with a very particular challenge. Although never a monolithic culture with a centralized government, one thing all ancient Celtic peoples seem to have in common is that they did not write down their myths, beliefs, or religious practices – preferring instead to entrust the sacred elements of their culture to a professional class of druids and bards who memorized them and transmitted them orally from generation to generation.

Because of this, other than what can be deduced from the archaeological record, our information about the divinities of the Celts is limited to secondary sources – particularly, what ancient Greek and Roman writers observed about the various Celtic tribes with whom they were in contact – and to the vernacular tales (stories told in the culture's native tongue) that started to be written down in in Wales and elsewhere in the Celtic world during the early Medieval period. While it may seem strange to look to medieval literature for information about Pagan deities, scholars believe that these early tales contain characters and story elements that originated in the pre-Christian period and were preserved in oral tradition.

The power of oral tradition is that it is living tradition – and living tradition allows stories to evolve and change over time, mirroring shifts in culture so that the tales are able to maintain their relevance. What is no longer relevant is no longer passed on. Considering that a span of almost 800 years passed between the complete Christianization of Britain and the period when the great treasures of early Welsh story tradition were set into writing, it is possible that the most ancient story elements in these tales had been transmitted in orality for at least eight centuries.

It is this organic process of evolution that makes early Welsh literature, like the Four Branches of *Y Mabinogi* and *Llyfr Taliesin* (*The Book of Taliesin*) so important to those who are interested in the Gods of Celtic Britain. There is evidence, for example, that the Four Branches were transcribed directly from orality in the 12th or 13th century, and so it makes sense that these tales reflect the contemporary medieval Christian culture of Wales. This explains why no extant sources directly identify any of the figures in these stories as Gods – but this does not mean that we are completely without evidence for their former divinity.

In 2015, almost three decades after first entering into devotional relationships with several divinities in the Welsh pantheon – including Rhiannon and Blodeuwedd – I completed my Master's degree in Celtic Studies from the University of Wales, Trinity St. David. Over the course of my formal studies, I learned how to read medieval Welsh literature from within its cultural context, discovered how to engage in academically sound cross-cultural comparisons, and came to recognize how the field of linguistics and the practice of literary and folkloric analysis can extract critical information embedded in tale. Taken together, this work and the new way of thinking it fostered within me, has greatly expanded my understanding and deepened my relationship with my Gods.

I approached the writing of *Rhiannon* and *Blodeuwedd* with three main goals: to gather in one place all of the extant source materials related to each Goddess; to undertake a deconstruction of these sources using a variety of analytical tools in order to broaden our understanding of these figures and their stories; and to offer lore-based devotional suggestions for present-day spiritual seekers wishing to establish relationships with these Goddesses. Although I am a long-time devotee of these divinities and a practitioner who follows a specific spiritual path, my over-all intention was to present these Goddesses and their lore in a way that would be relevant to all paths and practices. Further, it was my hope that the process of what I call "mythic archaeology" employed in these works would provide an example to readers on how they might engage in this sort of analysis for themselves.

Rhiannon: Divine Queen of the Celtic Britons is an exploration of one of the better known Welsh divinities. Connected to a complex lineage of deities found in other Celtic lands, Rhiannon is arguably the most fully realized example of the Sovereignty Goddess motif found in Welsh Tradition. She presents us with lessons concerning the power of our word, teaches us how to remain true to ourselves in the face of loss and injustice, and offers us comfort in times of tribulation.

Blodeuwedd: Welsh Goddess of Season Sovereignty is a deep dive into the mythos of a figure who is fairly unknown outside of her native Wales. A woman made of flowers to be the bride of a prince, she falls in love with a neighboring lord and conspires to kill her husband to gain her freedom. She is turned into an owl as a punishment for her choices. Modern readers often struggle to see Blodeuwedd's divinity, but examining her story from the perspective of its contemporary medieval audience helps us unlock its deeper meaning. Blodeuwedd can be seen as a feminist icon, teaching us the power of claiming our personal agency despite the risks, especially in the face of societal and familial expectations.

It is my profound hope that the information presented in these pages will assist you in building or fortifying bridges of connection with Rhiannon and Blodeuwedd. May you find echoes of your own experiences within their tales, and perhaps be inspired to embrace all that is powerful, transformative, and sovereign within yourself.

Jhenah Telyndru
September, 2024

About the Author

Jhenah Telyndru has always felt called to dance with joy in that liminal space that straddles the realms of history and myth, of individuality and collectivity, of the seen and the unseen. A creative mystic who loves science and values fact, Jhenah embraces the conscious co-creation of the future, while immersing herself in an impassioned study of the past. The path between, she believes, is where the mysteries are revealed and where true magic happens.

A formally trained Celticist, Jhenah holds an MA in Celtic Studies from the University of Wales, Trinity St. David, as well as a BA (Hons.) in Archaeology from Stony Brook University. She founded the Sisterhood of Avalon in 1995 and serves as Academic Dean and lead instructor of the Avalonian Thealogical Seminary. Jhenah hosts residential training retreats around North America and the UK, presents internationally at conferences and festivals, teaches online workshops and immersion programs, and facilitates pilgrimages to sacred sites in the British Isles through Mythic Seeker Tours.

A priestess in the Avalonian Tradition for over 35 years, Jhenah has been following a Pagan path since 1986. She is an Awenydd Druid of the Anglesey Druid Order (ADO), as well as a certified Amicus Mortis (Friend of Death) through the Order. As a member of clergy, Jhenah performs rites of passage in her community, has trained in herbalism and a variety of alternative healing modalities, and is in service as a Transpersonal Tarot Counselor and teacher.

In addition to her formal studies, Jhenah has delved into Hermetic science, Qabalistic philosophy, transpersonal astrology, archetypal tarot, and depth psychology in an ongoing quest to further her understanding of the Universe as it manifests within and without.

To learn more about her and her work, she invites you to visit her website: www.ynysafallon.com

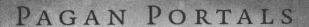

PAGAN PORTALS

RHIANNON

Divine Queen of the Celtic Britons

JHENAH TELYNDRU

Pagan Portals

Rhiannon

Divine Queen of the Celtic Britons

Jhenah Telyndru

What People Are Saying About

Rhiannon: Divine Queen of the Celtic Britons

Sophisticated and elegant, steeped in scholarship and passionately written, Telyndru's offering to Rhiannon will take you on a journey deep into the heart of mystery, sovereignty and connection. Within these pages you will discover the tools necessary to develop a lasting and meaningful relationship with Rhiannon. To connect to the Divine Queen we must ask her to stop and no tice us, Telyndru offers you a guiding hand to understand this process and move into relationship with the Goddess. What you hold in your hands is priceless, for this is a gift of inspiration.

Kristoffer Hughes, head of the Anglesey Druid Order and author of *From the Cauldron Born: Exploring the Magic of Welsh Legend and Lore*

Rhiannon: Divine Queen of the Celtic Britons is the perfect introduction to a Welsh Goddess who can be elusive and ephemeral as well as profound and present. In this slim introduction Jhenah Telyndru has combined solid academic information, myth, spiritual devotion and practical suggestions that anyone could incorporate into their own lives. The end result is a book that invites the reader to delve deep into the history of Welsh mythology and create a profound connection to this powerful Goddess. A must read for anyone interested in either Rhiannon or Welsh deities more generally.

Morgan Daimler, best-selling author of *The Morrigan* and *Fairies: A Guide to the Celtic Fair Folk*

Jhenah Telyndru's *Rhiannon: Divine Queen of the Celtic Britons* is a real treasure-trove of lore and wisdom regarding this beloved Welsh goddess. The first half of this book gives us a brilliant scholarly introduction to Her, while the second half offers insights into developing an immediate and first-hand relationship with this Sovereign deity. By combining the academic with the experiential this work really stands out in today's modern goddess literature. Another superb offering by Jhenah Telyndru.

Joanna van der Hoeven, Druid Priestess and Director of Druid College UK and best-selling author of *The Awen Alone: Walking the Path of the Solitary Druid* and *The Crane Bag: A Druid's Guide to Ritual Tools and Practices*

As both literary character and goddess, Rhiannon is hard to get to know. But Jhenah Telyndru's book brings her to life. Here you find the historical and literary sources studied with logical clarity and precision, as well as a gentle and loving present-day devotional interpretation. This book is not only an informative text: it is also a work of art.

Brendan Myers, PhD, author of *Reclaiming Civilization: A Case for Optimism for the Future of Humanity* and *The Earth, The Gods and The Soul — A History of Pagan Philosophy*

With a clear voice for storytelling and a deft hand at complex and multidisciplinary research, Jhenah Telyndru's love and devotion to her goddess shines through with every page. This book is satisfyingly academic while being deeply moving and practical for anyone looking to build or deepen into a relationship with this goddess. I highly recommend this book for new seekers and experienced practitioners alike.

River Devora, priest and founder of the Strong Roots and Wide Branches Polytheist Learning Community

A new entry in Moon Books' excellent *Pagan Portals* series, Jhenah Telyndru's *Rhiannon: Divine Queen of the Celtic Britons* presents us with an introduction to this enigmatic Goddess that is both lyrical and academic. Ms. Telyndru is well equipped to take on this challenge. The founder and leader of the Sisterhood of Avalon, with a Master's in Celtic Studies from the University of Wales Trinity Saint David, she is steeped in medieval Celtic literature, ancient archaeology, and Welsh culture – all of which enable her to read early sources with special clarity, and then relate those sources to the modern spiritual and cultural concerns of her readers. At once practical and poetic, mystical and scholarly, Jhenah Telyndru's *Rhiannon: Divine Queen of the Celtic Britons* teaches us much about a popular yet ill-understood deity, who we think we know, but don't really. In consequence, I recommend it highly.

Segomâros Widugeni, formerly Aedh Rua, author of *Celtic Flame*

So much more than brilliant, precise scholarship, *Rhiannon: Divine Queen of the Celtic Britons* is an exquisite melding of history, mythology and lore. Jhenah Telyndru entices a depth of historical insight out of rich range of resources to place it at your doorstep in an engaging, evocative manner and she takes dynamic relationship with Rhiannon out of ritual confines to place it actively in the nuances of everyday life. This important work is a linguistic archeological treasure; an invitation to hone awareness of how we know what we know; and an inspired guide for spiritual practice. Jhenah follows the trail of historical breadcrumbs to give us a feast, complete with ancient tales, poetry and song. Every morsel is a delight to savour.

Tiffany Lazic, author of *The Great Work: Self-Knowledge and Healing Through the Wheel of the Year*

Rhiannon: Divine Queen of the Celtic Britons is an excellent introduction to Rhiannon and Her world. Jhenah's warm, engaging style illuminates a mysterious Lady like a medieval manuscript, weaving history and mythology together like the worlds Rhiannon traverses: effortlessly and with grace. A well-researched and powerful aid to those who seek to know Her, at any level of engagement.

Rev. Tamara L. Siuda, founder of the House of Netjer and author of *The Ancient Egyptian Daybook* and *The Ancient Egyptian Prayerbook*

Contents

Acknowledgements xix

Introduction – Climbing the Mound xx

Chapter One – The Tapestry of Time 1
Chapter Two – Primary Sources 8
Chapter Three – Retelling the Myths 12
Chapter Four – Rhiannon and Divinity 31
Chapter Five – Aspects of the Divine Queen 60
Chapter Six – Seeking Her Within 84
Chapter Seven – Building a Relationship
      with Rhiannon 91
Chapter Eight – Rhiannon Speaks 104

Conclusion – The Journey Begins 110

Appendix 1 – Notes on Welsh Pronunciation 111
Bibliography 113

To the Mothers.

Acknowledgements

Nothing is created in a vacuum, and to enumerate everything and everyone that made up the matrix of support that assisted in the birth of this book will be impossible, so I will do my best to hit the highlights.

First and foremost, I would like to thank Trevor Greenfield for the trust he placed in me when he approached me to write this volume for Moon Books. His patience, guidance, and support, as well as those of the whole Moon Books team, are deeply appreciated.

I am incredibly grateful for the Gaulish expertise and open sharing of River Devora, whose devotion to the Matronae is inspirational. My gratitude for the generosity of Morgan Daimler similarly knows no bounds; her ability (and cheerful willingness) to point me towards the correct Irish resources, including those she herself has translated, has been of enormous assistance.

There are so many reasons for me to feel deeply blessed and appreciative for the presence in my life of my dear Sister and friend Lori Feldmann; in this case, I am grateful for her editing magic and for all of her support and feedback.

I am so very thankful for the Sisterhood of Avalon, for all of my beautiful Sisters, and to all who have shared sacred space with me – especially those times, under the Full Moon, when we call to the Divine Queen...

I am grateful to my family, both of blood and of choice. Thank you for your support, for your understanding, and for always gifting me with a soft place to land. Thank you especially to my children for being so understanding of my sometimes-crazy process. I love you both so!

Introduction

Climbing the Mound

Winding our way up the yew-lined pathway which led us deeper and deeper into a shadowland of overhanging trees standing in stark contrast to the ruins of Castle Narberth, whose stones were bare and hot in the summer sun, it was easy to feel as if we were passing into another world. That the long, uphill path required that we pass over a small bridge and under the spreading branches of an enormous hawthorn tree only reinforced the feeling that the borders of the Otherworld were close at hand. We stopped there and circled beneath the holy thorn, centering and chanting and pouring out a libation as an offering to the spirits of place, before we continued on to emerge from the shadow of trees and stand before the gentle rise of the rounded hill. Surrounded by a bramble hedge, the hill's green mantle was drenched in slanting sunlight beneath the bright blue sky.

A moment of silence. A breath. A heart-felt prayer before we continued forward. Step by intentional step, we made our way up to the crest of the hill, and saw the whole of the landscape spread out before us... an almost timeless patchwork of farmlands, the steeples of churches, and the peaks of centuries old buildings. There, a copse of trees... here, the stone ruins of the Norman castle we had just visited... always, the white embellishments of sheep grazing serenely against the verdant quilt of the countryside. It was a beautiful sight, but we were there with hopes of seeing something more. A wonder, perhaps, or a vision of what was. A glimpse of the Lady of this land, whom legend says emerged from this very mound, or perhaps one like it, in pursuit of that which she desired.

Where before we had circled beneath the tree, joined in chant and in intention, now this group of 20-odd women instead fanned out, organically seeking a place of their own on the hillside. Some sat, others stood. Still others chose to stay in motion, tracing the diameter of the hill. All maintained a space of sacred silence, keenly aware of the mythic import of the moment. For tradition teaches that the Gorsedd Arberth, the legendary mound that some identify with this very hill, was a place of magic... and those who came to stand upon this hill – especially a king... or in our case, a group of women actively seeking our personal sovereignty – would either experience a great wonder, or be subject to terrible blows. We all hoped for the former, but knew that even the latter – albeit in a more metaphorical sense – would have something to teach us about who we were and our work in the world.

There is something powerful about embodying myth, something transformational about seeking Source out in the world in order to discover that the sacred landscape exists both around and within us as we reflect those energies back upon ourselves. Joseph Campbell wrote, "myths are public dreams, dreams are private myths." Myths are the dreams of a culture, representing the needs and perspectives of a people in the same way our personal dreams help us to process and understand our own desires, the ways in which we see ourselves and, consequently, our place in the universe. To consciously come into alignment with legends and folktales is to see ourselves in more cosmological terms. We take ourselves outside of time when we move ourselves into a liminal space where all possibilities coexist, and where the truth of who and what we are is not limited to that which we are able to imagine. And so, a mythic tale of an Otherworldly woman who emerges from a magical hill astride a white horse can become our own story, its embedded symbols become vessels that we can fill with our most secret selves, and the twists and turns of the plot reflect the map of our own unfolding lives.

To understand Rhiannon, we too must undertake a journey into unknown lands to pursue that which we most desire. We must excavate the layers of her myth, decode the meaning of her symbols, and seek to restore the significance of her very name. We cannot pursue her directly, for the seemingly slow and steady gait of her magnificent white mount ever outpaces even the swiftest of steeds. Yet, if we but call to her and ask for what we need, she immediately stops and answers us, a generous and gracious Lady whose bag of plenty can fill us, and whose birds can soothe our deepest hurts and call us back to the lands of the living once more. And so, as we embark upon this reflection on Rhiannon, the Divine Queen of the Celtic Britons, let us call to her and speak our need with all of our hearts:

Lady Rhiannon, Holy Sovereign
Great Queen of the Otherworld:

> Teach us the way of the White Horse –
> That we may journey on the paths of this world
> With clarity of purpose and strength of heart,
> Holding fast to the Sacred Center of our inner truth
> Even in the face of all hardships and injustices.
>
> Teach us the way of the Three Birds –
> That we may find courage in times of darkness
> And relief from our burdens and cares.
> That the parts of ourselves we have thought long dead
> May arise in joy and gladness once more.
>
> Teach us the way of the Divine Mother –
> That we may nurture truth, birth understanding,

And act with endless compassion for ourselves and others.
Show us the ways of unconditional love and loyalty
That we may know when to hold tight... and when we must
let go.

Teach us the way of the Great Queen –
That we may walk in this world in our power,
In unflinching pursuit of our true purpose,
And unafraid to ask for that which we need
As we come fully into the light of our Sovereignty.

Lady Rhiannon, Holy Sovereign
Great Queen of the Otherworld:

Teach us to be free.

Chapter One

The Tapestry of Time

To write about Rhiannon is to undertake a journey. While she has a mythology around her, her origins are obscure. While she has many modern-day devotees, she is never identified as a Goddess in any of the primary source material. While she appears to have ancient Pagan attributes, her tales were written during the medieval period in a Christianized country that did not even exist politically when the Island of Britain was Pagan. There are no known ancient prayers or rituals in her honor. We have no known cult centers or devotional altars dedicated to Rhiannon. We 'have only a breadcrumb trail of clues to follow which are made up of syncretic resonances, embedded symbolism, and a mythic heritage which begs to be traced back through the Otherworldly veils of history. How then do we approach this revered Lady? How can we best know her as Goddess?

Neo-Pagans generally have come to expect to interact with divinities either from within a newly-created tradition that recasts them to work in a neoteric system like Wicca, for example, or else seeks to reconstruct the old ways with as much cultural authenticity as possible. The latter is possible because many ancient societies have left behind a rich corpus of written work detailing the stories, rituals, and observances to honor their Gods. Unfortunately, the Celts did not do the same, preferring to transmit their sacred stories through oral tradition rather than setting them down into writing. Caesar writes of this phenomenon in his *Gallic War*:

> They [the Druids] are said there to learn by heart a great
> number of verses; accordingly some remain in the course

of training twenty years. Nor do they regard it lawful to commit these to writing, though in almost all other matters, in their public and private transactions, they use Greek characters. That practice they seem to me to have adopted for two reasons; because they neither desire their doctrines to be divulged among the mass of the people, nor those who learn, to devote themselves the less to the efforts of memory, relying on writing; since it generally occurs to most men, that, in their dependence on writing, they relax their diligence in learning thoroughly, and their employment of the memory.

(Caesar, *Gallic War*, Chapter 14)

Regardless of the intention, the result of this practice is that unlike many other ancient cultures, the beliefs, religious practices, and myths of the Pagan Celts were not written down until relatively late, especially in areas that had been annexed by the Roman Empire, such as Gaul and Britain. It is important to note that Druidism – the priestly caste which performed the ceremonies and sacrifices, served as judges and mediators, acted as augurs and healers, and transmitted the lore as bards and poets – was outlawed in Gaul in the first century CE and finally wiped out in Britain during the siege of the Island of Anglesey by Roman troops in 61 CE. The primary keepers of religious knowledge in these areas, therefore, were mostly eradicated, and so it is posited that what may have remained did so as folk memory and practice which were passed down from generation to generation through oral tradition.

As time progressed, Britain, like almost all of Europe, became Christianized and endured wave after wave of invasion, first from Germanic tribes after Rome withdrew and then from the Normans. Eventually, several nations arose on the island: Wales, made up of a network of kingdoms to the west of Offa's Dyke, most retained the culture of the Celtic Britons, and resonated strongly with the other Brythonic people of Cornwall and Brittany; Scotland, which was more closely aligned culturally with the Irish and Manx; and England, which was primarily influenced by Germanic and Norman cultures, rather than those of the Celts.

When whatever myths and legends which had endured in oral tradition since Celtic Pagan times finally began to be redacted in the Welsh medieval period, we can assume that the tales had evolved over time, and, as written, we can see that they are greatly influenced by the laws and social mores of the contemporary medieval audience. The stories which comprise The Four Branches of the mythic cycle we know as *Y Mabinogi* were written down sometime between the 11th and 13th centuries, possibly by clerics, or otherwise by lay scholars interested in preserving Welsh culture at a time when Wales had lost its independence to Anglo-Norman England. Ostensibly, because of this desire to archive and preserve these tales, it is unlikely that the redactors themselves made any substantive changes to the stories as they had received them, and indeed, there are phrases included in the narratives which were typical of the mnemonic and onomastic devices known to have been used during oral recitation (Davies, 1993). If these tales have their roots in Pagan Celtic tradition, therefore, any shifts of characterization or symbolism are likely a natural result of evolution of the tales over time, and not reflective of any kind of political or religious agenda.

The characters we generally assume to be divinities are never identified as such in any existent tales; they are, however, often depicted as supernatural or larger-than-life figures. These stories feature a comfortability with magic and the Otherworld which may seem unusual to us when we consider that Wales was a wholly Christian country at the time they were committed to writing; the Four Branches are filled with faery queens, magicians, shape changers, giants, visits to the Otherworld, magical animals, and even the creation of a woman out of flowers. Textual references are made to religious traditions performed "in the custom of the time", which seem to refer to Pagan rites and rituals from the pre-Christian era. Where scholars of *Y Mabinogi* and contemporary tales embrace the theory that these stories have Pagan roots, they are careful to say that there is no direct proof of this connection, noting, for example, that the similarity of character names with divine figures in other Celtic mythos (such as Rhiannon's second husband, Manawydan fab Llŷr and the Irish God of the sea Manannán mac Lir) and the appearance of common international folk motifs (for example, the king obtains sovereignty by sleeping with a representative of the land) could instead be the result of cultural exchanges in the early medieval period; everyone likes to tell a good story, and these tales may well have been influenced by stories originating in Ireland or on the continent (Jackson, 1961).

There is a similar problem with concluding that British folk customs, such as the winter mumming tradition of the Mari Lwyd (Grey Mare) or those of the Hunting of the Wren, are remnants of Celtic Pagan practices that survived through time. While the symbol sets included in these traditions – a veiled horse's skull with a working jaw used as a pantomime in a ritualized exchange between mummers and individual households in turn, and the capture, displaying, and parading of a tiny, otherwise protected bird from house to house in order to confer luck and fertility – appear to be very Pagan in origin, they may simply reflect the unconscious needs of an agrarian people who worked the same land, with essentially the same technology, and faced the same survival challenges during the winter months as their ancient ancestors. Since these practices can only be attested to from the 17th century forward, there is again no direct proof of their ancient Pagan origins –

but this need not diminish the power of these practices, both psychologically and practically (Wood, 1997).

It is important to again stress that there are no known temples, altar inscriptions, or votive offerings dedicated to Rhiannon; the archaeological record simply does not directly support the idea of her divinity, nor that of any character in existent Welsh lore. However, if we consider the ways in which cultures change and grow over time, especially as new influences and challenges arise, it is possible that a similar process occurs when it comes to the form and even the name of a culture's gods. It is fairly well attested that in the process of becoming Christianized, the gods of a people often became local saints, not necessarily canonical as far as the Church of Rome was concerned, but honored and appealed to as intercessors nonetheless; oftentimes, these saints retained attributes or areas of influence from their godly past. Perhaps the most famous example of this is the transition of the Irish Goddess Brigid to the beloved St. Brigid; both shared a cult site in Cill Dara/Kildare, both were associated with the forge, healing, and creativity, and both had an eternal flame burning in their honor – a devotion that was extinguished during the Reformation, and rekindled in Kildare once more in 1993.

If we accept that this has happened during the transition from Paganism to Christianity, certainly then there have to have been other times when the Gods evolved and changed forms. In Western European traditions, we speak of a reconstructed Indo-European "mother culture" which is believed to have been the origin point for certain language groups and their attendant cultures. The Celtic language family is a branch off of this Proto-Indo-European language tree, and it is possible to trace the approximate times and places where new languages – and, ostensibly, their associated cultural forms – broke off from the main branch. As the Celtic peoples and their ideas began to spread across Europe from what is believed to be their origin points in the upper Danube valley in the 13th century BCE, their tribal nature saw distinct cultural groups develop depending on where they settled (Cunliffe,1997). These differentiations likely arose from a combination of integrating with the peoples who already inhabited these lands, the adoption of Celtic cultural ideas by other peoples, and as a result of the challenges presented by the lands themselves.

Although Celtic territories once spanned from as far east as Turkey, as far west as the Iberian peninsula, and as far north as the British Isles and Ireland at their greatest extent, the two major subgroups branching off of the Common Celtic language was Continental Celtic and Insular Celtic (Koch, 2006). These groups formed their own branches and according to one linguistic model, from Continental Celtic arose Celtiberian, Gaulish, Galatian, Leptonic, and Noric – all of which are extinct. Insular Celtic branched into two major groups: Brythonic (P-Celtic), from which came Welsh, Cornish, and Breton; and Goidelic (Q-Celtic), out of which evolved Irish, Manx, and Scots Gaelic – each of which had their own stages of development (Sifter, 2008). The modern iterations of these languages survive at various levels of success, despite long-term attempts by the English to suppress and extinguish them.

While this may seem like a strange side-track to a conversation about Rhiannon, it is a critical piece for understanding several key ideas. First, it underscores the reality that the Celts were not a monolithic culture; there were Celtic peoples whose languages had evolved so distinctively that although they were related linguistically, the speakers would not have been able to understand each other. Second, it is important to realize that not only were the Celtic peoples separated from each other in space, but also in time. Their cultures existed in various stages during the Pagan period for at least 1000 years, and their different historical experiences had great impact on the further development of their cultures (Cunliffe, 1997). For example, the Roman conquest of Gaul and Britain changed the trajectories of these peoples and their religious forms in a way that we do not see in Ireland, a critical distinction when attempting to study the mythos of any of these cultures. Lastly, it is important to realize that *Y Mabinogi* and contemporary tales were written down in Middle Welsh, a language which did not exist until the 12th century, and that the nation known as Wales didn't even come into being until the 6th century CE, which was approximately the same time that all of Britain had been Christianized (Sifter, 2008).

So, while it is true that Rhiannon is not identified as a Goddess in *Y Mabinogi*, nor have we found any artifactual proof of her worship, or any observation of her cultus by contemporary ancient writers, perhaps the conclusion that this is because she and other legendary Welsh figures are not divinities is incorrect. Perhaps we have found no shrines, images, or inscriptions dedicated to Rhiannon because there simply could not have been any as a consequence of the pre-Roman Celtic preference to worship in sacred groves and not to write sacred things down. Indeed, the very language of Rhiannon's name had not developed until long after the Pagan Celtic period in Britain had ended. Perhaps then, in order to explore the truth of Rhiannon's potentially divine nature, we must follow a more subtle route – one which requires a deep reading of her mythos, an examination of linguistic evidence, the identification of medieval elements in her tale to discern the provenance of what remains, and a comparative study of similar Goddesses both from adjacent and precursor cultures. What follows is an exploration of this very path, undertaken in hopes of gaining a deeper understanding of Rhiannon.

Chapter Two

Primary Sources

The primary mythological source for Rhiannon's story is from a collection of Middle Welsh narrative tales that has come to be called *Pedair Cainc y Mabinogi* or *The Four Branches of the Mabinogi* – often given as *Y Mabinogi* for short. There has been some confusion about the name of this collection of tales, as well as the names of the individual tales themselves since the source manuscripts do not provide titles for any of them. Of the stories collected, only four of them end with the formulaic "and so ends this branch of *Y Mabinogi*", leaving us to conclude that those particular tales are in some way related (Mac Cana, 1992). The word *"mabinogi"* is believed to come from the Welsh *mab,* which means "youth" or "son", and so could potentially mean "Tales of the Youth". This appears to be a Welsh iteration of a type of narrative tradition that relays a hero's youthful adventures, such as we see in the Irish *macnímartha* genre of tales. While the evidence is not entirely conclusive, it is possible that the youthful hero whose exploits unifies these *Four Branches* is none other than Rhiannon's son, Pryderi; we will explore this idea in more depth in chapter four.

The term *"mabinogion"* appears to have been a scribal error in one of the source manuscripts, and when Lady Charlott e Guest translated and published these tales in English for the first time between 1830 and 1840, she did so in multiple volumes which she called *The Mabinogion* – a convention that has remained to this day. Guest included additional medieval Welsh tales in this collection, all taken from the same source manuscripts, but the story cycle properly known as *Y Mabinogi* is formally comprised only of the four *cainc* or branches (Mac Cana, 1992).

The titles given to these branches by Guest are:

The First Branch – *Pwyll Pendefeg Dyfed* (Pwyll, Prince of
Dyfed)

The Second Branch – *Branwen ferch Llŷr* (Branwen,
Daughter of Llŷr)

The Third Branch – *Manawydan fab Llŷr* (Manawydan, Son
of Llŷr)

The Fourth Branch – *Math fab Mathonwy* (Math, Son of
Mathonwy)

The additional tales included in the source manuscripts
containing the Four Branches and came to be collected with
them, but are not part of *Y Mabinogi* proper are:

The Four Native Tales:

Culhwch ac Olwen (*Culhwch and Olwen*)
Lludd a Llefelys (*Lludd and Llefelys*)
Breuddwyd Macsen Wledig (*The Dream of Macsen Wledig*)
Breuddwyd Rhonabwy (*The Dream of Rhonabwy*)

The Three Romances:

Owain, neu Chwedyl Iarlles y Ffynnawn (*Owain, or The Lady
of the Fountain*)
Peredur fab Efrawg (*Peredur son of Efrawg*)
Gereint fab Erbin (*Gereint son of Erbin*).

The source manuscripts for these eleven tales are:

Peniarth 6 (The earliest source, dating to about 1250 CE,
which is unfortunately fragmentary)

Llyfr Gwyn Rhydderch (The White Book of Rhydderch, dating to around 1350 CE)

Llyfr Goch Hergest (The Red Book of Hergest, dating to around 1400 CE)

While most scholars believe that the tales themselves, as written, may date back as far 1050 CE, there are references to some of the characters in the poems of *The Book of Taliesin* (*Llyfr Taliesin*) which are believed to pre-date *Y Mabinogi*. Further, it is commonly accepted that these tales were redacted from oral tradition, and therefore the stories themselves are likely of much older origin (Davies, 1993). Is it possible that these stories, or at least the seeds of what they wound up becoming, originated in Celtic Pagan British times? Perhaps, but there is no definitive evidence for any direct lineage between them, especially when you consider the timeline involved.

The Iron Age Celts are believed to have come to the British Isles around 500 BCE; the Roman conquest of Britain was complete by 77 CE, and Roman rule lasted until 410 CE. The Roman Empire established Christianity as its official religion in 312 CE, and although there is some evidence of Christianity in the British Isles before this, due to the departure of the Romans and the subsequent invasions of Pagan Saxons, the religion didn't gain a firm foothold until the 6th century (Ross, 1996). As the Pagan Celts themselves held a prohibition against writing any of their sacred teachings down, we do not have any written materials contemporary with ancient Pagan practice in Britain, and since the stories of *Y Mabinogi* were not written down until a good 500 – 700 years later, it is very difficult to find any conclusive proof that these tales have their origins in Pagan British myths.

Rhiannon directly appears in the First and Third Branches of *Y Mabinogi*, playing a larger role in the First Branch than in the Third. She is referenced in the Second Branch, and the

Adar Rhiannon – the Birds of Rhiannon – make an appearance. These Otherworldly birds are also mentioned in *Culhwch and Olwen*, and potentially feature, albeit unnamed, in *The Lady of the Fountain*. The Adar Rhiannon are also mentioned in a Welsh Triad whose authenticity is contested, as it is likely the creation of Iolo Morgannwg, the Welsh writer and poet who reestablished the Eisteddfod in 1792, and who infamously passed off some of his own writing as translations of old, rare texts thereby casting doubt on the antiquity of all of his writings. Aside from mentions of her son and husbands in other places, including authentic triads from *Trioedd Ynys Prydein (The Triads of the Island of Britain)* and *Llyfr Taliesin (The Book of Taliesin)*, that is the sum of the literary primary source material that we have on Rhiannon. Considering the lack of material culture which attest to her myth or any known cultus directly concerning her, there really isn't very much information to work with, especially in comparison to other deities both within and outside of Celtic cultures.

Let us therefore embark upon a review of these sources so that we can establish a foundational context for understanding Rhiannon and for crafting a devotional practice in her honor. What follows is a straightforward retelling of her stories from all known literary sources; it is recommended that, in addition to these, you read a translation of the tales for yourself as well, as there are details and turns of phrase that cannot be transmitted through a retelling but which can provide important information to the seeker. Even the most direct translations lose something from the original Welsh; the redactors often made use of beautiful linguistic wordplay requiring a fluency in Welsh to appreciate, and therefore non-Welsh readers need to rely upon explanatory notes from the translators in order to understand them.

Chapter Three

Retelling the Myths

Rhiannon in the First Branch

The beginning of the First Branch recounts how Pwyll Pendefig Dyfed, prince of the Welsh kingdom of Dyfed, slighted Arawn, king of the Otherworldly kingdom of Annwn. In order to redress this insult, Pwyll and Arawn changed places with each other, and each noble ruled in the stead – and with the visage – of the other. At the end of a year spent in the guise of Arawn, ruling his kingdom wisely and respecting Arawn's marriage bed by not sleeping with the other king's unsuspecting wife, Pwyll defeated an enemy of Arawn that the Otherworldly king batt led every year at a ford. Thus, gaining Arawn's gratitude and friendship, Pwyll was given the name Pen Annwn (Chief of Annwn) and returned to Dyfed with many gifts to find that Arawn had ruled well in his place, and brought great prosperity to his kingdom.

Sometime later, after a feast at his court in Arberth, Pwyll and his men visit a nearby hill where, it was said, any noble who sat upon it would either see a wonder or be beaten by many blows. Unconcerned for his safety, and desiring to experience a wonder, Pwyll and his retinue make for the hill, called Gorsedd Arberth. When all are settled and seated, they are met with the sight of a veiled and golden horsewoman astride a tall and pale white horse; she rides along the road that passes in front of the hill, and her mount appears to be walking at a slow and steady pace. Pwyll is intrigued by this stranger, and sends one of his men after her to find out who she is. Thinking that her slow pace would permit him to catch up with her on foot, Pwyll's man runs after her, but he is unable to reach the horse and rider. He returns to the court to get the fastest horse available, but no matter how hard he rides, the horsewoman remains out of reach, and at last he gives up. Pwyll and his men return the next day with their fastest horse, hoping to encounter the mysterious rider once more. She appears almost immediately, again seeming to move at a slow and steady pace, but she again evades Pwyll's man; the harder he pushed his horse, the further away she became even though she never altered her pace. Undeterred, Pwyll and his retinue return the next day, and this time it is Pwyll who pursues Rhiannon on his own horse; just as before, the apparently slow-moving white horse and its rider remain out of reach regardless of how quickly they were pursued. Finally, Pwyll called out to Rhiannon:

> "For the sake of the man you love most, wait for me."
> "I will wait gladly," she said, "and it would have been better for the horse if you had asked that a while ago!"
> (Davies 2007, pg. 10)

Drawing her horse to a halt, Pwyll immediately catches up with Rhiannon who draws back her veil. Pwyll thinks to himself that he had never seen so beautiful a woman, and asks who she is and where she is going. She gives him her name, saying:

> I am Rhiannon, daughter of Hyfaidd Hen, and I am to be given to a husband against my will. But I have never wanted any man, because of my love for you. And I still do not want him, unless you reject me. And it is to find out your answer on the matter that I have come.
> (Davies 2007, p. 11)

Captivated, Pwyll responds that if he could choose from any woman in the world, he would choose no one but Rhiannon. Gladdened, Rhiannon arranges to meet with Pwyll at her father's court a year hence, where their wedding feast would be lain and the two of them would be married. As promised, Pwyll and his retinue arrive a year later to the Otherworldly court of Hyfaidd Hen, and the joyous feast commences, with Rhiannon and Pwyll seated side by side in their place of honor.

During the course of the merrymaking, a man approaches the bride and groom and asks a boon of Pwyll; overcome with goodwill, Pwyll immediately agrees to give the stranger anything within his power to give. Unfortunately, the man is no stranger to Rhiannon, as it is her former suitor Gwawl, who immediately asks for the hand of Rhiannon and the wedding feast besides. Forced, now, to keep the word he had too readily given in front of the entire gathering, Rhiannon takes Pwyll to task for his impulsiveness:

> "Be silent for as long as you like," said Rhiannon. "Never has a man been more stupid than you have been.'" (Davies 2007, pg. 12)

She then turns to Gwawl and informs him that the feast had been laid by her and gifted to the visitors from Dyfed, so it was not Pwyll's to give; however, should Gwawl return in a year's time, she would have another feast waiting and she would become his wife. Gwawl agrees and departs, leaving Rhiannon to comfort the devastated Pwyll. She gives to him a magical bag and a set of instructions and sends him on his way, counseling him to follow her directions exactly so they might yet become married with Pwyll's honor still intact. Promising to do so, Pwyll takes his leave of Rhiannon.

A year later, Pwyll returns to the court of Hyfaidd Hen. A new wedding feast is underway in honor of Rhiannon and Gwawl. Disguised as a beggar, Pwyll approaches the seats of honor and makes a petition for a boon from Gwawl. Cautiously, Gwawl replies that he would give what he could within reason, and Pwyll replies that all he desires is for his bag to be filled up with food from the feast. Eyeing the small bag proffered by Pwyll, Gwawl airily agrees to the boon, and gestures to the servants to fill the bag with food. However, this being Rhiannon's magical bag, no matter how much food is placed into it, it never becomes full. Gwawl's demeanor transforms from smug to concerned as he watches almost the entirety of his feast disappearing into the never-sated bag. Concerned there would not be enough food to feed his guests, Gwawl asks, "Will your bag ever be full?" To which Pwyll replies:

> "Never... no matter what is put in it, unless a nobleman endowed with land and territory and power gets up and treads down the food in the bag with both feet and says 'Enough has been put in here.'." (Davies 2007, pg.14)

Hastily, Gwawl rises up to do just that, and the moment he puts both feet in the bag, Pwyll pulls the sack up over Gwawl's head, then ties it securely shut. Trapped within the bag, Gwawl pleads for help as Pwyll's warriors emerge from hiding and begin kicking the sack about, thereby birthing a new game called "the badger in the bag." Rhiannon and her father are mortified by the ignoble treatment, and call upon Pwyll to bring his men to order. Once done, Rhiannon sets the terms for Gwawl's release, requiring him to give up his claim on her and to vow that he will seek no redress for the indignities suffered at Pwyll's hands. Gwawl agrees to these terms and is released, freeing Pwyll to finally wed Rhiannon and to enjoy the wedding feast.

The couple sleep together that night, and spend a second day in feasting, during which a humble and cautious Pwyll bestowed gifts upon all who asked for them. On the third day they departed for Pwyll's lands, taking residence at his court in Arberth. Rhiannon builds a reputation as a very generous queen, bestowing rich gifts upon courtiers and proving herself a model of hospitality. The couple are very happy, but after three years of marriage without an heir, Pwyll's advisors begin to suggest that he take another wife. He refuses to do so, asking them to let the matter rest for another year as much may yet happen. And indeed, before that year is over, Rhiannon gives birth to a son.

On the night of his birth, six nurses are sent into Rhiannon's chambers to watch over the mother and child, but one by one, they each fall asleep. Awaking before dawn, they realize to their horror that the baby is gone; search as they might, he is nowhere to be found. Fearing they would be put to death for their negligence, the nurses devise a plan to save themselves, knowing that the word of all six of them would win out against the word of Rhiannon. Taking and killing several stag-hound puppies, the nurses smear the blood on the sleeping Rhiannon's face and hands, and arrange the bones all around her. When Rhiannon awakens and asks for her son, the nurses reply that she shouldn't be asking them for him, that they tried and tried to stop her from destroying the baby, but she was too strong and overpowered them. Rhiannon replies that she knows this is a lie, and that they needn't be afraid – that they should tell the truth about what happened and she would ensure that no harm would come to them; but they would not be moved from their course.

As word of the incident spreads throughout the land, Pwyll's advisers beseech him to divorce Rhiannon because of the terrible thing she had done, but Pwyll refuses, preferring instead to punish her. Rhiannon, meanwhile, had gathered her own group of advisors, who recommended that she accept the punishment from Pwyll, rather than try to argue against the six nurses. She agrees to do so, and her punishment was this: for seven years she is to sit every day on a mounting block outside of Arberth's gate, where she is to tell the story of how she destroyed her newborn child to anyone who approached. Additionally, she was to offer any newcomer a ride to the court on her back, and all of this she did, although very few visitors took her up on the offer.

While all of this is going on, Teyrnon Twryf Lliant, the lord of nearby Gwent Is Coed, is vexed with an ongoing problem. Every year on May Eve, or Calan Mai, his fine white mare births a beautiful foal, and every year that foal mysteriously disappears without a trace that same night. Tired of losing such beautiful animals year after year, Teyrnon decides on this May Eve to bring the pregnant horse inside so that he can keep watch over her. When night falls, she gives birth to a beautiful foal, and just as it stands for the first time, an enormous clawed arm reaches through the window and grabs hold of the newborn's mane, seeking to spirit it away.

Teyrnon saves the horse by cleaving the monstrous arm off with his sword so that both foal and claw fall back into the house. He hears a horrible scream outside, and gives chase to the wounded creature as it attempts to escape into the night. Teyrnon doesn't get far before he remembers that he left the door open, and upon returning to ensure that the horses would not escape, discovers a newborn baby swaddled in silk brocade lying on the threshold of his home. He brings the child to his wife, with whom he has had no children, and the two decide to raise the boy as their own after she notes that his clothing clearly mark him as coming from noble lineage. They name the child Gwri Wallt Euryn, (Blooming Golden Hair) because of his blond hair.

Gwri was a strong child who grew incredibly quickly; by the time he was one, he was as developed as a three-year-old, and when he turned two, he looked and acted more like a six-year-old. By the time he turned four, he was pestering the grooms to permit him to ride a horse. Teyrnon's wife suggested that the boy be given the horse that Teyrnon had saved on the night he found Gwri; he agreed, and asked her to give it to the boy herself. It was about this time that Teyrnon became aware of the plight and punishment of Rhiannon, and he became filled with compassion for her loss. He then looked to Gwri, and for the first time realized the strong resemblance the boy had to Pwyll, who was known to Teyrnon through once having been Pwyll's vassal.

After conferring with his wife, they decide to make a trip to Pwyll's court the very next day in order to restore the boy to his family. When they arrive at the gate, they encounter Rhiannon sitting at the mounting block. She introduces herself to them and, as required, offers to carry each of them in turn to Pwyll's court. Everyone refused to allow Rhiannon to carry them, and together entered the court where a feast was being lain in celebration of Pwyll's return from touring the lands around Dyfed. During the feast, Teyrnon recounted the story of finding the golden-haired child, and turning to Rhiannon he said, "This is your son, my lady. And whoever told lies against you did you wrong." (Davies 2007, pg. 20)

Rhiannon replied, "what a relief from my anxiety if that were true!" and it is from this utterance that Pryderi, from the word *pryder*, meaning "anxiety", received his name from Rhiannon (Davies, 2007). Pwyll and Rhiannon are so overcome with gratitude for the way the boy had been raised by Teyrnon, they make assurances that Dyfed will forever support Teyrnon and his lands. They also offered rich rewards, strong horses, and hunting dogs – all of which Teyrnon refused. Pryderi was given as a foster child to Pendaran Dyfed, a wise member of Pwyll's court, and the boy preternaturally grew into adulthood. After Pywll passes away, Pryderi takes over the seven cantrifs of Dyfed, along with fourteen more, and rules them all well. He eventually takes a bride, a woman named Cigfa.

Rhiannon in the Second Branch

Rhiannon does not appear directly in the Second Branch, but her influence in the story is both deeply felt and memorable. A great war breaks out when the king of Britain, Bendigeidfran, or Bran the Blessed, brings an army to Ireland in order to rescue his sister Branwen from the mistreatment she is suffering at the hands of her husband Matholwch, the king of Ireland. The devastation resulting from this war leaves Ireland populated only by five pregnant women who each give birth to sons, and together they repopulate the island and establish Ireland's five provinces. Of the warriors who came from Britain, also known as the Island of the Mighty, only seven survivors return. Branwen, whose young son is killed in the maelstrom, regards the devastation on both sides of the conflict, dies of a broken heart, and is buried in a four-sided grave on the island of Anglesey.

Bran himself is struck with a poisoned spear during the battle, and before he dies, instructs his men to cut off his head and to bring it to White Hill in London, where they are to bury it facing France. This act is immortalized in a Welsh Triad as one of the Three Fortunate Concealments, for as long as Bran's head is buried there, its talismanic power would ensure that Britain could never be conquered by anyone from across the sea. A complementary Triad is that of the Three Unfortunate Disclosures, which relates how King Arthur himself had the head of Bran removed from White Hill because he thought it was unseemly that anyone but he, Arthur, himself should protect the Island of Britain.

However, before the burial of the head, the seven survivors of the war – who counted among them Pryderi son of Rhiannon, and Manawydan son of Llŷr and brother to Bran and Branwen – brought the head with them to Bran's court at Harlech, following their king's instructions. When they arrived and sat at the feast that had been laid out for them, the Adar Rhiannon (the Birds of Rhiannon) began to sing, as Bran foretold:

> As soon as they began to eat and drink, three birds came and began to sing them a song, and all the songs they had heard before were harsh compared to that one. They had to gaze far out over the sea to catch sight of the birds, yet their song was clear as if the birds were there with them. (Davies 2007, p. 33)

Thus attended, the band of men feasted together for seven years, with Bran's head never becoming corrupted; it kept them company the same as it had when it was still upon their king's body. After seven years in Harlech, they departed for Gwales where there was a royal household high above the sea. There, the seven men along with Bran's head, dwelt together for eighty years. All of their needs were met, all of the sorrows of what they had experienced faded away and were forgotten, and they spent that time filled with great joy, with none of them aging and the head of Bran never knowing decay. The group became known as The Assembly of the Noble Head, and it is only when one of their number opened the door Bran had warned them against opening and they looked out towards Cornwall that their memories returned, and they were overcome with sorrow for all that they had lost. They immediately took up Bran's head, which would only remain uncorrupted while the door was closed, and made for London, burying it at White Hill as he had instructed.

Rhiannon in the Third Branch

The story of the Third Branch picks up immediately where the Second Branch leaves off, with the burial of Bran's head in London having been accomplished. Pryderi son of Pwyll and Rhiannon, and Manawydan son of Llŷr had become fast friends.

With their memories restored and eighty years having passed, Manawydan lamented that he had nowhere now to go. As the brother of Bran, Manawydan had a claim to the throne of the Island of the Mighty, which had been usurped by his cousin Caswallon during the events of the Second Branch; however, Manawydan chose not to challenge him, lest a new war begin. By not claiming his birthright, Manawydan was counted as one of the Three Undemanding Chieftains, another of the Triads of the Island of Britain.

Pryderi invites his friend to come to Dyfed with him, and along with offering him rule over the seven cantrefs he had inherited from his father Pwyll, he also offers him the hand of the now-widowed Rhiannon. Manawydan decides to visit Dyfed with his friend, and agrees to meet Rhiannon there. When the men arrive in Arberth, they find that a great feast had been readied for them by Rhiannon and Pryderi's wife Cigfa. Rhiannon and Manawydan sit to talk with each other, and the son of Llŷr is overcome with tenderness for her, thinking he had never encountered such a well-spoken and beautiful woman. Manawydan tells Pryderi that he agrees to his friend's proposal that he marry Rhiannon, and upon learning of the offer, Rhiannon readily agrees to the union. The two are wed that very night.

Soon after the wedding of Manawydan and Rhiannon, Pryderi visits Caswallon at his court in Oxford to pay homage to the king. Upon his return to Dyfed, there is a holy day feast at the main court in Arberth; between courses of food, and along with other feasters attending the celebration, Rhiannon, Manawydan, Pryderi, and Cigfa climb the Gorsedd Arberth, the same hill from which Pwyll first spied Rhiannon on her horse many years ago. Once the four were seated upon the hill, they heard a terrible noise and a blanket of mist descended upon them; it was so thick they could not see each other. Suddenly the mist disappeared and everything became bright again, and with the return of the light the four looked around and saw that every person, every domesticated animal, every dwelling place, and every sign of life aside from them had completely disappeared.

They searched everywhere in the court and eventually searched throughout the countryside, and found that, aside from wild animals, the four of them were utterly alone. After working through the provisions at hand, the two couples sustained themselves by hunting and fishing, spending two contented years together, before deciding that they no longer wished to live alone in this way. Upon Manawydan's suggestion, the four traveled to England, which had not been affected by the strange magic that had rendered Dyfed uninhabited, and in the town of Hereford, took up the craft of saddle making to sustain themselves. Their saddles were so excellently crafted and in such high demand, that the other saddlers banded together and decided they were going to kill them. Warned of this threat, Pryderi suggests that they kill those who were going to come after them, but Manawydan grew worried about their reputations, and counseled that it would be better for the group to leave town and take up a new craft elsewhere.

Following Manawydan's advice, the four take up residence in a new place and begin to create shields of incredible quality. The demand for these shields was so great that the local shield makers became furious and decided to kill the four of them for taking all of their business. Once more warned, Pryderi again suggests that they should go after their enemies and kill them first, but Manawydan expresses concern that Caswallon would hear of it and come after them with his army, and so the four again uproot and move to a new town. This time, they decide to become shoemakers, hoping that any competition would be too meek to try to come after them. Manawydan teaches the others how to make shoes out of fine Spanish leather, and himself learns how to guild the buckles for the shoes – earning himself the reputation of being one of the Three Golden Shoemakers of the Island of the Mighty. However, the group was once more threatened by the other shoemakers whose profits they were impacting. Pryderi again expressed that they should kill those who would try to kill them, but Manawydan's mild nature was once more victorious, and upon his advice that they return to Dyfed and leave England altogether, the four of them do just that.

After a long journey that brought them back to Arberth, the group began to hunt for their food once more, spending a year contentedly in this way. One morning, Manawydan and Pryderi gather their dogs to go hunting when they notice several of them run ahead of the group and into a thicket, only to return with their hair standing on end in terror. The two men investigate the area for themselves, and discover a pure white wild boar hiding there. Along with their now-emboldened dogs, Pryderi and Manawydan give chase until the boar and the dogs run into a strange and enormous towering fort that had never before existed where it now stood. The two men climb the hill upon which the fort had been built, waiting for the dogs to return. But after some time had passed and they did not hear a sound coming from within the fort, Pryderi decides he is going to go inside to find the dogs.

Always cautious, Manawydan counsels against this action, concluding that whoever had built the fort was also the same person who had put a spell on the land. Pryderi insists that he will not abandon his dogs, and ignoring his friend's advice, he enters alone. He soon discovers that the fort is completely empty; there is no sign of habitation, of his dogs, or of the boar. What he does notice, however, is a well at the center of the space, ornamented with fine marble work. Hanging over the edge of the well was a finely wrought golden bowl which was suspended from four chains that extended so high up into the sky that Pryderi could not see where they ended. Drawn to the beauty of this bowl, Pryderi reached out to grab it with both hands and was immediately frozen into place, unable to speak; he could neither move his feet, nor could he release the bowl.

Unaware of his friend's fate, Manawydan waited for him outside until almost evening, finally returning alone to the court at Arberth. Noticing his solitary state, Rhiannon inquired after her son and the dogs, and Manawydan explained what had transpired. Scolding him as a faithless friend, Rhiannon set out to find the mysterious fort for herself, seeking to rescue Pryderi. Upon discovering the gate of the fortress left open, Rhiannon entered to find her son still holding onto the golden bowl, completely immobilized. In an attempt to free him, Rhiannon grabbed hold of the bowl herself and was immediately rendered silent and paralyzed as well. The two stood there motionless until night fell, and as had happened on Gorsedd Arberth many years before, they heard a terrible noise and a blanket of thick mist fell upon the tower before it – with them inside – disappeared.

When Cigfa and Manawydan discovered that they were alone, Pryderi's wife was overcome with grief and worry until Manawydan assured her that he would not seek to dishonor her in any way. As they had lost their hunting dogs and could not obtain food for themselves, the pair made for England, with Manawydan setting up shop to be a shoemaker once again. Cigfa argued that this craft was both below his station and his skill set, but he insisted that this was the work he wanted to pursue. They lived in the town where they settled for a year until, as before, the local shoemakers began to plot against them. This time it was Cigfa who urged Manawydan to act against their persecutors, but he decided it was better for them to return to Dyfed, and they did.

Bringing with him a bundle of wheat, Manawydan and Cigfa settled in Arberth once more, and he learned how to fish and trap wild animals for their food. He also began to till the soil, and planted three fields' worth of wheat. When the time of the Harvest arrived, he visited his fields and found that they were ripe, and he committed to reap the first of his fields the next day. However, when he arrived in the early morning, he found that the entire field had been decimated and every stalk of wheat had been cut down and the grain carried away. Concerned, he checked on his second field, and found that it was ripe and intact and committed to reap it the next day. When he arrived the next morning, he discovered that the second field had now become emptied of grain, and he lamented his terrible fortune while also recognizing that whoever was responsible for the destruction of his fields also had set the enchantment upon the land and had carried away Rhiannon and Pryderi.

Discovering that his third field was ripe and still intact, Manawydan returned home to gather his weapons and to keep watch over the fields during the night, with the hope that he could protect his harvest and discover who had been acting against him. Thus, armed and vigilant, Manawydan returned to the last field. Around midnight, he heard an incredibly loud sound, and suddenly an entire army of mice descended upon the field, breaking every stalk and carrying away every head of grain. Manawydan tried in vain to stop them, but there were too many and he could not grab hold of them before it was too late and the field was bare. He was able, at last, to capture one little mouse who was fatter and slower than the rest; he placed it in one of his gloves and tied it up so the mouse could not escape. He brought it back to court with him and told Cigfa that he intended to hang the mouse as a thief the next day. She at first tried to dissuade him, as it was below his status to bother with such a lowly creature, but he was adamant and since she could come up with no other reason for him to release the mouse, she relented.

Manawydan then made for the Gorsedd Arberth, and at the very top of the hill, he began to create makeshift gallows by pressing two forks into the ground. As he was doing so, he caught sight of a cleric approaching him – the first person, other than his three companions, that he had seen in Dyfed in seven years. The two exchanged greetings and the cleric said he had come from England and was passing through Arberth. When the cleric asked what Manawydan was doing, he replied that he was going to hang the mouse as a thief in accordance with the law. The cleric tried to convince Manawydan to let the mouse go, even offering him money, but he would not, and so the cleric continued on.

Manawydan was affixing a crossbeam over the two forks when a priest approached him and asked what he was doing. He again replied that he was going to hang the mouse as a thief and refused to be paid off or convinced otherwise by the priest, who likewise continued on his way. Manawydan began to tie a rope around the neck of the mouse when he became aware of a bishop and his retinue approaching. Like the others, the bishop tried to convince Manawydan to release the mouse or else allow him to pay money for it; Manawydan refused. The bishop tried again, offering a much larger sum of money, but Manawydan would not be moved. The bishop then promised that in return for the release of the mouse, he would give him the seven horses that had accompanied his retinue as well as the seven bags of riches on each of the seven horses besides. Once more, Manawydan refused.

Finally, and desperately, the bishop asked what Manawydan's price was to release the mouse, to which he replied, "The release of Rhiannon and Pryderi." The bishop assured him he would have that, but it was not enough for Manawydan, who also demanded that the enchantment be lifted from Dyfed. That too was promised to him, but it was still not enough as Manawydan wanted to know who the captive mouse was. The other man replied that she was his pregnant wife, and with prompting from Manawydan, the "bishop" explained everything:

> "I am Llwyd son of Cil Coed, and it is I who placed the enchantment on the seven cantrefs of Dyfed, and I did so to avenge Gwawl son of Clud out of friendship for him; and I took revenge on Pryderi because Pwyll Pen Annwfn played Badger in the Bag with Gwawl son of Clud and he did so unwisely at the court of Hyfaidd Hen. And having heard that you were living in the land, my retinue came to me and asked me to turn them into mice so they could destroy your corn... the third night my wife and the ladies of the court came to me and asked me to transform them too, and I did that." (Davies 2007, p. 45)

Llwyd asked for his wife to be released once more, but Manawydan wisely refused to do so until he received assurances that there would be no other spell ever cast upon Dyfed; that there would be no further vengeance taken against Rhiannon and Pryderi, or any on him because of what had occurred; and that Rhiannon and Pryderi be returned to him before he released the mouse. Praising the good bargain that Manawydan had made, especially that it avoided any further action against Manawydan himself, Llwyd agreed to all of the conditions. Rhiannon and Pwyll appeared, and they gratefully embraced each other, and the enchantment over Dyfed was lifted, with all of the people, homesteads, and livestock returned to their proper places. Manawydan released the mouse to her husband who changed her back to her proper form with his magic wand.

Satisfied that all things had been restored to their proper place, Manawydan made one last inquiry about the nature of the captivity that had been endured by Pryderi and Rhiannon. Llwyd replied:

"Pryderi had the gate-hammers of my court around his neck, while around hers, Rhiannon had the collars of the asses after they had been hauling hay. And that was their imprisonment." (Davies 2007, p. 46)

And so concludes the Third Branch of the *Mabinogi*.

Rhiannon in *Culhwch and Olwen*

As with the Second Branch, Rhiannon does not directly appear in this story, which is the oldest prose Arthurian tale; its earliest redaction is believed to date to somewhere in the 10th or 11th centuries CE (Bromwich, 1992). The tale, in brief, recounts the exploits of Arthur and his knights on behalf of his cousin Culhwch who has fallen in love with Olwen, the daughter of the giant Ysbaddaden Bencawr who is fated to die when his daughter marries. Because of this, Ysbaddaden sets a series of incredibly difficult and seemingly impossible feats before Culhwch and his allies, all of which needed to be accomplished before the giant would grant permission for the marriage to occur. One of these requirements was to obtain for him the Birds of Rhiannon, "they that wake the dead and lull the living to sleep" (Davies 2007, p.196), so that they will sing for Ysbaddaden on the night of the wedding, which would also be the last night of his life. Ultimately, with the help of his warriors and from Arthur himself, Culhwch is able to complete all of the challenges set before him by Olwen's father. Ysbaddaden keeps his word, and gives his daughter to Culhwch; the giant is then beheaded by one of Arthur's men, who takes over his lands and holdings.

Rhiannon in the Welsh Triads

Believed to be a creation of Iolo Morgannwg, rather than an authentic triad, this is nevertheless included here for the sake of completion as it is often referenced in regards to Rhiannon:

There are three things which are not often heard: the song of the birds of Rhiannon, a song of wisdom from the mouth of a Saxon, and an invitation to a feast from a miser. (*Trioedd y Cybydd*, cited in Guest, p.209)

The Mythic Landscape

Y Mabinogi is filled with references to the contemporary landscape of the medieval redactors, perhaps as a reflection of the nationalistic spirit of this transitional time in Welsh history – a deliberate effort on the part of the Welsh to preserve their culture in the face of losing their national autonomy during the Anglo-Norman conquest. The tales may have reminded the Britons of a time when they were independent kingdoms, at times unified under the aegis of a high king, especially in times of strife and against the threat of invasion. Happily, many of the sites mentioned in the text still exist and are accessible enough to be directly experienced today.

Whereas many sites are named directly in the narrative of the Four Branches, and there are many inferences through onomastic tales which explain why a place bears a particular name, it is still difficult to discern what came first, the name or the tale. Perhaps some of the sites are included because they carry faint mythic memories of cult sites sacred to a particular deity, or perhaps the tale came afterwards, in an attempt to provide a retroactive explanation for why things were named or built, or why certain artifacts or ruins exist long after their original uses had been forgotten over time. Either way, the energies of the tales have come to rest in particular landscape areas, and many modern locals are aware of folk traditions which surround the sites, even those which have not been directly recorded in the myths themselves. Further, the study of Welsh toponyms or place names is a worthwhile pursuit, as it can deepen one's understanding of how very important was the land of Wales itself to its mythic heritage.

The main setting of the First and Third Branches is Dyfed, an historical kingdom believed to have once been the territory of the Demetae, a Brythonic Celtic tribe from whom the region got its name. In *Y Mabinogi*, Dyfed is comprised of seven cantrefs, a political unit used in medieval Wales that refers to an area made up of one hundred settlements (from the Welsh *cant* (hundred) and *tref* (town)) (Bollard, 2006). Dyfed is in south-west Wales and its territory was roughly comprised of today's Pembrokeshire and part of Carmarthenshire (Davies, 2007). Arberth in Dyfed was the chief court of Pwyll, and later also that of Pryderi and Manawydan. It is here that Rhiannon gave birth to Pryderi, and where she was sentenced to sit at the gates and offer travelers a ride on her back as penance for her unjust accusation of infanticide. Near to the court was Gorsedd (meaning "tumulus" or "burial mound", or else "throne" or "court") Arberth (Bollard, 2006), the mysterious mound from which Pwyll first encountered Rhiannon, and from where the enchantment of Dyfed in the Third Branch both came down and was lifted.

It is believed that Arberth once existed where modern-day Narberth now stands. There, one can visit the ruins of a Norman motte and bailey castle, believed to have been built in the 12th century CE. While this date is problematic for this having been the court of Pwyll and Rhiannon, the Normans were known for building castles upon older sites, likely because both were chosen for their strategic position. Indeed, not far from the ruins of Castle Narberth, there is a place called Camp Hill which features the remains of an Iron Age enclosure; this appears to be the location most favored to have once been Gorsedd Arberth, and it is the setting for the introduction to this book (Bollard, 2006).

Chapter Four

Rhiannon and Divinity

With what is directly known about Rhiannon from primary source materials as our foundation, we can now work to seek a greater understanding of her. We shall do so through an exploration of her symbols from a cultural perspective, through an examination of her trans-cultural associations with potentially related divinities, by identifying the international folk motifs that are present in her tales, and by investigating the nature of the relationships she has with other mythic characters. Although this kind of analysis is, by nature, much more subjective than any face value reading of her mythos, the tools and process are based in solid academic and scholastic inquiry and so can be used to build a bridge of connection to Rhiannon with some degree of objectivity.

Although Rhiannon is neither directly identified as a divinity in the text of *Y Mabinogi*, nor have we discovered to date anything in the archaeological record that proves that the Pagan Britons worshiped a figured named Rhiannon, the question of whether or not she is a Goddess can be addressed through a thorough exploration of older figures in Celtic tradition who are clearly attested to be divinities and with whom she appears to have correspondence and relationship. There are several streams of investigation to consider, and while their interrelatedness appears to present as a tangled skein, when taken collectively, the areas of differentiation and those of redundancy paint a picture which permits us to conclude that Rhiannon may well be a complex divinity who embodies and inherits a rich corpus of tradition in her person, albeit subtextually. How much the contemporary medieval Welsh audience may have recognized these aspects of her character as having ancient Pagan roots is unknown, and perhaps beside the point, although there are some medieval writings where Pagan and Christian traditions are depicted together quite comfortably.

Britain had been solidly Christian for at least 500 years when the Four Branches began to be written down, and yet the stories are overflowing with magic and supernatural beings. Sojourns into the Otherworld – strongly believed to be a remnant of Pagan British cosmology – are common, and references to pre-Christian religious practices are made in the text without judgment. Although it may seem odd that a Christian society would have been so accepting of the supernatural, medieval Welsh culture embraced these fantastic story elements and did not appear to find any contradiction in this. There is a phenomenon observed through the analysis of myth called "reverse euhemerization" which posits that larger-than-life heroes or supernatural beings found in myths, such as fairy women or giants, had once been divinities whose stature – literally and metaphorically – diminished over time. It is possible therefore that characters in Welsh Mythology who have associations with the Otherworld were once divinities, a theory which helps us better understand Rhiannon as a Goddess, rather than solely as an example of the international folk motif of the Fairy Bride.

In these tales, the Indigenous Otherworld of Britain – called Annwn or Annwfn in Welsh mythos, and believed to mean "Un-World" or "Very Deep" – seems to exist side by side with the human world, and the boundaries between them sometimes become blurred. There are subtextual markers throughout the tales which would have functioned to allow the contemporary medieval audience to understand that the Otherworld was near, or that the threshold into the magical world has been crossed. One of the functions of myth is that it presents a cosmological template both for the society which birthed it and for the place each individual has within that society; it defines the sacred order of things and serves as a cautionary tale for what happens when something or someone upsets the balance and moves outside of this order. The Otherworld therefore provides a mythic arena within which characters and situations that are outside of the constraints of society can be explored. This is important because it is safer to explore what happens when a woman chooses to circumvent her family's choice of a mate for her, for example, when she is a Fairy Woman, because she is already outside of the natural order and her choices, therefore, do not serve to inspire contemporary women to make the same choices. If going outside of the natural order of things is an action reserved for supernatural beings, no ordinary woman could do the same without dire consequences.

There needs to be a balance with this perspective, however. The idealization of women or depictions of women holding power or privileges not known to contemporary medieval women are often attributed to an earlier narrative strata representing a time period featuring different cultural norms when it comes to women. The Irish Queen Medb and the Welsh Arianrhod are examples of this; they are both rulers who display an enormous amount of personal agency and autonomy, to a degree that a regular medieval woman would never know. While some scholars, like Proinsias Mac Cana, suggest this inconsistency may be proof of pagan Celtic mythological remnants entering the narrative through oral folk tradition, others, like Joanne Findon, warn against making broad generalizations of this kind. She argues that seeing Goddesses in all Celtic depictions of women act to further marginalize the depiction of real women rather than to empower them:

> Common among scholars of Celtic literature to assume strength and prominence of female characters... must represent the residue of an earlier mythic discourse... disproportionate emphasis on mythological analysis therefore quest for survivals from a presumed base

overshadow the possible concerns of the text's 'present' – that is, the time(s) in which it was composed and transmitted. The result is a radical dehistoricizing of the text, its characters, and concerns. Women are not read as themselves but as archetypes in disguise, bearing the weight of a mythic past that can be glimpsed only dimly at best. (Findon, 1997, pg. 8)

The magical, Otherworldly origins of Rhiannon might have been enough to make her stand out in the Four Branches, but her actions are themselves remarkable even if she were but a mortal queen of her time. It may well be that her boldness and autonomy are a memory of a former social paradigm where women held more power. If she herself comes from the Otherworld of a past or fading culture, her disempowerment upon marriage and childbirth might be symbolic of what happens when women are absorbed into the new order – one of patriarchal constraint and societal limitation for women. Yet:

...while Rhiannon is evidently aware of the inequalities of contemporary society, she has not embarked upon a struggle against it so much as within it. This is a crucial distinction since unlike Aranrhod, who refuses to accept social patterns, Rhiannon seeks to improve her lot by working with the system. Thus Rhiannon does not flee from the obligation to marry but simply chooses a type of man to suit her best. (Winward, 1997)

Determining which characters possess attributes that point to their past divinity and which are simply meant to represent inspirational women and men who are powerful in their own right is a task which requires discernment; relying upon only one stream of data can be limiting in this regard. It is therefore important that, in addition to the mythic narrative itself, we take multiple factors into consideration when deciding if a figure is indeed, at the core, a devolved representation of a divinity. The approach I take is one which considers characterization and function in primary source materials, identification of international folk motifs, cultural context, name etymology, the presence of linguistic theonyms, syncretism, material culture in the archaeological record, iconography, and symbolic analysis. Even with all of these, it is critical to stress that without direct primary proof that a figure is a divinity – for example, a proven archaeological discovery of a devotional altar inscribed with the divinity's name – we cannot say with complete and utter certainty from an academic perspective that the mythic character in question is definitely a god. The standards for accepting a figure as a deity are different, however, when it comes to modern day Neo-Pagan devotional practices; indeed, there are whole magical and religious traditions which have arisen around figures and philosophies of modern cultural origins. There is no question that Rhiannon is greatly beloved and honored as a Goddess by modern devotees around the world regardless of whether she was once worshiped as such by ancient Celtic Britons. The final section of this book suggests ways to build a relationship with, and craft devotional practices around Rhiannon, but for now, let us explore the evidence we do have of Rhiannon's divinity from the context of the culture which birthed her.

Etymology and Linguistics

One of the first clues to Rhiannon's true nature is her very name. Most Celtic scholars agree that Rhiannon is the medieval Welsh reflex of the Old Celtic *Rīgantona, a Gallo-Britt onic Goddess whose name means "Great Queen" or "Divine Queen." In fact, Koch calls *Rīgantona the "preform of the Welsh Rhiannon" (Koch, p. 1490). *Rīgan is the Proto-Celtic word for "queen", which is the etymological root from which the Welsh word *rhiain*, originally meaning "queen", but has come to mean "maiden" or "lady" is derived. *Rīgantona is also believed to be the antecedent of the Irish Goddess Mórrígan whose name also means "Great Queen" or, alternatively, "Phantom Queen" (Beck, 2009). This is the first of several connections that Rhiannon has with the Mórrígan, as we shall see.

Another clue can be found in the terminal deific which is present at the end of Rhiannon's name. The suffix "-on" appears in the names of many Welsh mythological figures including Modron, Mabon, Teyrnon, Gwion, and Gwydion. This is a direct reflex of the "-onos" and "-ona" terminations, meaning "Great" or "Divine", which mark the names of known Gallo-Brittonic deities such as Epona, Sirona, Maponos, and Matrona (Hamp, 1999). Similarly, the "-wen" suffix, which means "white, shining, holy" in Welsh can be found in the names of mythological female characters like Ceridwen, Branwen, and Olwen; the male counterpoint to this is "gwyn", which has the same meaning, and can be seen in the names of Gwyn ap Nudd, and Gwion. The practice carried on into the Christian period, where some Welsh saints' names are constructed with the addition of an honorific prefix "ty", meaning "your."

Connections to Other Goddesses

While Rhiannon is only known to us from the relatively late sources of the Welsh medieval literary tradition, the etymology of her name and her associated symbol sets are shared with older figures who are clearly Goddesses in their own right. While similarities with other divinities are something to note, it in no way implies that these Goddesses are all the same Goddess. There are several possibilities present, several of which may have happened concurrently: 1) That the medieval Rhiannon evolved into her literary form from that of a Celtic British Goddess over centuries of oral tradition. 2) That she is the Welsh reflex of older Celtic Goddesses, possibly from the

Continent, which speaks to a Gallo-Brittonic tradition. 3) That she represents a local aspect of a divinity type which is found in many Indo-European cultures, especially those in the Celtic cultural branches. 4) That she is a purely literary character in alignment with several international folk motifs found all over Europe. There are arguments for and against each of these possibilities, and it is impossible to say for sure what the ultimate truth is, based upon the information we currently possess. However, an exploration of the Goddesses which have commonalities of mythos, etymology, and iconography can serve to broaden our understanding of Rhiannon, and deepen our relationship with her.

The Matres and Matronae

One of the richest sources of information about Celtic Goddesses comes to us from continental Europe, where an abundance of epigraphic and iconic evidence supports the existence of a widespread cultus centered on the veneration of Mother Goddesses. Found primarily in Gaul and the Rhineland, and later spreading throughout the Roman Empire to eventually find its way to Britain through the devotion of the Roman soldiers garrisoned there, inscriptions called these Goddesses variously *Matres*, *Matronae*, and *Deae Matronae* – simply, "The Mothers" or "The Divine Mothers." These names are believed to be Latinized forms of the Celtic Gaulish word for mother (*mātīr*) – which itself derives from the Indo-European **mātēr*, as does *mētēr* in Greek and *māter* in Latin (Beck, 2009).

It is challenging to ascertain the cultural origins of this cultus because we don't have clear archaeological evidence of their worship until after the Roman annexation of Germany and Gaul. As the Celts did not commit their sacred things to writing, and it appears that they did not create images of their divinities, it was only in the Gallo-Roman period that we begin to see dedicatory altars to the Mothers as well as syncretic imagery that depicted these Goddesses with some of the iconography of Roman deities. It is generally accepted that while their names derive from a combination of Gaulish and Latin, the oldest epigraphic evidence we have for the Mothers is in Gaulish, which suggests that they were a Celtic religious form rather than a Roman import (Beck, 2009).

The Matronae were typically depicted in triune form, but not in the way some modern Pagans conceptualize the Triple Goddess. These were the Mothers – granters of abundance, fertility, and sovereignty – and their cultus was popular and widespread. While there are many examples of formal devotional shrines and temple stele dedicated to the Matronae and Matres across Europe (with the latter name being preferred in Celtic areas, and the former more common in Germanic territories), the archaeological record has also yielded examples of mass produced Matronae statuary crafted from terra-cotta and other inexpensive materials; it is likely therefore that these deities had also been honored in household shrines (Beck, 2009).

They were often depicted seated, and many featured them wearing distinctive headdresses or rounded bonnets which are believed to reflect the traditional dress of the Germanic Ubii tribe, along with crescent-shaped lunulae necklaces and centerpinned cloaks. Occasionally, the central figure of the three was depicted with their hair down, which is believed to indicate her unwed status. The Mothers held various objects in their laps all of which underscored their roles as granters of fertility and abundance. Some scholars believe that the triads of Goddesses bearing the name Matronae are somewhat different from those who are called Matres. The Matronae appear to be reflective of women who are more mature and hold a higher social authority, like the Roman matrons who are heads of households, and are depicted holding objects that convey abundance within the domestic sphere such as baskets of food, spindles, and bags of coins. The Matres, on the other hand, appear to be concerned more directly and literally with motherhood and child rearing, and are shown nursing infants, holding children, and folding diapers. (Garman, 2008).

These Goddesses are likely not the same figures in all depictions, as the iconography associated with them appears quite variable, and where there are inscriptions, we can observe that many have been given attributive bynames or epithets that describe the nature, origin, or function of the divinities. For example, Matronae often bear toponyms which connect them to a specific area, ostensibly the area from which they originated, that they serve to embody, and is directly under their care. The bynames have also been used to describe the Goddesses' connection with or authority over different animals, trees, and other natural phenomenon like springs and rivers. Ethnonyms were also used, honoring them as ancestresses of specific tribes, although it is unclear if the tribes were named after their deities or if the Goddesses were given the names of the tribes. Some Matronae are named by their functions, like the Nutrices who feed and care for children, while others are named for the attributes they embody, and still others appear to be tutelary divinities, perhaps hinting at local ancestral worship (Beck, 2009).

It is possible that a folk memory of the worship of these divine mothers persists in Southern Wales where a common appellation for the fairy folk is "Bendith y Mamau" – the Blessings of the Mothers (Hamp, 1999).

Matrona

In singular form, this Goddess was called Matrona, meaning "Divine Mother". This Gaulish deity was likely the personification of the river Marne in France which once bore her name; a Gallo-Roman sanctuary dedicated to Dea Matrona was erected in the 1st century CE near the source of the river at Bellesmes, although votive offerings have been found at this sanctuary which date from the Late Bronze through to the Roman period. As the Marne region is also the area where the distinctive La Tène art style developed in concert with other cultural manifestations that spread through the Continental Celtic and British areas, Koch posits that, "the Marne country had been the epicenter of the cult of the mother goddess called Matrona, that this cult had originally been linked to the depositional rituals in the river itself, and that it then spread from there – to Britain and the Rhine – with the dominant Marnian culture" (Koch, 2006, p. 1279). This is an important piece of information to consider as we explore roots of Rhiannon's divinity, as we will see.

Although it is uncertain, the cult of Matrona was likely associated with that of the Three Mothers, and references to her have been found in Gaulish and British dedications; her mythos has not survived, however. What is known is that Matrona had a child called Maponos ("Divine Son"), and that this dyad was widely revered by the continental Celts. The Romans came to associate Maponos with Apollo, the perpetual youth, and like his mother, his cultus spanned Northern Europe both in his syncretic and indigenous forms. Maponos was especially revered among Roman soldiers garrisoning Hadrian's Wall, and there is evidence of a concentration of his worship in the north of England, particularly in the area north-west of the Wall (Bromwich, 2006).

Epona

The Gallo-Brittonic Goddess Epona ("Divine Mare") is a unique figure as she is ostensibly the only Celtic deity to have been widely worshiped by the Romans without having been overlain with a Roman deity with similar characteristics and functions, as was the general Roman practice. Her myths have been lost to us, but we know her from devotional inscriptions and cult images found throughout the Roman Empire. In addition to Celtic Gaul, she appears to have been a very popular Goddess in

Britain, and we have found devotional images of the Goddess as far north as Hadrian's Wall. She is not considered to have been a pan-Celtic deity; it is rather more likely that her worship spread because she was particularly revered by the Roman cavalry, a large portion of which was made up of Celtic horsemen (Wood, 1997). Despite her soldier following, Epona does not seem to have had a directly martial function, unlike the equine Irish Goddess Macha, who is often discussed in relation to both Epona and Rhiannon.

In addition to formal temples and dedicatory stele, contemporary Roman writings tell us a bit more about the ways that Epona was honored. For example, in his immortal work *The Golden Ass*, Apuleius writes:

> [3.27] These thoughts were interrupted by my catching sight of a statue of the goddess Epona seated in a small shrine centrally placed, where a pillar supported the roof-beams in the middle of a stable. The statue had been devotedly garlanded with freshly picked roses.

Of her birth, we have this Roman account from the first century, CE:

> Fulvius Stellus hated women and used to consort with a mare and in due time the mare gave birth to a beautiful girl and they named her Epona. She is the goddess that is concerned with the protection of horses. (Plutarch, *Parallela Minora*, p.299)

Some scholars believe that Epona was a specialized Matrona figure (Gruffydd, 1953), set apart by iconography of which there are two main types. The "Side-saddle" type is more common throughout Gaul, and depicts Epona seated peacefully side-saddle on a still or gently moving horse; she is facing forward towards the viewer, while the horse is presented in side-view – typically, right-facing. The "Imperial" type is generally found outside of Gaul but within a Roman context, and shows the Goddess seated (or sometimes standing), and facing forward while flanked by two or four sideview horses; often they face towards the Goddess between them and eat from her hand or from a basket in her lap (Beck, 2009). Depictions of Epona sometimes show her accompanied by a foal whom she often feeds from a cornucopia or other vessel in much the same way the Matronae were often rendered with baskets of food or loaves of bread in their laps; however, unlike these other Divine Mothers, Epona is never shown with a human child.

She is sometimes depicted holding a key, which may point to Epona possessing a psychopomp aspect; that is, she acted to guide the souls of the departed to their rest in the Otherworld, and indeed, she is depicted on funerary stele as well. This perspective is in alignment with the theory that horses, in addition to being symbols of sovereignty in Celtic lands, were also seen as threshold guardians, and were able to cross the boundaries between this world and the next (Ross, 2001). We will explore both of these concepts later on in the text.

Primarily because of their shared equine associations, Rhiannon is generally accepted to be a Welsh reflex of Epona; the two are related but were likely not the same Goddess. That they both can be traced back to the Matronae, albeit by different paths, may be significant, as are the commonalities in some of their symbol sets. There is even one extant inscription where she is referred to in the plural, "Eponabus", in what appears to be a direct mirror of the Matronae (MacCulloch, 1911). Epona exhibits a fertility aspect as represented by the cornucopia or dish of food she sometimes carries, and she was often depicted holding a bag; the latter may be related to the magical bag Rhiannon gives to Pywll which can never be filled to capacity with food, unless a nobleman pushes it down with his feet.

Epona's relationship to sovereignty is also present on several levels. The most obvious is, of course, her status as the Divine Mare and all of the attendant connections to sovereignty that brings. Further, the unhurried pace of Rhiannon's horse when we first meet her in the First Branch appears to correspond with the calm and peaceful depictions of Epona's mount. Finally, in some dedicatory inscriptions, the Goddess is called "Epona Rigani" – the Divine Queen Mare (Koch, 2006). The epithet *Rigani*, meaning "queen", is clearly a connection etymologically to *Rīgantona and, by extension, to Rhiannon herself.

Modron and Mabon

Another thread that connects the Matronae to Rhiannon is Modron, the Welsh reflex of Matrona, whose name also simply means "Divine Mother." Likewise, Modron's son Mabon is a reflex of the divinity Maponus. This Divine Mother-Son dyad appears to be a recurring theme in several Celtic cultures. In addition to Gaulish inscriptions to Matrona and Maponus, and the tales of Modron and Mabon from Welsh narrative tradition, in Ireland we see the pattern manifest in the personages of Boand, who is a river Goddess like Matrona, and her son Oengus Mac ind Óc. His epithet, meaning "Young Son", is thought to have derived from the Old Irish *Maccan Oac, leading scholars to believe that he too is related to the same Proto-Celtic God as Maponus and Mabon (Hamp, 1999).

Modron is present both directly and indirectly in Welsh tradition, and the evolution of her story can be traced from early Welsh literature to Arthurian legend and through to later Christian hagiographies. Modron features anecdotally in the tale of her son Mabon that appears in the early Welsh story *Culhwch and Olwen,* which is also the earliest extant Arthurian prose tale. In *Culhwch*, we learn that, "Mabon son of Modron, was taken when three nights old from his mother. No one knows where he is, nor what state he's in, whether dead or alive" (Davies

2007, p.198). The eponymous Culhwch, with the help of his cousin King Arthur and his knights, must find Mabon as part of a Herculean series of quests that must be completed so that Culhwch can marry the woman he loves.

Mabon's imprisonment is further attested in Triad 52 of *Trioedd Ynys Prydein*, which records the following:

> Three Exalted Prisoners of the Island of Britain: Llŷr Half-Speech, and Mabon son of Modron, and Gwair son of Geirioedd. (Bromwich, 2006, p. 424)

After a long search, Mabon's whereabouts is discovered and he is freed from the tortures of his prison; he is then able to aid Culhwch in his quest to hunt down a giant boar named Twrch Trwyth. Mabon was the only huntsman in the world who could hunt with a dog so strong it needed a special collar and leash, while on a horse so fast it was as swift as an ocean wave – both of which were necessary to bring down the boar. Mabon is mentioned in several other early Arthurian tales as a member of his court, and is believed to have been integrated into the later Arthurian corpus in the guise of characters named Mabonagrain, Maboun, and Mabuz – all of whom also have story lines associated with imprisonment (Bromwich, 2006).

It is easy to see the parallels between the stories of Mabon and Pryderi: both sons are taken from their mothers as newborns; after their disappearances, no one knows if they are dead or alive, and if alive, their whereabouts are unknown; both Mabon and Pryderi are imprisoned in fortresses, and are punished or made to suffer; they are both hunters and are seen pursuing magical or Otherworldly boars; and they both have connections to dogs and affinities for horses. Celticist W.J. Gruffydd believed that Gwair, one of the three prisoners mentioned in Triad 52, is the same person as Gwri – the name that Teyrnon gave to the infant Pryderi; Gwair also appears as the prisoner mentioned in

The Spoils of Annwn (Gruffydd, 1953). These similarities do not prove that they are both the same deity, but certainly Mabon and Pryderi are reflexes of each other. "The suspicion is that, like Pryderi, these figures represent localized variants of the Magical Prisoner archetype, all of which perhaps stem back to Mabon ap Modron" (Parker, 2005).

There is a theory that the word *Mabinogi* translates as "Myths Pertaining to Mabon or Maponos" (Hamp, 1999). Pryderi's connection with Mabon suggests the possibility that he was once the central figure of *Y Mabinogi*; indeed, he is the only character who appears in all Four Branches, even if only in a supporting role. We see Pryderi born in the First Branch; come into his manhood as a warrior in the Second Branch; inherit land and title, but share rule of his lands with Manawydan and Rhiannon in the Third Branch; and then finally, fully in his sovereign power in the Fourth Branch, we see Pryderi lose his life to Gwydion in single combat. These are incredibly evocative slivers of what appears to have been a rich heroic cycle that is now lost to us, save for these tantalizing glimpses.

Returning now to Modron, she is mentioned again in Triad 70 of *Trioedd Ynys Prydein*, which enumerates the Three Fair Womb-Burdens of the Island of Britain; the second of which is:

Owain, son of Urien and Morfudd his sister who were carried together in the womb of Modron, daughter of Afallach. (Bromwich, 2006, pg. 449)

The father of the twins mentioned in the above triad is Urien Rheged, a 6th-century semi-historic warrior-king who ruled the early Northern British kingdom of Rheged; the area today is part of Scotland, but during Urien's reign, it was culturally Brythonic like the region which ultimately became Wales. A story preserved in Peniarth Ms. 147 tells how in Llanferran all of the dogs of the countryside kept gathering on the banks of a river which came to be called "The Ford of Barking" because of the din they raised. No one except Urien was brave enough to investigate this strange phenomenon, and when he arrived at the ford, all he saw was a woman washing in the water. The barking suddenly ended, and Urien, "seized the woman and had his will of her" (Bromwich, 2006, pg. 449). When he was done, she blessed him and revealed to him that she was the daughter of the King of Annwn, and that she had been fated to wash in the river until she was delivered of a son by a Christian man. She implored him to return at the end of the year so that she could give to him their son. He does so, and finds that he has sired both a son and a daughter: Owain, who was a famous Welsh hero, and Morfudd, who was renowned for the devoted love she shared with her husband.

There are several points here to note. The washer woman is not named in this story, but in almost every other sense the tale is identical in detail to Triad 70, allowing us to conclude that she is Modron. She identifies herself as the daughter of the King of Annwn, whose name is Afallach in Triad 70. Afallach is the son of Beli Mawr, a British solar deity married to Dôn, the ostensibly divine ancestress of a lineage of divinities called the Children of Dôn, which included Arianrhod, Gwydion, and Gilfaethwy, whom we know from the Fourth Branch of *Y Mabinogi*. It appears to have been common for British ruling families of Urien's time to claim lineage from divine or historically significant ancestors. It is meaningful therefore to consider that the family of the historical Urien Rheged claimed descent from Afallach, a fact that exists independently of Triad 70 (Koch, 2006).

The name Afallach means *"Place of Apples"*, and is one of several pieces of lore which connected Modron's father to Ynys Afallon, the Otherworldly Island of Apples, also called Avalon. Because of this we can confidently say that at the very least Modron would have been recognized by the contemporary medieval audience as a fairy woman. Her connection to Avalon goes even deeper. In later Arthurian tales, King Uriens of the North is married to Arthur's sister, and she bears him a son whose name, depending on the provenance of the tale, is given either as Owain or Yvaine – both great Arthurian heroes. And what is the name of Urien's wife, who is also Owain's mother, and Arthur's sister? Morgan le Fay – a powerful healer and wielder of magic, who also appears to be a reflex of the Goddess Modron. And while their names are not cognate, as Morgan is an Old Welsh name meaning *"Sea-born"*, both Morgan and Modron are powerful figures with strong water associations (Bromwich, 2006).

Another female figure associated with water is represented by the international folk motif known as the Washer at the Ford; this motif has iterations present both in narrative tradition as well as the folk beliefs of almost every Celtic culture. It typically manifests as a Goddess or Otherworldly woman washing the bloody clothing or limbs of a warrior who is fated to die in battle. While this existent story of Urien doesn't have the death omen component, and seems to rather be about the granting of Sovereignty through sexual congress with a Goddess (which often occurs at liminal places like river banks, and at liminal times like dusk or Samhain), there is a very similar tale from Irish tradition that incorporates both themes (Bromwich, 2006). In *The Second Battle of Moytura* (*Cath Maige Tured*), it is close to All Hallow's or Samhain when the Dagda – who is the High King of the Tuatha Dé Danann – meets up with the Mórrígan at an appointed place they arranged a year and a day earlier. Her hair is wild and she is standing over a river with one foot on one bank and one foot on the other. The two of them speak and then unite as lovers, and the place where they were was henceforth called "The Bed of the Couple." Afterwards, the Mórrígan tells the Dagda details of the battle to come between his Tuatha De and the Fomorians, whom she pledges to fight against. In this way, she gives both prophecy and Sovereignty, for in mating with the Dagda, she has empowered the leader of the warring faction she has favored to win (Gray, 1983). We will discuss the Mórrígan in more detail later on in this chapter, and it is important to keep the mirror roles of Modron and the Mórrígan in mind.

The essence of Modron's own divinity is preserved in this tale in several ways. Her Otherworldly connections support the reverse euhemerism of divinities that is common in Celtic mythos. Her association with the river is a symbolic call-back to her continental reflex Matrona, who is a river Goddess and divine personification of the river Marne in France. Modron is best known as the mother of Mabon, the Divine Youth or Divine Son, and it is thought that Owain and Morfudd are his half-siblings by a different father. On the other hand, it is intriguing to consider that a potential etymological root for the name Owain is the Welsh word *eoghunn,* which means "youth." Further, Morfudd's name is potentially derived from the Welsh *morwyn,* which means "maiden." Finally, Modron is mentioned in the poem *Cad Goddeu,* "The Battle of the Trees" from *Llyfr Taliesin,* and in it she is paired with someone named Euron. Koch posits that this is a scribal error, and that the redactor meant to write "Gwron", which itself is derived from *Uironos,* which means "divine man, husband, hero" – a possible etymological root for Urien (Koch, 2006). Perhaps, then, Owain is a reflex of Mabon instead of being his half-brother, and the rest of his kin represent a primal and sacred family group: Divine Mother is married to the Divine Man, and she gives birth to the Youth and the Maiden. If such a Divine Family did once exist, their mythos – like that of Matrona and Maponus – has been lost to us.

An intriguing point of information: the archaeological record in the areas along and to the north-west of Hadrian's Wall is rich with artifactual evidence of a strong devotional cultus to Maponus; this north-western area is believed to be the location of Rheged, the Brythonic kingdom ruled by the historical King Urien and his son Owain, after him. The historic Taliesin, considered the greatest of the Early Welsh poets, was a contemporary of Urien and the king was believed to be his patron. The bard wrote praise-poems in honor of Urien and Owain, and Bromwich suggests that some of the poetry in *Llyfr Taliesin* alludes to the name Mabon being used as a pseudonym for Owain. She also points out that during this time period, both in Ireland and in Wales, the attribution of a divine birth for an important historical personage is common, and that it would only serve to further elevate the status of Urien and Owain for the father to have mated with the local sovereignty Goddess, and for the son to be the semi-divine fruit of that union (Bromwich, 2006).

It is quite possible that the story of Modron does not end here. There are multiple sites, churches, and towns in Wales and Cornwall dedicated to, or named for, a saint (or possibly, multiple saints) whose name is variably given as Madron, Madrun, Maderne, and Materiana. In all cases, these names are linked etymologically to Modron and Matrona, and the sites themselves may once have been places where the cultus of the Goddess Modron was strong.

Hagiographic information about St. Modrun tells us she was the granddaughter of Vortigern (the famous, semi-historical 5th century British king), and that her husband and three children were all also saints; like Modron, she had two sons and a daughter. One of the key elements of her story focuses on her fleeing Wales with her youngest son after the battle that killed Vortigern and her husband, the chieftain Ynyr Gwent, before finally settling in Cornwall. (Vermaat, 1999). Madron Well in Cornwall is especially renowned as healing well for children; its waters also had the property of being cool and refreshing for those who are true, while becoming scalding hot at the touch of a traitor (Dunbar, 1905).

It is said that she and her handmaid St. Annun founded a church, which would later be dedicated to them, based on a directive they both received in separate dreams while on pilgrimage to Ynys Elli (Bardsey Island). (Vermaat, 1999) This is an interesting piece of lore, as Ynys Enlli is a potential real-world location for Ynys Afallon, an island of the Otherworld; both islands have strong associations with apples, with the dead, and are places where religious communities were established. As we have seen, Welsh lore states that Afallach is the king of Ynys Afallon – and Modron is his daughter. The feast days of St. Modrun are given as April 9 and October 19.

The Mórrígan

The Mórrígan is a threefold Irish Goddess, whose name, like that of Rhiannon, means "Great Queen" and can also be traced back to the Gallo-Britt onic Goddess *Rigantona. The Mórrígan is known primarily as a Goddess associated with batt le and prophecy, and as her name suggests, she also embodies the Sovereignty of the land. Like Rhiannon, the Mórrígan chooses her mate of her own accord, and as a Sovereignty Goddess, she has the power to grant and rescind kingship over the land (Beck, 2009).

She is made up of a collective of three sisters, and while there are variations on the Goddesses who comprise the Mórrígan, and their areas of divine influence overlap with each other, the most well-known grouping is made up of Mórrigu ("Great Queen") who is primarily concerned with battle, fate, and magic; Babd ("Battle Crow") who often appears as the Washer at the Ford, and who incites warriors to battle; and Macha ("Of the Plain") who is a granter of Sovereignty, a bringer of fertility, and a fierce warrior deity. Of these, it is Macha who holds the most resonance with Rhiannon, as she too possesses equine characteristics.

The Mórrígan is very strongly associated with crows and ravens, and is known to assume their forms. Rhiannon, too, has black birds associated with her, and while their species is never directly identified, the Adar Rhiannon are renowned for the beauty of their song, such that they can lull the living to sleep and bring the dead back to life. Crows are not exactly known for the sweetness of their song, so there appears to be a departure in attendant symbolism. As carrion birds, crows are often found on battlefields, a further reflection of the Mórrígan's martial aspect; this is another difference from Rhiannon, whose extant mythos does not reflect any connection to war, save for the sending of her birds to soothe the souls of those seven warriors who survived the war with Ireland fought in the Second Branch of *Y Mabinogi*.

Interestingly, although Epona was widely worshiped in the Roman military, and was especially revered by the cavalry, she herself is never depicted with any trappings of war; rather, she is almost universally shown seated serenely on a horse with a very calm and peaceful stance, and the majority of the symbols with which she is depicted underscore her connection to fertility and abundance. It is here, however, that the aspect of Epona as a psychopomp may forge a connection between her and the Mórrígan. We shall discuss the symbolism of the horse in detail in chapter five, but for now it is enough to say that it is a potent symbol of Sovereignty as well as a threshold guardian. The liminal nature of the horse therefore makes it a perfect ally to a Goddess that gathers the souls of the war dead to bring to the Otherworld. Perhaps Epona represents a gently aspected psychopomp; as a reflection of her association with the Matronae, she is a comfort to the dying, while the Mórrígan is an inciter, whipping up a battle fury that embraces war as an honorable death.

Differences aside, it is of great importance to note that unlike Rhiannon and other figures from Welsh legends, the Mórrígan and other prominent figures are specifically identified as divinities in early Irish literature. For example, in *The Metrical Dindshenchas*, which was written down during the 11th century, but which is believed to have existed in oral tradition since at least the 5th or 6th century (Westrop, 1899), we have the following:

ben in Dagda,
ba samla día sóach.
...in Mórrígan mórda,
ba slóg-dírmach sámda.
Metrical Dindshenchas: Odras
the wife of the Dagda
a phantom was the shapeshifting goddess
...the mighty Morrigan
whose ease is trooping hosts
(Translation by Morgan Daimler)

That the Gods are still identified as such in early literary works and are not simply Otherworldly figures is significant; it is likely the result of Ireland, unlike Britain, remaining free of Roman annexation, its attendant early Christianization, and the subsequent societal collapse and waves of invasion that resulted after Roman withdrawal from the British Isles 400 years later. The Irish therefore held on to their Pagan beliefs and social structures longer than the Celts of Britain and the continent, and began to write them down sooner. The happy consequence of this is that of all the Celtic cultures, the Irish possess the largest corpus of myth and lore; and while all of the Celts possessed distinct, yet related cultures, it is possible to look for parallels both in story and with divinities to help fill in some (very strongly-qualified) blanks in the Brythonic traditions, especially when there are also similarities in Gallic cultures.

Macha

Although she is one of the three sisters who make up the tripartite Goddess Mórrígan, a separate consideration of Macha reveals some evocative connections with Rhiannon specifically and perhaps reveals some of the root Indo-European religious constructs surrounding the sacred function of the Horse Goddess in general. There are several stories in Irish lore about Macha, although it is unclear if these are all the same person, or if, indeed, they are all divinities. The most famous story of Macha comes from the *Noinden Ulad* (*The Debility of the Ulstermen*).

In this tale, Macha is married to an Ulsterman named Crundchu mac Agnomain, and her presence in his life brings him abundance and wealth. She becomes pregnant by him, and though she is close to her term, he tells her that he is going to attend the great assembly of the Ulstermen. She implores him not to go, saying that if he were to speak of her at the assembly, their union would be ended. He promises to keep silent about her, and leaves to attend the festival. He is unable to keep his word, however, and boasts to all assembled that his wife could run faster than the king's pair of champion horses.

The king has Crundchu imprisoned, and sends his men to bring Macha to the assembly to prove her husband's boast by racing his horses. She asks for a delay because she is about to give birth, but the king refuses and threatens to kill Crundchu on the spot if she will not race. Macha appeals to the crowd for their help, but her plea for mercy is once more rejected, so she tells the king to bring up his horses, and the race begins. She easily outruns them both, and with a cry of pain, gives birth to twins at the finish line before the horses even arrive. The place of the assembly was from then on called Emain Macha – the Twins of Macha. Those who heard her cry of pain themselves became overcome with the pains of a birthing woman and so she lays her curse on them:

From this hour the ignominy that you have inflicted upon me will redound to the shame of each one of you. When a time of oppression falls upon you, each one of you who dwells in this province will be overcome with weakness, as the weakness of a woman in childbirth, and this will remain upon you for five days and four nights; to the ninth generation it shall be so. (Hull, 1989, pg. 100)

This curse has terrible repercussions during the *Táin Bó Cuailnge* (*Catt le Raid of Cooley*), as it delays the Ulstermen from entering the battle.

The king in this tale of Macha is the famous Conchobar, who was so highly regarded by his people that he was given the *droit du seigneur* to sleep with a bride before her wedding night and also to have the right to sleep with the wife of whoever was providing hospitality to him. On one such occasion, he demanded this right from a woman named Dechtire, whom he did not recognize as his sister at the time; she too asked for a delay as she was in labor – which Conchobar granted. Dechtire, nevertheless, gave birth to a child that looked like Conchobar – a child who would grow to be the great hero Cú Chulainn. At the moment of his birth, a mare in the household gave birth to two foals, and these were gifted to the boy; they would later pull his chariot in battle, and one of them was called Liath Macha, or "Grey of Macha" (Hull, 1989).

There are several parallels between the stories of Macha and Rhiannon. Both are forced to take on the role of a horse; Macha, by racing horses, and Rhiannon by offering to carry visitors on her back from where she sat on a mounting block. Both of them give birth to twins of a sort. Rhiannon doesn't directly do so; her giving birth to Pryderi is paired with the foaling of Teyrnon's white mare which is, in many ways, her avatar. Both Irish and Welsh myth feature the gifting of the horse born at the same time as them to a hero, and even though Cú Chulainn is not the child of Macha, that one of his "twinned" horses nevertheless bears her name is worthy of note.

Dexter believes that the twinning is an important element of these tales, as they harken back to the Indo-European mythos of the divine twins, sometimes manifesting as a divine horseman and his brother, or as twin horsemen, or else as a human and a horse birthed together from the same mother, who is most certainly a Goddess. She also posits that the mytheme of a hippomorphic Goddess who is punished after childbirth is really a memory of the Indo-European horse sacrifice. This rite was not undertaken lightly; horses were too valuable and of high status to be sacrificed with any regularity. Instead, the intention of the ritual was to renew the power of the kingship, and most often included sexual congress between the king and a mare, although some Indian iterations involved the queen and a stallion (Dexter, 1990).

Gerald Cambrensis, also known as Gerald of Wales, relates an Irish version of this horse sacrifice in his 1187 work *Topographia Hiberniae*, which is significant not only because this was a kingship ritual granting Sovereignty, but because it also takes place in Ulster – whose royal seat is none other than Emain Macha:

When the whole people of that land has been gathered together in one place, a white mare is brought forward into the middle of the assembly. He who is to be inaugurated, not as a chief, but as an outlaw, has bestial intercourse with her before all, professing himself to be a beast also. The mare is then killed immediately, cut up in pieces, and boiled in water. A bath is prepared for the man afterwards in the same water. He sits in the bath surrounded by all his people, and all, he and they, eat of the meat of the mare which is brought to them. He quaffs and drinks of the broth in which he is bathed, not in any cup, or using his hand, but just dipping his mouth into it round about him. When this unrighteous rite has been carried out, his kingship and dominion have been conferred. (O'Meara 1951, 1982, p. 109 – 110)

Dexter believes that the mythological memory of this act is present wherever there are Horse Goddesses, especially when their fecundity is signaled by the birthing of twins. Because these are Goddesses, they cannot die as a sacrificed animal would, and so they are shown mythically to undergo a punishment instead (Dexter, 1990). We will look further at the symbolism of the horse in chapter five.

International Folk Motifs

If we look at the story of Rhiannon from a purely literary perspective, we find that she serves as a clear example of several international folk motifs, a fact that may be of some consequence when it comes to determining the status of her potential or former divinity. An international folk motif is a narrative element that can be found both across stories and across cultures. These are identifiable patterns which appear in international popular tales that may not have any direct relationship to each other, but which nonetheless employ similar identifiable plot devices. The Stith Thompson *Motif-Index of Folk-Literature* is a six-volume collection of these motifs, originally gathered primarily from European stories, which have been classified and cataloged numerically using the Aarne-Thompson tale type index. This, and its modern expansions, is an invaluable tool for the study of folklore and mythology, and it is especially useful for comparative literary analysis.

Although the entirety of the First and Third Branches, and Indeed, the whole of *Y Mabinogi*, feature many folk motifs, there are three which apply specifically to Rhiannon and her story. On the outset, she represents a variant of the Fairy Bride motif, which has very specific manifestations in Wales especially (Wood, 1992); she is an Otherworldly maiden who falls in love with and marries a mortal. She does not quite fit into his world, however, and through careless action, he loses her and she returns to the Otherworld. In Rhiannon's case, Pwyll loses her more than once. The first time is when he promises Gwawl anything he desires, and Gwawl asks for Rhiannon's hand; she must remain in the Otherworld for a year without Pwyll until she can set a new feast and Pwyll can convince Gwawl to give her up again. The second time is after the disappearance of their newborn son, which sets the stage for the next motif – that of the Calumniated Wife.

The Calumniated or Falsely Accused Wife is a very well attested international folk motif, with many sub-motifs, several of which are present in Rhiannon's story. She is an innocent woman who has been accused of killing her newborn child – worse, the First Branch infers that she is accused of having devoured the child, and puppy bones are planted as evidence of what she has done (Jackson, 1961). That these story elements appear in other tales as well is somewhat shocking, but Hemming believes that while Rhiannon's tale is very likely to have been influenced by other tales with the same motifs, it on its own cannot fully explain her story, especially taking the horse elements into account (Hemming, 1998).

Lastly, we have the motif of Sovereignty personified, which is a prominent motif in Celtic legend that takes many forms over the course of the literary traditions of Ireland, Wales, and Brittany. In the case of the Four Branches, this motif is symbolic and subtextual, and is something we will be examining at length in Chapter five.

When we consider the existence of international folk motifs, we need to ask why it is that popular tales – tales which likely have their origins in oral tradition – feature narrative elements that can be found in different cultures separated both in space and in time. There are several explanations for why this might be so. The first takes into account the origins of the motif, and posits that 1) either the motif in question reflects a human experience so common across cultures that the motif is *polygenic*, that is, it arose independently in different areas, or 2) the motif originally arose as part of the story tradition of an ancestral culture, and as people and ideas migrated to different places, they took the stories with them; these stories then evolved to reflect the changes in culture over time, but still held on to some of the core narrative elements.

In addition to origin, we must also consider that the method of a tale's diffusion will also impact the story. In the case of horizontal transmission, neighboring areas and cultures influence each other, sharing stories and infusing them with details and narrative shifts that ripple outward and come to reflect local cultural relevance. Vertical transmission, on the other hand, sees one generation passing its stories down to the next generation, and the changes in the tale reflect the shifts in the social, political, and cultural landscapes within which it comes to dwell as it descends down the lineage of tradition. These can both happen simultaneously and therefore may be one way to account for the spread of international folk motifs.

The Big Picture

These considerations around transmission may be what we can use to ultimately account for Rhiannon's subtextual divinity – whether from a literary or mythological perspective. She is clearly connected to the Goddess Epona, who is believed to be a specialized reflex of Matrona – a Gallo-Roman Divine Mother Goddess who may be a singular iteration of the typically triform Dea Matronae, believed to be of Continental Celtic origin. Matrona has a Welsh cognate in Modron, the Divine Mother, whose Divine Son Mabon is a cognate of Matrona's son Maponus. This mother/son dyad is considered to be the template for the story of Rhiannon and Pryderi, as they both share in the mytheme of the stolen and imprisoned child. Another potential pathway of connection exists when we look at Rhiannon's connection to *Rigantona. There is, of course, an etymological link, as their names both mean "Divine Queen", a fact which also connects them to the Irish Mórrígan, who is directly attested to be divine in Irish mythos. It may also be of note that one of Epona's Roman appellations is Epona Regina, meaning "Divine Horse Queen", underscoring her connection to Sovereignty (Hemming, 1998).

With all of these considerations we can comfortably say that Rhiannon is a Goddess, although her divinity is subsumed from an earlier form than that which was eventually set into writing during the medieval period in Wales. While shifts in culture, evolution of language, and influences from foreign lands shaped the Divine Queen of the Celtic Britons into the being that we know as Rhiannon, the fierceness of her spirit, the enormity of her heart, and the strength of her noble bearing persist. No matter what name we call her, no matter how much of her story we have remembered or have forgotten she is the Divine Mother, the Sovereign Mare, and the Great Queen. And she has much yet to teach us.

Chapter Five

Aspects of the Divine Queen

Now that we have recounted her stories and established the potential lineage of her divinity, let us look to the mythic and cultural roles played by Rhiannon, and examine the areas of her concern.

Lady of the Otherworld

Rhiannon has strong associations with the Otherworld, both directly through her person, and indirectly through the animals, items, and events connected with her. When we first see her in the First Branch, she rides out from the Gorsedd Arberth – a wondrous mound that promises to any noble who sits upon it either that they will be witness to a wonder, or else receive many wounds and blows. In Celtic lore, mounds and fairy hills are considered liminal places which serve as portals to the Otherworld, and are often portrayed in legend as places where the Fair Folk would come to feast, or where humans could pass through into the Otherworld for what they thought was a night, only to return to find that a hundred years had passed, or where someone could dare to sleep under the hill with the fate of either returning with the poetic gift or else becoming consumed by madness.

These beliefs may perhaps be a reflection of the Neolithic indigenous British practice of burying their dead in artificial earthworks, such as megalithic long barrows and single chambered dolmen tombs which were covered with earth to form hill-shaped tumuli. It was to these burial places that the ancient Britons would bring offerings of food to their beloved dead, and it is possible that they practiced a form of ancestor worship. It is a testimony to their belief in an afterlife that many of these burial mounds had seasonal solar (and occasionally lunar) alignments, where on certain astronomically significant days, such as the Winter Solstice, a beam of light would enter the dark earthen chamber to illuminate a carving on the back wall or central upright stone, or else serve as a visual metaphor of the revitalizing energies of the sun piercing the darkness of the tomb to symbolically implant new life.

It's difficult to say with any certainty that there is a direct connection, but it is possible that the folkloric associations of hills and mounds with the Otherworld remained even after the names and cultures of those who may have been interred within them had fallen away. Perhaps a vague sense of the original function and purpose of these mounds may have lingered to inform the belief that transformed these ancestral burials into magical portals into the Otherworld; indeed, there appears to be a hint of cultural memory which underscores the folk beliefs around fairy mounds, some of which persist into the present day. It is likely, then, that the contemporary medieval audience would have understood the significance of this magical hill, and would immediately have seen Rhiannon's emergence from the mound as a clear proclamation of her Otherworldly origins. Even if this were not the case, there are other signs that Rhiannon is no ordinary human woman, and they are immediately apparent.

When we first meet her, Rhiannon is described as, "wearing a shining golden garment of brocaded silk" (Davies, 2007, pg. 8). Earlier in the First Branch, the exact same description is given to the clothing that Pwyll is dressed in when he takes on the likeness of Arawn, king of Annwn; Arawn's unnamed wife and Queen is also garbed in this fashion. When Gwawl, Rhiannon's rejected suitor, comes to the wedding feast of Rhiannon and Pwyll, he too is dressed in silk brocade. Later on in the story, Rhiannon's infant son is found swaddled in a mantle of brocaded silk. Very few characters are described in the First Branch as wearing what, in the middle ages, would have been an incredibly expensive and high-status fabric, and while this detail may have been included in the story to simply mark the noble stature of these figures, that the garb appears to have been reserved only for those characters who are associated with Annwn is potentially significant, and may serve as another marker for the Otherworld.

Another potent characteristic of the Otherworld is that where its influence is present, the normal rules governing the passage of time and the measure of space do not apply; the unchanging and unhurried gait of Rhiannon's white horse, which nevertheless could not be overtaken no matter how long or how hard another rider pursued her, is a clear example of this kind of distortion and is probably the defining experience of our introduction to her. It is likely that the magical speed of her horse, or perhaps its ability to warp the passage of time in a way that prevented anyone from catching up with them, would have marked Rhiannon as an Otherworldly figure to the contemporary medieval audience. This phenomenon is also present in the Second Branch where the British survivors of a terrible war in Ireland spend almost 80 years feasting in a grand hall on what appears to be an Otherworldly island, where they never aged, and dwelt with joy and without memory for the tragedies they had endured – even feasting and communing with the head of their dead king.

In addition to the Otherworld's ability to distort time, it also had a tendency to disregard the limitations of distance and volume with its magic. Later in the First Branch, Rhiannon gives Pwyll a small bag that would never run out of room no matter how much food was placed in it until a wealthy and landed nobleman trampled down the food with both feet, and declared, "Enough has been put in here" (Davies 2007, pg. 14). And again, in the Second Branch, the Adar Rhiannon appear to the feasting war survivors, and sing to them a song so beautiful that every other song in the world was unlovely in comparison. The birds appeared to be across the water and very far away from the island, but simultaneously, they felt and sounded as if they were in the feasting hall with the men.

Perhaps related to the Otherworld's ability to warp physical limitations, or else as a byproduct of the reverse euhemerization process examined earlier, Rhiannon is depicted as having superhuman strength when she accepts Pwyll's unjust and perhaps bizarre judgment that she be punished for the destruction of their infant son; she was required to sit on a horse block outside of Arberth for seven years, telling all comers the story of her alleged crime, and offering to carry them into the court on her back. While the First Branch is quick to say that very few visitors accepted her offer, the subtext is that some did and no mention is made of her inability to do so. Further, Rhiannon's nurses concocted an apparently believable story that their queen, who had just given birth, was able to fight all seven of them off as they tried to prevent her from destroying her son, and finally, in the Third Branch, Rhiannon is said to have carried asses' collars on her shoulders as she labored in the Otherworld. This is no fragile human woman, clearly, and her strength seems to mirror the larger-than-life appearance of Bendigeidfran in the Second Branch; indeed, the king of the Island of the Mighty was described as a giant for whom no house was ever built that could contain him.

Goddess of Sovereignty

The quest for Sovereignty is a well-known international folk motif which is an important element in many tales from Ireland and Wales, and which also plays an important thematic role in Arthurian legends. This popular narrative theme features a candidate for kingship entering into a *hieros gamos*, or sacred marriage, with a representative of the land. Sometimes the Sovereignty was embodied by a tutelary Goddess who appeared to the would-be-king in the form of a woman, while other traditions utilized symbolic or totemic representations of Sovereignty as seen with the mating of Irish kings with a white mare, which was later sacrificed and eaten.

The Sovereignty figure is quite overt in Irish lore, often appearing as a hideous hag who tests potential kings; when they mate, she is transformed into a beautiful maiden, and the land is likewise transformed by the energies of the new king. In Welsh mythos, the figure of Sovereignty shifts to be more subtextual, while in later Arthurian legend the quest for Sovereignty becomes purely symbolic in some tales – as with the quest for the cauldron or grail – and in other stories, shifts from a Goddess granting a king rulership over the land, to a man in authority granting a woman sovereignty over herself.

Seeming to bridge these two manifestations of tradition – the direct identification of Sovereignty in Irish lore and the indirect symbolism of the cauldron or grail quests in Arthurian legends – the Welsh materials require that we rely upon an analysis of subtext to find the representations of Sovereignty in the Four Branches and their associated tales; it is worth wondering if these thematic undercurrents would have been obvious to the medieval Welsh audience of these stories.

There are several archetypal parameters defining the personification and function of Sovereignty:

1. She is a representative of the land, often a tutelary deity or spirit.
2. She is encountered at liminal places and times – such as bodies of water, land boundaries, areas associated with the Otherworld, dusk and dawn, holy days.
3. She presents challenges to the would-be king, determining his worth and initiating sexual contact.
4. She enters into a *hieros gamos,* or sacred marriage, with a kingly candidate, sealing the fortunes of the land to the

health and actions of the man she has, through this act, made king.

5. She has the power to grant, and rescind if circumstances require, sovereignty over the land.

6. She has the ability to change shape, often as a reflection of the status of the land in relationship to the righteous king.

Let us briefly examine these points as they concern Rhiannon's marriages.

Rhiannon and Pwyll – Sovereignty in the First Branch.

1. Rhiannon is not directly stated to be a representative of the land, although she is coded with Otherworldly associations through her magical white horse, her fine garb, her greater-than-human strength, and magical objects like the bag she gives to Pwyll.

2. She rides out from the Otherworld on a white horse, itself a symbol of Sovereignty and a threshold guardian, and she is associated with a magical mound.

3. Rhiannon tests Pwyll by remaining out of his reach as they ride until he asks for her to stop. Pwyll's loss of Rhiannon to her former suitor, and then (with her assistance) clever retrieval of her a year later is also a test – one he passes – as he defeats his rival and frees Rhiannon of the obligation to wed him. Pwyll's worth was initially tested by the powers of the Otherworld when he faced off Arawn's enemy at an Annuvian ford, possibly a re-enactment of the seasonal sovereignty motif of one king overcoming the other, and being chosen by Sovereignty to rule over the next season or seasonal cycle.

4. Pwyll finally weds Rhiannon in her father's Otherworldly court, before they return to his own land. While Pwyll

was already a Pendefig Dyfed (a prince), and obtained a second name Pen Annwn after his year in Annwn, it is possible that his marriage to Rhiannon granted him true authority over his lands.

5. Rhiannon rejects Gwawl, and choses to marry Pwyll instead – an act that could be seen as Sovereignty choosing her mate based on his worthiness. She also gifts Pwyll with a magical bag that cannot be filled in order to assist him in defeating Gwawl. This bag is a possible symbolic reflex of a womb in the same way a cauldron can be, therefore representing the underlying sexual nature of the granting of Sovereignty.

6. When Rhiannon is unpartnered or in a position of imbalance with her partner, she is seen either riding a horse, or taking on an equine aspect by inviting others to ride her like a horse. She is also seen as a double of Teyrnon's magnificent white mare, as both of them give birth on the same day, and both lose their offspring almost immediately after birth.

Rhiannon's first husband was Pywll, whose name means "discretion", "good sense", or "wisdom" (McKenna, 1980). He was Pendefig Dyfed, the prince of Dyfed, a kingdom in South Wales. The First Branch of *Y Mabinogi* is named for him, and the first act of the tale demonstrates what could only be considered an enormous *lack* of "good sense" on his part. While out hunting with his dogs one day, Pwyll comes upon a stag that had been felled by a pack of white dogs with red ears; he calls those dogs off and sets his own animals to feast upon the deer. Unfortunately for him, the strange dogs belong to Arawn, the king of Annwn, and Pwyll's actions cause great insult to the Otherworldly king, who soon arrives in search of his dogs.

After realizing he was in the wrong because, as a crowned king, Arawn outranked him and therefore had greater claim to the deer, Pwyll sought to make amends with him. The two agree upon an arrangement whereby they would switch places with each other for a year with each taking on the visage of the other and ruling their respective kingdoms in their stead. At the end of the year, Pwyll – still in the guise of Arawn – would go to a ford in Annwn where he would engage an enemy of Arawn in one-on-one battle. Arawn and Hafgan, a neighboring Annuvian king, had battled each other annually in this place, with one never able to get the better of the other. Arawn instructs Pwyll to strike only one blow with his sword, no matter how Hafgan would plead to be finished off by another; it is only through dealing the singular blow that Hafgan could be defeated.

The details of the battle evoke the ancient motif of the eternal struggle between the light and the dark, or between summer and winter. Arawn, whose name is thought to mean "He of the Sown Field" forever battles Hafgan, whose name means "Summer Light" or "Summer Song", the king of the lands adjacent to his in Annwn. The battle taking place at a river ford is significant as it is one of those magical liminal places we see so often in Celtic myth – places that are boundaries between the worlds. Too, when we see Pwyll exchange places with the Lord of Annwn, the two meet at a boundary between the two lands, and share a wife, although Pwyll chooses not to consummate with her. It may be that these elements are remnants of sovereignty rites where the Lord of the Winter supplants the Lord of the Summer, only to give way again in six months' time – each taking turns as mate to the Goddess of the Land.

It is also possible that Pwyll's keeping chaste with Arawn's wife may have been a test. Described in the text as an exquisitely beautiful woman next to whom Pwyll slept for the entirety of a year – a woman who believed that Pwyll was in fact Arawn, her husband – he nevertheless did not engage with her sexually, even after Arawn had explicitly told Pwyll he could lie with her. This loyalty surprised Arawn greatly and further endeared the

Prince of Dyfed to him. This test of purity is mirrored in the late 14th-century tale, *Sir Gawain and the Green Knight*, which also contains a coded Sovereignty figure.

Although the narrative is fairly clear that Pryderi's father is Pwyll, in a mythic context he has more than one father – all of whom appear to have complex and symbolically overlapping relationships with Rhiannon. Ostensibly a mortal prince at the onset, Pwyll's relationship with Arawn and his victory over Hafgan in the Otherworld shifted his domain somewhat, rendering him a Lord of Annwn – Pwyll Pen Annwn. It is after he receives this name and forges an alliance with Arawn that Rhiannon rides forth from the Otherworld, seeking to marry him. The strong connection that Pwyll has with the Otherworld appears to underscore this union; even their marriage takes place in an Otherworldly realm, at the court of Rhiannon's father.

Stolen from Rhiannon on the night he was born, the infant Pryderi was inexplicably found, swaddled in golden brocade, on the threshold of the house of Teyrnon Twryf Liant, a nobleman who was a vassal of Pwyll. Teyrnon possessed a beautiful mare who gave birth every May Eve, and whose foal always disappeared that very night. It is not difficult to see the parallels between Teyrnon's horses and the circumstances of Pryderi's birth, and there are several other connections of note.

Rhiannon and Teyrnon's horse are essentially doubles for each other. They both give birth and lose their offspring on the same day – and it is May Eve, a portal day that blurs the boundaries between this world and the Otherworld. Although the horse has apparently lost several foals in the past, it is on this particular night that Teyrnon keeps vigil, and because of this, he is able to rescue both the newborn horse and the infant Pryderi – who is discovered in yet another liminal place: the threshold of the house. Teyrnon brings the child to his unnamed wife, and together they decide to raise the boy as their own.

The child grew preternaturally quickly, reaching a height and displaying a skill level of children twice his age. He possessed an incredible affinity for horses, and when he reached four years of age, although appearing and acting much older, Teyrnon's wife suggested that the boy be given the colt that had been born on the same night as he; in effect, the boy and the colt are mirrors of each other as well.

On the surface, the fosterage by Teyrnon of Rhiannon's missing son seems fairly straightforward. It was a common practice for members of nobility to foster their children in other courts as a way to forge bonds of friendship, to shore up alliances, and to share wealth between them. Aside from the supernatural intervention that brought the boy that he named Gwri Wallt Euryn ("Blooming Golden Hair") to his literal doorstep, this fosterage would have resonated as a cultural expectation for the contemporary Welsh audience. However, when we look a little deeper, there appears to be something else going on here, the explanation for which scholars have sought to resolve for a very long time (Koch, 2006).

To begin with, Teryrnon's very name is intriguing. Featuring the terminal deific "-on", which we've already seen in the names of Rhiannon, Modron, and Mabon, we are immediately alerted to the idea that Teyrnon is not an ordinary supporting character (Hamp, 1999). Ford gives Teyrnon Twryf Liant's full name to mean "Lord of the Tempestuous Sea" (Ford, 1982) His first name appears to be the Middle Welsh form of the Celtic name *Tigernonos, meaning "Divine or Great Lord" – a direct mirror of Rhiannon's "Divine or Great Queen" derivation from "*Rigantona" (Davies, 2006). While we have no direct proof of the existence of *Rigantona and *Tigernonos as early Celtic deities aside from their reconstructed names, it is difficult to consider it purely a coincidence that the names of Pryderi's birth mother and foster father are such perfect reflections of each other. This is what led influential early Celticists, Sir Edward

Anwyl and William John Gruffydd, to posit that Teyrnon, and not Pwyll, was Pryderi's father (Hutton, 2011). Gruffydd further developed the theory that the story of Pryderi's birth and childhood as depicted in the First Branch is a very garbled version of the original story which the medieval redactor struggled to reconstruct using fragments of the tale, which Gruffydd believed ultimately had its source in Irish mythos (Gruffydd, 1953).

While Gruffydd's ideas are fascinating, and the various pieces of information that he weaves together are worthy of study by scholars and Brythonic Pagans alike, current scholarship discounts most of his conclusions, in large part due to lack of supporting evidence. Modern scholar Patrick K. Ford finds it difficult to believe that the redactor of *Y Mabinogi* was writing down something they didn't understand; given the amount of time involved as well as the expense of the vellum used, Ford feels that what was retained – and the form in which it was preserved – was intentional and purposeful (Ford, 1981/1982).

Rhiannon and Manawydan – Sovereignty in the Third Branch.

1. Although Rhiannon is not directly stated to be a representative of the land, Pryderi offers his friend, Manawydan, rulership over the seven cantrefs he inherited from his father Pwyll as well as the hand of Rhiannon in marriage; the linking of the two may subtextually signify Rhiannon's role as a tutelary Goddess of Dyfed.

2. Manawydan's first encounter with Rhiannon was without a doubt, solidly Otherworldly. Both he and Pryderi were two of the seven survivors of the war in Ireland that was fought in the Second Branch, and they both experienced the Adar Rhiannon – the Otherworldly Birds of Rhiannon – sing for them while they were feasting at Harlech.

3. While perhaps not directly challenging Manawydan to test his worthiness, the now-widowed Rhiannon does meet with him at her son's suggestion, and apparently finds him worthy to be her mate as she chooses to marry him that very day.

4. Rhiannon and Manawydan sleep together after feasting, and he takes over administration and enjoyment of the seven cantrefs of Dyfed.

5. Pryderi maintains legal lordship, however, and travels to the court of Caswallon to give homage to the British king. When he returns, and sits upon the Gorsedd Arberth with his mother, wife, and Manawydan, the Otherworld intervenes and all of Dyfed is divested of people, human habitation, and domesticated animals. The land has reverted to a wild state, and has become a Wasteland of sorts. This may relate to the imbalance of rule both in Dyfed and in Britain as a whole: the ruler of Dyfed has given power to another, and the one who should be king of the Island of the Mighty has not taken up his throne. The Wasteland theme in later grail mythos is a reflection of the lame or wounded king, and something similar may be happening in Dyfed subtextually.

6. Manawydan's inaction around rescuing Pryderi caused his relationship with Sovereignty to be negatively impacted, and coupled with his failure to assert his right to the throne he may not have been considered the right candidate for the role he had undertaken. Manawydan earns the right to rule by correctly, and ethically, restoring Dyfed to its abundant form; in the end, his wisdom and patience wins the day in contrast to Pryderi's impetuous nature. When Rhiannon and Pryderi are restored to Dyfed, along with the people and animals that were previously gone, we see that Rhiannon had once again "shapechanged" while out of right relationship with her

husband: she was required to wear asses' collars after bailing hay. Rhiannon returns to him, no longer laboring like a work horse in the Otherworld.

Rhiannon's second husband is Manawydan fab Llŷr, the son of the Sea, who is brother to Bran and Branwen. We know very little about Llŷr, who is himself the son of the solar deity Beli Mawr, although the etymology of his name suggests that he was once a Brythonic sea deity. Although Manawydan's name is almost directly cognate to Manannán mac Lir, the Irish Sea God who dwells upon the namesake Island of Man, there is very little else that directly ties him to Manannán. There is nothing of the ocean about Manawydan, who is instead a master craftsman, an agriculturalist, and one who embodies critical thinking and strategies, rather than the fire of a warrior. Named as one of the Three Golden Shoemakers in the Trioedd Ynys Prydein, some believe that his name derives from the Brythonic word for awl, a shoemaker's tool.

There is, however, a strong connection between water, or water divinities, and horses in many Indo-European cultures; Poseidon created the horse in Greek mythology, for example. In Celtic traditions, there are several connections between horses and the sea: Macha is the daughter Sainreth mac Imbaith, "Nature of the Sea" (Ford, 1977); Manannán mac Lir's chariot is pulled across the waves by Enbarr, a horse with a flowing mane; after the death of Cú Chulainn, Liath Macha, one of the twin horses born at the same time as the hero, returns to the water; and in Welsh lore, Teyrnon Twryf Liant, a horse lord and another potential mate to Rhiannon, is also associated with water as suggested by the meaning of his name: "Lord of the Tempestuous Sea." Perhaps the association between water and horses has something to do with their shared property of liminality. We will discuss this aspect of the horse further later on in this chapter and we've already seen several examples of the ways in which bodies of water, especially rivers and fords, are considered threshold places where this world meets the Otherworld. It is probably not coincidental that one of Manannán's functions as a Sea God is to guard the gateway to the Otherworld. Indeed, in Irish mythology especially, one must undertake an Immrama, or journey across the water, in order to reach the Islands of the Otherworld.

While Rhiannon does not figure as prominently in the Third Branch as she does in the First, her subtextual identity as a Sovereignty Goddess is clearly present, albeit tempered by the filter of contemporary medieval Welsh society. The story of the Third Branch is a direct continuation of the events of the Second Branch, wherein the great war in Ireland saw only seven of the British warriors dispatched to Ireland survive the war; Pryderi, son of Rhiannon and Pwyll, and Manawydan among them.

When the two men, who are fast friends, return to Britain, they retreat to Dyfed where Pryderi offers both the hand of his now-widowed mother and rulership over his seven cantrifs to Manawydan. This demonstrates a key point of inheritance law: Rhiannon does not gain ownership of her husband's land after his death; it passes down through him to her son. However, Rhiannon is shown to have some say in the matter of her remarriage:

> Then Manawydan and Rhiannon sat together and began to converse; and as a result of that conversation, his head and heart grew tender towards her, and he was delighted that he had never seen a woman who as fairer or more beautiful than her.
>
> 'Pryderi,' he said, 'I will agree to your proposal.'
> 'What was that?' said Rhiannon.
> 'My lady,' said Pryderi, 'I have given you as a wife to Manawydan son of Llŷr.'
> 'I will agree to that gladly,' said Rhiannon.

'I am glad too,' said Manawydan, 'and may God repay the man who gives me such firm friendship.' Before that feast finished, he slept with her. (Davies 2007, p. 36)

While it may seem odd that Pryderi would act as a matchmaker for his mother, this is consistent with medieval Welsh convention, and illustrates the standing of women in medieval Wales. A woman is under the legal authority and protection of the men in her life: when she is single, she is under the authority of her father or brothers; when married, she is under the guardianship of her husband; and when widowed, she is either under her son's protection, or the responsibility for her reverts back to her kin group if she is without sons (Valente, 1986). However, this authority has some limits, and the Welsh Laws of Women are explicit in stating that women cannot be given in marriage against their will (Van der Linden, 2007).

All of this is illustrated clearly in the exchanges between Pryderi, Manawydan, and Rhiannon. It is the gifting of lordship over the seven cantrifs of Dyfed that stands out as an oddity here, and its apparent bundling with the offer of marriage to Rhiannon may suggest that rulership over these lands is a consequence of receiving the blessing of the tutelary spirit of the land – by entering into a sacred marriage with the local sovereignty Goddess who is, in this case, Rhiannon. It is noteworthy that as Bran's brother, and in the absence of an heir in Bran's lineage, Manawydan should have assumed the throne of Britain. That he did not contest the kingship of Caswallon because he did not want to start yet another war is a testimony to the measured wisdom of Manawydan, which is a feature in the events of the Third Branch; because of this, he is remembered as one of the Three Undemanding Chieftains in a Welsh Triad.

The Great Horsewoman

Rhiannon's association with horses in the narrative of the Four Branches is well attested; it is deliberate, symbolic, and repetitive. When she arrives in the First Branch, we see her astride a magical white horse that, even when walking, could be overtaken by no other horse. Later, when her newborn son is spirited away by a monster, the child is found on the threshold of a stall with a mare whose own foals disappear annually on the first of May, a significant and liminal feast day marking the beginning of summer.

Falsely accused of having destroyed the missing baby, Rhiannon is sentenced by Pwyll, her husband, to a bizarre punishment involving her sitting on a mounting block outside of the castle for seven years. While there, she must recount the details of her alleged crime to strangers and offer to bear them on her back into the court. In the Third Branch, when she is imprisoned in an Otherworldly fortress with her son Pryderi, she is made to wear the collars of asses after they had been out been hauling hay. The repetitive horse imagery is significant in that it ties Rhiannon to the equine Sovereignty Goddess with whom the king must mate to legitimize his kingship both in Celtic and in other Indo-European traditions. "The worship of and connection between the horse and the fertility goddess, known among the continental Celts as Epona, has been documented as common practice in Europe" (McKenna, 1980, p. 317).

The symbol of the horse ties into the Trifunctional Theory of influential mythologist Georges Dumézil. He posited that Proto-Indo-European culture was made up of three groups, which in turn, performed three separate social functions: Sovereignty, consisting of kings, judges, and priests; Military, concerned with war and protection; and Fertility, which was connected to food production, craftsmanship, and general prosperity. In this schema, the horse symbolizes the first function, although it relied greatly on the other two functions to be effective. This is why the Horse Goddess is often considered a transfunctional figure (Lyle, 1982).

The significance of the horse has a long history in Wales, dating back to pre-Christian times. As we have seen, horse divinities such as the Gaulish Epona, the Irish Macha, and the Welsh Rhiannon are prominent in Celtic culture, and these goddesses appear to be concerned with healing, fertility, and death. The horse also figured markedly in a Romano-Celtic divine horseman cult, where these divinities seem to have played roles both as protectors and healers (Green, 1997).

Furthermore, there are what appear to be sacrificial burials of horses evidenced all over the Celtic world. The association of these cult deposits with locations which had liminal qualities – that is, which straddled two different worlds, such as land boundaries or areas marking the transition between sacred and profane space – may indicate that the horse was thought of as dwelling in both worlds, perhaps because they were part wild and part domestic. This seems to be consistent with the later Welsh custom of burying the heads of horses under the thresholds of houses, under hearths, or straddling the chimney in order to prevent evil spirits from entering the home (Green, 1997). This connection with the liminality of threshold places further underscores the horse's association with sovereignty since Sovereignty figures themselves are bridges between states of being.

The Welsh folk practice of the Mari Lwyd ("Grey Mare") may also be a reflection of the liminal quality of the horse. Although it is tempting to see this winter tradition as a remnant of ancient Pagan practice, we only have proof of it dating back to the 18th century. The Mari Lwyd is thought to have been a wassailing tradition, which was a ritual of communal drinking believed to impart abundance, increased fertility, and good fortune to all who partook of the drink. In the Mari Lwyd tradition, a man wearing a horse costume fashioned from the skull of a horse traveled with a retinue which visited homes and public houses, and sought entrance to each by engaging in an *ex-tempore* battle of verses with those within; if the Mari party won, they were let inside to join a feast (Owen, 1985). While this may have been an example of sympathetic magic, which brought fertility and abundance to the household, the Mari Lwyd also served a practical purpose: bringing communities together during the more isolated winter months, and sharing food with neighbors at a time when, especially in rural areas, it had become scarcer.

It is significant, however, that the practice was tied into the liminal qualities of the season, the transitional time between the old year and the new – between the barrenness of late winter at Christmas, and the first signs of spring celebrated at Candlemas. One can see this as a reflection of the desire of the Mari Lwyd party to want to cross over the more literal threshold into the home (Wood, 1997). This echoes the Celtic conception of the horse as guardian and psychopomp, and its presence at this interstitial time assists in bridging this world and the Otherworld, in order to allow new and fertile energies to replace the fallowness of the dying year. Some modern Pagans see an echo of Rhiannon in the Mari Lwyd, interpreting the journey from house to house of this Otherworldly, skeletal horse as representing her frantic search for her missing son. Ghostly and frightening during in the darkest time of the year, the mourning Divine Mother seeks the Divine Son, whose restoration to her is represented by the increasing light marked by the solstice.

That Rhiannon's horse was white is also significant, as there is almost an entire language of colors in medieval tales, and white was indisputably connected to the Otherworld; it is almost certain that the medieval audience would have immediately understood its connotations (Davies, 1997). As threshold guardians, white horses and their riders often play the role of psychopomp, and there are images of Epona from the continent which depict her riding a horse and holding a key, which is symbolic of her chthonic role, leading the deceased to the Otherworld.

However, Wood argues that unlike Epona or other equine divinities, Rhiannon's association with horses are related with punishment, rather than empowerment or queenship: she rides forth at the beginning of the First Branch in order to escape a marriage she does not want; for having allegedly eaten her newborn son, Rhiannon is punished by having to sit at a mounting block every day for seven years, where she offers to carry strangers on her back as a horse would; and in the Third Branch, she is abducted to the Otherworld and forced to wear an ass's collar around her neck – all of which was retaliation for the mistreatment of her rejected suitor Gwawl in the First Branch. These punishments, according to Wood, therefore disqualify her as being considered a sovereignty figure (Wood, 1997).

On the other hand, if we were to consider that the equine qualities exhibited by Rhiannon during these challenging episodes are not a mirror of her punishment but rather an indication of an imminent change of state or status, a different picture emerges, especially if we factor in the idea that the way in which the horse aspects manifest themselves is a reflection of where Rhiannon's power lies.

Winward proposes that, in general, the extent of power possessed by women as well as the strength of their presence in the narrative of *Y Mabinogi* is directly related to their marital status and life stage: when a woman is unpartnered or unmarried, she is at her most powerful, and not only do we hear her speak, we see her take an active role in the story. When she is married, both her personal power and the degree to which she speaks in the story are observably diminished. Finally, when she has become a mother, she possesses the least power, and she is more apt to be talked about than to speak for herself – if she doesn't disappear from the narrative completely, as women who become mothers in the *Mabinogi* tend to do (Winward, 1997).

These states of presence in the narrative are somewhat paralleled by the degree of autonomy a woman has at different points in her life, according to the medieval Welsh Laws of Women, which state that an unmarried woman is under the legal authority of her father, a married woman is under the legal authority of her husband, and if widowed, she comes under the legal authority of a son; should a woman not have one, legal authority over her reverts back to her father or family group (Cartwright, 2012).

When it comes to Rhiannon, we clearly see that when she is unmarried, she is at the height of her power, both in word and deed. She defies the wishes of her father and takes action to ensure that she marries the man of her choosing. She reaches this goal after overcoming several challenges, including the complicated issue of honor that arose for Pwyll at their first marriage feast when he recklessly promised to give a supplicant anything within his power to give. Rhiannon deftly guides Pwyll to a clever solution in this situation which both keeps his honor intact as well as secures Rhiannon as his wife. During this transitional time between maiden and wife, Rhiannon's relationship to the horse is that she is its mistress and rider.

After Rhiannon's marriage to Pwyll, she goes to live with him in Dyfed, and becomes known as a very generous queen because of the gifts she bestows upon their courtiers. However, public opinion of her changes in time, and after three years of marriage without Rhiannon having birthed an heir, Pwyll's men encourage him to put her aside, something he refuses to do. And yet, even after she does give birth to a son, her nurses turn against her when the infant goes missing, and frame Rhiannon for the child's murder.

We clearly see here that after her marriage to Pwyll, Rhiannon exhibits less power. Where before Rhiannon was able to resolve complex issues of honor and hospitality through diplomacy and wit, after she is married has become a mother, she is unable to convince those who framed her with infanticide to tell the truth of what happened. It is also significant that we do not see any conversation between Rhiannon and Pwyll regarding the loss of their child.

Instead, as required and expected, Rhiannon accepts the strange cruelty of Pwyll's punishment, which reflects both that she is now under the legal guardianship of her husband, as well as her relationship to the horse; by sitting daily at the mounting block and offering to carry strangers on her back, she performs the functions of a horse and so has effectively become one. Rhiannon transitions from wife to mother, and then from mother to childless mother in this part of the story. Her association with the liminal qualities of the horse are further underscored by the mirroring of the annual loss of Teyrnon's mare's foal, as well as the discovery of Rhiannon's newborn baby on the threshold of his home. The child himself is a mirror of the foal as they were both born on the same night – the threshold time of May Eve.

There is an international folk motif that features an Otherworldly "devouring mother" and a doubling of the "cannibalized" child with dogs. This plot point may have been an inclusion from outside influences from continental Europe, although it is more typical for this motif to feature the actual eating of animals instead of just the pretense of it having happened (Hemming, 1998). It is also interesting to note that images of Epona from the continent never depict her with a human child, but oftentimes depict the Goddess feeding foals, and sometimes her images also include dogs.

Finally, in the Third Branch, while Rhiannon does not feature as centrally to the tale, her sovereignty aspect is underscored by her acceptance of Manawydan as her husband. When

Rhiannon and Pryderi are stolen away to the Otherworld, they experienced unusual punishments. Pryderi was made to wear door hammers, while Rhiannon was yoked with the collars of asses. This latter again alludes to her equine nature, and it is interesting that she again appears to embody the animal when she is separated from her mate, either by circumstance or by the status of their relationship. Not only had Rhiannon been kept in captivity and away from Manawydan for over a year, but the last time they saw each other, Rhiannon scolded Manawydan for being an unfaithful friend to her son before storming out to find the missing Pryderi, angry at her husband. That she found her voice to speak after her relative silence throughout the Third Branch recalls the agency and power of her maidenhood which she exhibited in the First Branch; yet her single-minded quest to rescue her son in the face of Manawydan's reticence mirrors both what she endured with her initial loss of Pryderi in infancy, as well as the gulf between herself and Pwyll during the course of her punishment for a crime she did not commit.

One of the hallmarks of the Sovereignty figure is that her form is a reflection of the status of the king to the land. When Rhiannon is out of synch or physically separated from her husband, she tends to exhibit equine characteristics which allude to her nonhuman origins and signify that there is an imbalance between the king and the land. That Dyfed undergoes a transformation that is similar to that of the Wasteland in the grail mythos is telling, as the grail itself is a proxy symbol for Sovereignty. Rhiannon's connection with the horse therefore is not a function of her punishment so much as it is a reflection of the status of her personal autonomy and marks her transition from one state of being to another. When Rhiannon exhibits her equine nature, it signifies that Sovereignty is starting to withdraw back into the land and, through it, to return to the Otherworldly origins of her power.

The Divine Queen

As modern readers, we may wonder why Rhiannon chose to abide by Pwyll's judgment of her, to ask why it is she didn't simply return home to the Otherworld. She was likely physically strong enough to do so; after all, she ostensibly carried some travelers on her back like a horse, and the story of the nurses that all six of them could not stop her from destroying her newborn baby was apparently believed by Pwyll and the judges, so clearly, the subtext is that she possessed some Otherworldly strength – strength enough, perhaps, to escape back to her own lands. That she chose to accept this judgment may be a reflection of the medieval layer of the narrative; this likely would have made perfect sense to the contemporary audience for several reasons.

One of the functions of myth is to illustrate, typically by means of cautionary example, the proper order of things, whether that concerns society, cosmology, or interpersonal relationships. When things become disordered, when people especially act in a way that puts them outside of social balance and expectation, calamity is sure to strike. These tales, then, function as a moral template where the heroes strive to illustrate proper behavior in a given situation. As a queen, it would be expected for Rhiannon to obey the law of the land, and as the recipient of an unjust punishment – indeed serving as the very embodiment of the Calumniated Wife motif – Rhiannon not only illustrates lawfulness, but further distinguishes herself as someone of high moral character, even in the face of loss and injustice.

While the particular punishment enacted against Rhiannon is strange to the point that it likely can only reflect deep mythic origins, that Rhiannon was assessed this kind of redress at all is in keeping with medieval Welsh laws. It is interesting to note that Pwyll does not divorce Rhiannon, even at the behest of his court advisors; it appears therefore that she is still queen despite her daily requirement to sit by the mounting block outside of the gate of Arberth for seven years. There is no mention of imprisonment, and indeed, when Teyrnon, Gwri, and their retinue come to court, Rhiannon goes with them even though they refuse her offer of a ride on her back. Once there, she is seated beside Pwyll at the feast given in their guests' honor – even before Gwri is revealed as their missing son.

As we saw with Pwyll's misstep at his first wedding feast by too-readily agreeing to grant the supplicant Gwawl whatever he asked for, Rhiannon understands that there are social forms and contracts which must be adhered to, and it is especially important for the nobility to abide by these rules. Rhiannon illustrates an ability to work within the limitations of societal expectations, instead of breaking away from them altogether, which is the kind of behavior we see from both Aranrhod and Blodeuwedd in the Fourth Branch. Even when she appears at the Gorsedd Arberth to ask Pwyll if he would marry her, rather than having to marry someone she didn't love, Rhiannon was perfectly within her legal right to do so, as medieval Welsh law did not permit families to give women away in marriage against their will.

It is this shrewdness of understanding that the law is in place for a reason and that everyone, noble or otherwise, is beholden to it that reflects so well on Rhiannon's moral character. It follows to say that as a Sovereignty figure, Rhiannon is the very embodiment of this social construct, and so can do nothing less but to adhere to it. And so, resigned to her fate, Rhiannon chooses to work within the social construct and accept her punishment, proving herself to be a great and noble lady, whose perseverance is rewarded when her child is at last returned to her and her innocence proven. Rhiannon, as a wife and mother, is no longer the autonomous woman of her maidenhood, and now demonstrates by example, the behavior that is expected of the medieval Welsh woman. "The virtues to be fostered are patience, modesty, wisdom, chastity, loyalty – these are the virtues that will ultimately win the day" (Davies, pg. 80, 1993).

Chapter Six

Seeking Her Within

Throughout this book, we have explored the myths, symbols, and attributions of Rhiannon. It is my belief that this information is crucial to help build a relationship with this beautiful divinity, especially since her stories were not written down by those who actively worshiped her. In one respect, this puts modern Pagans and Polytheists who are drawn to work with Rhiannon and other British divinities at a disadvantage because we do not have access to the types of resources available to Pagans who work with Gods and Goddesses from cultures who themselves have recorded the myths, rituals, prayers, and details of worship of their divinities.

On the other hand, because myth depicts Rhiannon as a fairy queen – less than a Goddess but ostensibly more than a human – her story is somewhat more relatable than those of divinities who are engaged with more cosmological concerns. In Rhiannon, we see a woman in process. She experiences challenges, trials, and losses just like anyone, and certainly many of us have experienced the same losses that she has. This relatability permits us to connect with Rhiannon in a way that reflects her ability to understand the human condition. This accessibility allows us to call to Rhiannon in times of need.

She is the Great Mother whose understanding and compassion is infinite and whose love is fierce and unconditional. Hers is the broad back of the mare that bears us through the darkest of times and over the rockiest of terrain. It is she who teaches us how to endure the challenges of life and bears us forth into the presence of our Sovereignty, permitting us to shift from one reality to another. She is the guardian of the liminal threshold that moves us from one situation to another, from one life stage to another... and from the present manifestation of who we are to one that is in deeper alignment with the Sovereign Self within.

Reflecting Sovereignty Within

Shakespeare said that art is a mirror held up to nature. And that's what it is. The nature is your nature, and all of these wonderful poetic images of mythology are referring to something in you. When your mind is trapped by the image out there so that you never make the reference to yourself, you have misread the image. Joseph Campbell, *The Power of Myth*

While the type of refection Campbell is speaking about doesn't mean that the Gods exist only (or simply) as archetypes or psychological constructs, it can nevertheless be very informative to reflect their tales inward. This provides us with a process that helps us discover what parts of any myth resonate with our own stories, as well as insight as to how these sacred stories can help inform our spiritual paths and catalyze our personal process.

One way of looking at Rhiannon therefore is as a representation of our Sovereign Self that comes up into consciousness from the subconscious realm of the Otherworld, pursuing that which it most desires. We can try to track our authentic selves down and chase after our dreams, but it is only in truly engaging them – naming these goals and asking for what we need – do they reveal themselves to us. It is a long process to manifest and integrate our Sovereign Self – to wed it to our "good sense" and help to develop the ability to hear the truth of its wisdom – because there are challenges to overcome. We have to process loss, and mourn for what we had hoped our lives would be, and we often find ourselves trapped in destructive patterns that cause us to feel "othered" or disconnected from the core truth of who and what we are.

We can become so invested in carrying the heavy loads of our emotional and physical responsibilities, which often include bearing the needs and expectations of others, that we allow our strengths to be drained and our resources to be used up, leaving nothing left for ourselves. What Sovereignty wants and needs when it does rise up from the Otherworld of the unconscious, is to dwell completely in a person's consciousness; it seeks to be to be embodied. It is a great test of personal Sovereignty for us to learn how to remain authentically who we are, no matter the challenges or circumstances around us.

Just as Rhiannon is sought after by Pwyll, the active mind seeks to integrate the wisdom of the lessons it has learned – it is our conscious self-seeking an authentic experience, no matter the potential risks to the status quo of the present moment. Pryderi can be seen as the result of the union of Sovereignty and consciousness, the wondrous child that represents the birth of the new self, when that which is sought has come into manifestation. The challenge here lies in keeping present in this new life… keeping grounded in a new sense of self, and centered in self-worth. Rhiannon teaches us to endure in the face of persecution, regardless of the of lack of support from those who will not themselves take responsibility for their own lives, and despite those doubts and fears that rise up from within us – trying to convince us that we are not worthy of what we seek to have, who we strive to be, and all we hope to accomplish.

When we can do this, and live from this powerful and conscious center, nothing can move us from our mark.

We will be Sovereign.
We will be free.

The Functions of Rhiannon

Based upon what we have glimpsed both explicitly in the stories where she appears, and implicitly through a close reading of these same texts – and perhaps with a sprinkling of folk tradition mixed in, even if there is no proof of any direct lineage to ancient Celtic Pagan practices – here are some of the spiritual functions of Rhiannon and ways in which to approach her.

Rhiannon as Lady of the Land

In this iteration, she is a Sovereignty Goddess, testing and choosing the candidate who would best serve as king. She rides forth on a White Mare, indicating her Otherworldly origins, while also keeping watch over her domain. She connects this world with the Otherworld, and as such, serves as a bridge or a threshold between the two. By reflecting these ideas within, we can see the liminal qualities of the horse as bridging the conscious, waking world with the unconscious, intuitive world. Rhiannon not only guides our way from one state of being to another, she also carries us on her back if we need support during difficult times. She teaches us how to obtain our Sovereignty – which I defi ne in the context of the inner landscape as "fully-conscious self-determination" – by learning to ask for that which we need. Rhiannon also demonstrates the importance of being true to what you know to be your authentic and Sovereign self, even in the face of doubt and persecution from the outside world. As Lady of the Land, Rhiannon is a granter of abundance, and her magical bag which cannot be filled is, in many ways, a proxy both of the dish or cornucopia filled with food that we see in images of Epona, and a resonance of the Cauldron of Abundance and Transformation.

Rhiannon as Lady of the Otherworld

In this more subtle iteration, Rhiannon is a faerie bride who brings great magic with her to this world. She rides out from the Gorsedd Arberth, a mound where one will receive blows or see a great wonder – exactly the type of mound that would be considered a doorway to the Otherworld. Rhiannon is dressed in a silk brocade that symbolizes her Otherworldly origins, and she appears to play the role of the psychopomp – a guide who assists the spirits of the dead to cross the threshold into the Otherworld. The latter ties into the liminal qualities of her white mare, whose very color is a hallmark of the Otherworld, as well as with the Adar Rhiannon, the three magical birds which, like most things associated with the Otherworld, appear able to warp human perceptions of space and time. In "Culhwch and Olwen" these same birds are said to be able to soothe the souls of the living and awaken the souls of the dead. When reflected within, Rhiannon's role as Lady of the Otherworld calls us to transform those parts of ourselves which no longer serve us, to dare to pass over the threshold that leads us from one state of being to the next, all the while promising us that, even in the face of our greatest pain and deepest sorrow, the song of her birds will bring us comfort and the blessing of forgetting our troubles – even if for a little while.

Rhiannon as the Divine Mother

Perhaps the most poignant and relatable attributes of Rhiannon are connected to her role as Mother. It is after the loss of her newborn son, and the unjust punishment she receives when the child's negligent nurses blame her for his loss, that we witness Rhiannon's deeply sympathetic character and endless compassion. She assures the nurses that no harm will come to them if they tell the truth of what happened to the child, and when they refuse, Rhiannon bravely and with dignity accepts Pwyll's punishment. Here, then, is a divinity who is intimately acquainted with the loss of a child, and who knows what it means to have to carry an unjust burden.

We can also imagine Rhiannon's pain in the Third Branch when she learns that her son has disappeared again. She takes Manawydan to task for having lost Pryderi and leaving him behind, before setting forth to find him for herself. Although her attempt to free Pryderi from the magical fortress results in her own entrapment, and they are both are taken to the Otherworld for punishment, we see in Rhiannon a fierce and selfless mother figure whose love for her child transcends all. Reflecting this within, whether one is a literal parent or someone who is devoted to birthing a project or a life which is in accordance with their greatest desires and highest purpose, Rhiannon models our need for dedication to our work and loyalty to our vision. She embodies the pureness of unconditional love, and, as her children, gathers us up into her arms, and holds us as we move through the pain of our losses. She opens our hearts, and teaches us to love and mother ourselves as fiercely as she, the Divine Mother, loves us.

Rhiannon as Calumniated Wife

Gentle but firm, Rhiannon shows us that she knows what it is to be "Other", knows how to endure an unspeakable loss, and knows what it feels like to suffer an unjust punishment. When reflected within, we can see how Rhiannon also demonstrates that regardless of what challenges and life situations come our way, if we can endure the hardships and the heartaches while staying true to who and what we are from a place of inner sovereignty and personal authenticity, then in the end, our faith in ourselves will pay off and we will obtain that which we most desire.

The Lessons of Rhiannon

Rhiannon teaches us that:

- We have the power to choose our Sovereign natures over our learned fears.
- We have the strength to endure in the face of grave injustice.
- We have the ability to change our shape – to transform ourselves and our lives.
- We have the vision to be able to move through suffering and loss and into redemption.

Rhiannon encourages us to:

- Ask for what we need.
- Stay committed to our truths.
- Persevere in the face of challenge.
- Pursue what we love and what will make us most fulfilled.
- Seek comfort and solace to ease our way; the lap of the
- Mother welcomes all.
- Bear our burdens with grace, and ask for help when needed; we need not carry them alone.

Chapter Seven

Building a Relationship with Rhiannon

If we step outside of the realms of mythology and history, it is clear that the memory of Rhiannon persists in modern pop culture. Most people are familiar with the Stevie Nicks song "Rhiannon", which was inspired by a novel called *Triad*, by Mary Leader. While the book itself only made vague references to Welsh myth, Nicks was stunned at how well the song she wrote reflected the story of Rhiannon when she read the *Mabinogi* after the fact. Nicks wrote another song, called "Angel" which she said is directly influenced by the Rhiannon of the *Mabinogi*. Other groups, including Faith and the Muse and Faun, have written songs inspired by Rhiannon, and she features in the movie *Otherworld*, an animated retelling of the Four Branches. But perhaps the most well-known retelling is that of Evangeline Walton, whose *Mabinogion Tetralogy* lays out Rhiannon's story in *The Prince of Annwn* and *The Song of Rhiannon*.

The modern Pagan movement has played a huge role in restoring Rhiannon to a place of honor by recognizing her divinity. She features prominently in the pantheons of established traditions such as the Anglesey Druid Order and the Sisterhood of Avalon, as well as being honored in the devotional work of Brythonic Polytheists, Welsh Reconstructionists, Druidic practitioners, and individual Pagans of many types and traditions. There are many ways to approach this Goddess, both in the context of a formal tradition as well as on the path of an inspired individual. What follows therefore are some devotional practices that anyone who feels drawn to Rhiannon can use in order to build or deepen a meaningful and authentic relationship with the Divine Queen.

Shrines and Altars

Setting up a devotional shrine or creating a place to honor Rhiannon on your working altar is a powerful way to invite her presence into your life. When creating any shrine, it can be helpful to meditate on the symbols associated with the divinity you are seeking to honor, and begin to gather those items or images together in a space dedicated to them. The Hermetic Principle of Correspondence which teaches that "like attracts like" underscores this practice; the more the images, symbols, and cultural components hold or replicate your understanding of the deity in question, the more the shrine can act to build a connection between you and the God/dess to whom it is dedicated.

Shrines can be of any size, ranging from an elaborately carved piece of furniture, to a shelf on a wall or in a bookcase, an assemblage of wall art, or even a collage of meaningful images. You can decide if you want to include an image of Rhiannon on her shrine, perhaps in the form of a piece of devotional art or sculpture made by you or purchased elsewhere. There are several commercially available statues of Rhiannon to choose from, including reproductions of ancient Epona statuary which may resonate with you. Alternatively, you may find something depicting a horsewoman that speaks to Rhiannon's energy for you, or else choose instead to represent her with an image of a white mare.

My personal shrine to Rhiannon incorporates several statuary images of her, a large banner with an image of her from the "Avalonian Oracle" deck; a small pottery figure of a white horse that I purchased in Wales, a resin box carved with white knotwork horses which contains a vial of a vibrational elixir I made on pilgrimage at the site of Rhiannon's court in Narberth, a leather bag embossed with knotwork, a stone with triple black birds intertwined with knots, a rock I picked up on the Gorsedd Arberth, an antique horseshoe, a small iron cauldron with a triple horse broach leaning against it where I burn herbs in her honor, and a pottery dish to receive offerings I leave for Rhiannon. For me, the difference between shrines and working altars is that shrines serve as a daily reminder of our devotion to our Gods. Whenever I pass my Rhiannon shrine, the images and energies I've build up there help me to connect and fortify my relationship with her, reinforce the intentions of the work I've been doing with her, and remind me to take a moment to be present in her presence, no matter how hectic my day may be.

Here are some correspondences for Rhiannon primarily gathered from her stories in *Y Mabinogi* which may be of use to you in putting together your own shrine to the Goddess:

- *Symbols*: White mare, three black birds, bag, golden veil, mare and foal, hanging cauldron, horse block, yoke, moon, torc.
- *Animals*: White mare, three black birds, dogs and puppies, badger.
- *Colors*: White, gold (attested in text); red (fertility, smeared blood, associated with the Otherworld along with the color white).

Offerings

A powerful way to give thanks to the Gods and to show them honor is to present them with an offering; these offerings can take many forms. As in ancient days, offerings can be gifts in the form of food, libations, herbs, flowers, stones, and other items. These can be placed on house altars and shrines and later brought outside and placed under a tree, in a body of water if appropriate, committed to a bonfire, and even buried in the ground. Choosing what to give as an offering can be as simple as giving what feels right to you, or as involved as researching the kinds of things ancient peoples would have gifted these Gods and then seeking out those items, or their modern equivalents.

The Celts were known to create votive deposits, often gifting high status items such as swords, horse trappings, and cauldrons to the Gods; as they believed that water was a gateway to the Otherworld, we have found large collections of offerings in lakes or at the source of rivers. Often, these offerings were created specifically to be given to the Gods, and were broken before being deposited, likely as part of the ritual, rendering them useless to humans. In Wales, one famous votive deposit was discovered in the lake waters of Llyn Cerrig Bach. It is also believed that in times of great need, the Celts performed human sacrifices in hopes that the departed would bring the appeal of the people before the Gods directly.

While of course we would never perform human sacrifice today, the idea of an offering representing a sacrifice is a powerful one. The very word means "to make sacred", and we can transform something into a sacrifice when we imbue it with intention and make it meaningful. Some say that a sacrifice should have an impact on the one who is offering it; this can be achieved by gifting something one has worked hard to obtain or an item which holds great emotional attachment. Tossing a tumbled stone one has just purchased into a lake with intention as an offering can be meaningful, but thanking the Gods for a blessing they have given you with the gift of a pinky ring you've worn since childhood, for example, holds a different devotional impact.

Offerings do not always have to be things; one can thank or honor the Gods with the gift of your time and energy. Creating a devotional piece of art or music is a powerful offering, as is volunteering your time in support of a charity or donating goods and services to a cause which is in alignment with the divinity you are seeking to honor. You can commit yourself to learning a skill, engaging in an activity, or adopting a moral code which you feel would please the Goddess. Offerings of the self are the most powerful ways to engage with the divine because they are often the most intimate. I personally tend to not see offerings as part of an exchange economy, where they are given in order to procure a desired outcome with the help of deity; rather, I think offerings are best used as a method of building a relationship with our Gods – a show of dedication, discipline, and devotion.

Here are some ideas for offerings you can gift to Rhiannon:

- *Food*: Welsh cakes, apples, honey, mead, apple cider.
- *Plants*: Rose, red clover, lady's mantle, and motherwort. These can decorate the altar, be placed in a dish as your offering, or burned together on a charcoal disk as a devotional incense.
- *Items*: Horse trappings, horse shoes, black bird feathers, bag.
- *Service*: Rehabilitating and rescuing horses (or supporting organizations that do this work); working to help missing and exploited children; sharing music therapeutically with those in need of serenity and joy; working with or donating to organizations that advocate for women's rights, safety, and well-being; working with dogs at an animal shelter.

When I am actively working at my shrine, I light candles and burn incense to empower my intention and to honor the Goddess, and I will often leave seven- day candles burning on the shrine to represent whatever intention I placed before Rhiannon in my work. I sometimes place live flowers on my shrine as a gift or a token of gratitude, and often place things like herbs, stones, and pieces of fruit in the offering dish; depending on what is in it, I have an outdoor shrine where I eventually place the offerings I've left for any of the deities I work with. I do this once a moon for non-perishable offerings, and the next day when I leave offerings of food.

Journey Work: Rhiannon Trance Posture

Inspired by the work of Felicitas Goodman, ecstatic trance postures are inner journeying tools that permit seekers to have an experience which leads to understanding through the embodiment of a figure, artifact, symbol or even natural phenomenon, such as a landscape feature or a tree.

While there are no known ancient depictions of Rhiannon, the abundance of devotional images of the goddess Epona have a very strong resonance with our initial meeting with Rhiannon in the First Branch: that of a noble female figure serenely riding a horse with an unhurried gait. Although in the *Mabinogi* Rhiannon is not described as holding anything as she rides before the Gorsedd Arberth, images of Epona often depict her holding a basket of food or a torc of sovereignty. Rhiannon is described as riding with her head covered with a golden veil, and later on in the First Branch she gives a magical bag to Pwyll which can never be filled. While Rhiannon's riding style is not specified in the text, almost every image of Epona depicts her as riding side-saddle; she presents with her entire body facing forward, while her mount is viewed from its side beneath her.

None of this is meant to infer that Epona and Rhiannon are the same divinity, but there is little question that they have many similarities, and may perhaps be related. That said, even without drawing upon the iconography of Epona, the author of the *Mabinogi* certainly provides us with enough of a descriptive image of Rhiannon that we can easily imagine her as an unhurried horsewoman astride her gently walking, white horse. For this embodiment exercise, you can choose to rely solely upon the textual description of Rhiannon, or research and emulate one of the various icons of Epona to use as the basis for this posture. In the latter case, instead of a bowl or basket of food, you can choose to hold or visualize yourself holding a bag or sack in order to tie more fully into the energies of Rhiannon specifically. You may also consider draping a scarf or wrap over your head to represent Rhiannon's veil.

There are many ways to approach trance posture work, and many types of information which this tool can provide. Primarily, trance postures are a powerful way to come to understand the image, symbol, or in this case, personage being embodied. When taking a posture journey, setting up your intention beforehand will set the tone of your work and specify what you are seeking to learn.

Performing a Rhiannon trance posture can help you to connect with the Goddess so you can ask her questions directly: you can enquire about her and ways to honor in order to deepen your relationship with her; you can ask her for clarity about her symbols or parts of her story – for example, asking why she accepted the unjust punishment for a crime she did not commit; and you can ask her for guidance in your own life and spiritual process.

Embodying this posture can help you integrate some of Rhiannon's lessons and bring insight into ways you can be sovereign in your own life; teach you how to bear the burdens of life and its injustices with grace and inner strength born of certainty, anchored in your own truth; comfort you in times of deep loss and sorrow; and help you to connect with the inner strength necessary to support others in your life with as much unconditional love as possible.

The Map of the Journey
Follow these steps to undertake a trance posture journey:

1. Set aside quiet time to yourself.
2. Wear loose and comfortable clothing.

3. Work in your sacred space, surrounded by those things that trigger entrance into the realm of the spiritual. The simple act of spreading a sarong on the ground dedicated solely for use in these workings can help move you into a receptive space for journeying.
4. Be sure you know how to embody the posture before you begin.
5. Have any necessary props or posture aids gathered and accessible.
6. Clear and center, coming to a neutral energy space before beginning your work.
7. Sit and clear your mind by paying attention to your breath for at least 15 minutes before embodying the posture.
8. Embody the posture as detailed below. If you are going to wear a veil, place it over your head before you begin.
9. Accompany the posture with an audio recording of 15 minutes of Trance Drumming. These are readily available on the internet; be sure to choose one that has a call-back beat at the end so that you know it is time to complete your work. Research has found that a drumming rhythm of 200-210 beats per minute seems to trigger the nervous system to enter the altered state of consciousness desired for these postures. If you cannot find a drumming track that you like, or if you prefer silence, focus on the rhythm of your breath as you journey and set a gentle alarm for 15 minutes from your starting time.
10. Start the drumming track, and be sure to keep your focus clear as you journey, while still allowing insight to flow. Spend the entire length of the 15 minutes of drumming (or breathing) remaining as clear and as open to the experience as you can. Pay attention to any and all visions, scenes, emotions, insights or information presented to you.

Rhiannon Posture Instructions

- Sit on a chair or couch with knees bent, legs closed and parallel to each other, and both feet flat on the floor.
- Envision your seat as a serene white horse upon which you are sitting side saddle. Her head is on your left side and she looks steadily forward in that direction, with her left leg raised as if ready to take a step.
- Your back is straight, your torso upright, your shoulders back, and your head facing forward.
- Your left arm is outstretched and your hand is resting on the "neck" of your "horse". A high pillow or bolster placed beside you can make this position more comfortable as well as help it feel more real.
- Your right-hand rests lightly in your lap, or alternatively can be holding an apple, a bag, a bowl, or a torc.
- Start the drumming track.
- Close your eyes. Suspend disbelief. Release expectation. Ask Rhiannon to be with you as you journey. Go…

After the Journey

It is always important to ground and center after every posture session. Release any excess energy or emotions that may have come up for you during the posture process. Place your hands on the ground and breathe those energies out until you feel centered and balanced. If you find it hard to get grounded, breathe up some rich, green Earth energy from the planet to help you find your center. It is unusual for people performing these postures to feel imbalanced, but it is better to know what to do than to feel unprepared.

Be sure to journal your experiences; make a written record of everything you heard, saw, and felt during your journey. These self-reflective questions can help you process your experience:

- How did the posture make you feel?
- What would you name this posture?
- What is the lesson of this posture?
- How does it relate to you and your process?
- What does this posture bring up for you?
- What did you learn about Rhiannon from performing this posture?
- What did you learn about yourself?
- In what way has this posture helped you to connect with Rhiannon?
- What is your next step in building a relationship with her?
- Know that this posture is something you can do over and over again. It is a powerful and effective tool, and it is worth developing this skill through practice. Each time you perform this posture, you can bring a different question with you, setting up your intention clearly before you begin. Remember one of the great lessons that Rhiannon has to teach us: ask for what you need.

Devotional Chants, Prayers, and Invocations

While I have collected a few of these devotional writings and songs, I encourage you to create your own as you move into relationship with Rhiannon.

Invocation to Rhiannon

Holy Rhiannon, Lady of the Otherworld, fill me with your boundless Love and endless compassion. Great Queen, teach me to ask for that which I most need and to endure the trials set before me on the path to obtaining that which I most desire. Nurturing Mother, help me to bear my burdens with strength and grace so that, empowered and empowering, I may in turn serve others.

Affirmation of the Divine Queen

I know who I am, what I need, and what I have to give. I live from my sovereign center, and take strength from the truth of my inner wisdom. I meet every challenge with clarity, and can see the gifts of growth they bring to me. There is nothing I cannot endure, and no place I must go alone. Broad-backed Rhiannon gives me the strength I need to move through any challenge, while her sweet singing birds comfort my soul.

Rhiannon Chant

(Em) The White Mare (D) dances in the (Em) Ninth Wave's foam
(G)Call out Her (D) name and (Em) She'll bear you (D)home
To the (G)Other (D)world where (Em) Her birds still (D)sing,
(Em) soothing your (D)soul with their (Em) song
The (G) Silver (D) Branch is the (Em) Scepter of the Great Queen, (D)Rhiannon. (Em)

Swift White Horse
by Tammi Boudreau

Chorus:
(Em) Ride a (D)swift white (Em) horse, oh (D)Mother,
(Em)Ride a (D)swift white (Em)horse.
(Em)Though the (D) path seems (Em) dark and (Am)troubled
(C)Stay fast (D) to your (Em) course.

Once You wed a king, dear Mother,
Once You wed a king.
Bore a son and bore a burden,
So the Three Birds sing.

Chorus

Truth comes in full time, my Mother,
Truth comes in full time.
Harvest now the seeds we've planted,
Branch and earth and vine.

Chorus x 2

Though the path seems dark and troubled –
Stay fast to your course.

Invocation
by Kelly Woo

Rhiannon, Divine Queen,
Lady of Manifestation and Mystery,
Bathed in Golden Light,
You ride forth from the Otherworld,
Strong in Self, Rooted in Love,
Untameable as the wind,
Upon which your birds fly high.
I ask that you stand with me,
Supporting me in my struggles,
And lending me your strength and grace,
That I may overcome and uncover the Great Queen Within.

Chant to Rhiannon
by Kelly Woo

Lady, please listen
Stay for awhile
Challenges burden
And Shadows beguile

Great Queen of Mysteries
Through thick and through thin
Help me stand true
To the Sovereign Within

Chapter Eight

Rhiannon Speaks

I have been a priestess in service to Rhiannon for over 20 years, and I consciously worked to make the writing of this book a devotional act. When the first draft was complete, I stood at my altar and invoked Rhiannon. With pen and notebook in hand, I asked her if there was anything more she wanted for me to include; if there was anything she wished to say to those who would read this book... to YOU, now holding it. What follows is the result of what became an automatic writing session; I have only edited it slightly for clarity, and tried to retain the shape of it as much as possible. I humbly submit this to you, recorded as accurately as possible, and ask that you keep in mind that this has come through a flawed vessel who has tried to get out of her own way in order to hear the words of the Divine Queen, and beloved Mother, as clearly as possible. And so...

Rhiannon Speaks:

I come to you in this Now time, the threshold Between where all is sacred... always on that precipice between what Was and what may Be. What Is, is that place – that time – the Now where all changes go. To pursue the fair prize of the Wonder is to never touch it, for you cannot by its nature; to remain in fear of the Blows, you cannot escape its sting. Caught in dream, lost in fear, the Now slips by and the bag can never be filled.

You who would follow me must be prepared to wear the ass's collar... to be whisked away into the Otherworld of pain and growth and silence to forge a self with many hammers. The Wondrous Youth is your sovereign self – the next king to be – the next part of the self that needs to be birthed forth.

I am the Great Divine Mother. The Nurturing One. The Threshold Guardian. I birth and I receive: the womb and the tomb are mine. My strength carries you through each portal, stands waiting for you at each threshold – not just those of death and of life, but also of new beginnings and of the releasing of old ties.

The steady gait of the milk-white Steed of the Moon, of the Bounty of the Breast – this is the elixir that heals the Wasteland. This is what frees the prisoner, for it is when you leave my breast, it is when you have forgotten who you are, that you dwell in the ancient prison of your own design.

You must move through the sentries of these layers, through the threshold of these mysteries: the blackbird, the stag, the owl, the eagle, and the salmon.

This last is the wisdom that will unlock the gate and set the prisoner free. That prisoner is the Wondrous Child... YOU. Heir of the Abundant Mother of the Earth. Next in line from the lineage of Ancestors, from the Otherworld of their memory.

Your father, also Wisdom, the King of the Otherworld, Master of the Past, of what lies Within, of what has come Before. He battles himself at the ford, in the waters of the Within... there at the threshold of summer and winter, of knowing and wisdom, of consciousness and unconsciousness. One blow is all that is needed. The Sword, the Spear, the Blade of Truth rings through, and you emerge victorious. Child of the Father... your own child, your own father.

And I... I will sanctify you, reinforce your victory, reconsecrate your sovereignty. The cost is constant renewal, oh my child! The battle is yearly, for the next prisoner needs to be freed. Seek out the Guardians of the inner temple: the Oldest Animals, the inner instinct that knows, if not the truth of who you are and where dwells your sovereignty, but then at least the places you can find them – where to look.

Temper your impulse with wisdom. Do not jump too quickly into the unknown, but also do not deprive yourself of opportunity for fear's sake. The greatest wisdoms lay in the Cauldron of Rebirth – four chains uphold it. And when you've entered its fortress, you must pause. You cannot speak of the Mysteries. They are for you alone. Be aware of the signs and follow your instincts. Learn the difference between fear of change and growth, and the fear that is triggered because of danger and deception.

Think too on that which you truly need: how big of a bag must you carry? There is honor in hard work and your crown is not tarnished by it. It is only when you bow to the fear and illusions of others that the torc begins to unwind. When you can make peace, make peace. Your personal sovereignty is threatening to others when you do not play by their rules, when you excel and succeed because you have been true to who and what you are. Be wary, but be compassionate. Do not turn the tools of Art into weapons, for even if you defeat your enemies in combat, it is they who will have won.

Honor yourself by honoring your word. Fulfill your commitments as best you can and do not be afraid to ask for help. Even if the world shifts and you no longer recognize the landscape around you, seek to be grounded in the landscape within you. Find the tools you need to re-craft your life.

Be generous with your bounty.
Be clear and careful with your words.
Be true to your vision.
Be honorable in your actions.
Be grounded in your sovereignty.
Be welcome in my presence.
    I of the broad back to carry you.
    I of the sweet song to comfort you.

I of the wide lap to nurture you.
I of the deep bag to fortify you.
I of the threshold to
    LEAD YOU HOME.

Love yourself and others.
Forgive yourself and others.

The past is your teacher.
The future is your student.

The present is the threshold between.

Step through every moment.
Step through each breath.
Step through the space between each heartbeat.

Where you stand is ever the bridge.
    How you cross this moment,
    What you choose to bring with you,
    Where you land on the other side...
        This is the burden of sovereignty.

And if where you land has pain unavoidable – loss, hurt, injury, death – how we step through is what we can control:
    the way we carry the burden,
    the companions we choose to walk with us,
    the tools within us to help us move through,
    the release of the struggle so that we are open to learn,
        open to yet love, open to face the truth of the prison,
        and seek how to set our wonder child free once
        again.

We are not born to suffer, to carry shame, to live in fear.
We are born to remember our sovereignty, to find healing
in the pain, release in the shame, love in the fear.
To harness the challenges – he disappointment, the loss,
the hurt, the fear, the pain.
To move through them.
To use them as a bridge to understanding, a pathway to
increased sovereignty, a KEY to unlock the door of
your inner prison.

The challenges are not the endpoint. We aren't meant to
dwell there.
They are the THRESHOLD over which we are meant to
step, the bridge we are meant to cross, the boundary
we are meant to break through.

For on the other side of it is the joy of release, of freedom,
of the renewal.

the reunion of Mother and Child,
of self to source,
of emptiness to wholeness.

The burden is lifted.

And we are free.

And sovereign.

I am the swift steed.
I am the law of right rule.
I am the door that swings into life and into death.
I am the pathway to the chieftain's court.

I am the key that frees the sacred prisoner.
I am the mother that births the warrior.
I am she who receives him home again.

Who receives YOU home again.

Conclusion

The Journey Begins

Through overgrown pathways of history that twist and bend, and lead out of sight, we have sought her. Through the living words captured in the black finality of ink on the candlelit illumination of precious vellum, we have chased her down. Through a webbed lineage of far-flung divinities, some anchored in a past unknowable, some revealing themselves in layers like a nesting doll with the truth of her at its core, we have made desperate pursuit.

And through it all, in the end, the lesson remains this: No matter the provenance. No matter the proof. No matter the mastery of the lore, or the availability of the resources, or the correctness of the translation. In order for Rhiannon to reveal herself to you... for you to come to know the truth of her... for you to be in right relationship with the Divine Queen and with your own Sovereignty... only one thing is needed. Only one thing must be done.

Ask.
And she will stop.
And she will answer.

Appendix 1

Notes on Welsh Pronunciation

VOWELS

a short: pronounced as in pan.

a long: pronounced as in father.

e short: pronounced as in pen.

e long: pronounced like the first element of the diphthong in lane.

i short: pronounced as in pin.

i long: pronounced as in machine.

o short: pronounced as in cot.

o long: pronounced like the first element of the diphthong in note.

u: pronounced (approximately) like the French u in sur.

w short: pronounced like the oo in wood.

w long: pronounced like the oo in wooed.

y: pronounced sometimes like u in but, and sometimes (approximately) like the French u in sur.

DIPHTHONGS

They may be pronounced by giving to each of the component vowels the value indicated above.

CONSONANTS

c is always pronounced as k, chi as in the Scotch loch, dd as th in breathe, f as v, ff as f, s is always hard, as in loss; ll represents a spirant l, a very difficult sound to represent in English – Englishmen generally render it as thl.

ACCENT
The accent is nearly always on the last syllable but one (or penult) as Elidyr, Seithényn.

EXAMPLES
Gwyddno = Gwithno, th as in breathe; Gwenhúdiw = Gwenhidue; Syfáddon = Syváthon, th as in breathe; Dwt = D?ot, oo as in wood; Pwca = P?oka, oo as in wood; Ardúdwy = Ardid?oi; Llwyd = Ll??id, ll the spirant l, oo as in wooed.
(From *The Welsh Fairy Book,* by Jenkin W. Thomas)

Bibliography

Primary Sources

Apuleius, Lucius, Adlington, W., trans., *The Golden Ass: being the metamorphoses of Lucius Apuleius* (London: William Heinemann, 1922).

Babbit, Frank Cole, trans., *Plutarch's Moralia* (Cambridge, MA: Harvard University Press, 1936).

Bollard, John K., trans., *The Mabinogi: Legend and Landscape of Wales* (Llandysul: Gomer Press Limited, 2006).

Bromwich, Rachel, ed. and trans., *Trioedd Ynys Prydein: The Welsh Triads* (Cardiff: University of Wales Press 2006).

Bromwich, Rachel and Evans, D. Simon, trans., *Culhwch and Olwen: An Edition and Study of the Oldest Arthurian Tale,* (Cardiff: University of Wales Press, 1992).

Coe, Jon B., and Young, Simon, The Celtic Source for the Arthurian Legend, (Felinfach: Llanerch Publishers, 1995).

* Davies, Sioned, trans., *The Mabinogion* (New York: Oxford University Press, 2007).

Ford, Patrick K., trans., *The Mabinogi and Other Medieval Welsh Tales* (California: University of California Press, 1977).

Gray, Elizabeth A., *Cath Maige Tuired: Second Battle of Mag Tuired* (Dublin: Irish Texts Society, 1983).

Guest, Charlotte, trans., *The Mabinogion* (London: Richard Clay and Sons, Ltd., 1906).

Gwynn, Edward, trans., *The Metrical Dindshenchas,* (Dublin: Royal Irish Academy House, 1903).

McDevitte, W.A, trans., Bohn, W.S., trans., *Caesar's Gallic War,* (New York: Harper & Brothers, 1869).

O'Meara, John J., *Gerald of Wales: The History and Topography of Ireland,* (Dundalgan Press, 1951).

Parker, Will, trans., *The Four Branches of the Mabinogi* (California: Bardic Press, 2005).
*Preferred academic translation.

Secondary Sources

Beck, Noémie, "Goddesses in Celtic Religion, Cult and Mythology: A Comparative Study of Ancient Ireland, Britain and Gaul", (Unpublished Ph.D. Thesis, University College Dublin, 2009).

Breeze, Andrew, *The Origins of the Four Branches of the Mabinogi* (Herfordshire, Gracing Press, 2009).

Cartwright, Jane, *Women in the Middle Ages: Sources from the Celtic Regions*, (Lampeter: University of Wales, 2012).

Cunliffe, Barry, *The Ancient Celts*, (Oxford: Oxford University Press, 1997).

Davies, Sioned, *The Four Branches of the Mabinogi* (Llandysul: Gomer Press, 1993).

Davies, Sioned, "Horses in the *Mabinogion*", *The Horse in Celtic Culture: Medieval Welsh Perspectives*, Jones, Nerys Ann, and Davies, Sioned, eds., (Cardiff: University of Wales Press, 1997), 121–140.

Derks, Ton, *Gods, Temples and Ritual Practice: The Transformation of Religious Ideas and Values in Roman Gaul (Amsterdam Archaeological Studies)*, (Amsterdam: Amsterdam University Press, 1998).

Dexter, Miriam Robbins, "The Hippomorphic Goddess and Her Offspring", *Journal of Indo-European Studies*, (1990), 285–307.

Dunbar, Agnes B.C., *A Dictionary of Saintly Women*, (London: George Bell and Sons, 1905).

Ford, Patrick K., "Prolegomena to a Reading of the "Mabinogi": 'Pwyll' and 'Manawydan'", *Studia Celtica, 16/17* (1981/1982), 110.

Findon, Joanne, *A Woman's Words: Emer and Female Speech in the Ulster Cycle*, (Toronto: University of Toronto Press, 1997).

Garman, Alex, *The Cult of the Matronae in the Roman Rhineland: An Historical Evaluation of the Archaeological Evidence* (New York: Edwin Mellen Press, 2008).

Green, Miranda Aldhouse, "The Symbolic Horse in Pagan Celtic Europe: An Archaeological Perspective", *The Horse in Celtic Culture: Medieval Welsh Perspectives,* Davies, Sioned and Jones, Nerys Ann, eds., (Cardiff: University of Wales Press, 1997), 1–22.

Gruffydd, W.J., *Folklore and Myth in the Mabinogion* (Cardiff: University of Wales Press, 1958).

Gruffydd, W.J., *Math Vab Mathonwy, An Inquiry into the Origins and Development of the Fourth Branch of the Mabinogi, with the Text and a Translation* (Cardiff: University of Wales Press Board, 1928).

Gruffydd, W.J., *Rhiannon: Inquiry into the First and Third Branches of the Mabinogion* (Cardiff: University of Wales Press Board,1953).

Hamp, Edward, "Mabinogi and Archaism", *Celtica 23,* (1999) pp.96–110.

Harrison, Henry, *Surnames of the United Kingdom: A concise etymological dictionary, Volume 2* (London: Morland Press, Ltd., 1918).

Hemming, Jessica, "Reflections on Rhiannon and the Horse Episodes in 'Pwyll'", *Western Folklore, Vol. 57, No. 1* (Winter, 1998), 19–40.

Hull, Eleanor, *The Cuchullin Saga in Irish Literature: being a collection of stories relating to the Hero Cuchullin,* (London: David Nutt, 1989).

Hutton, Ronald, "Medieval Welsh Literature and Pre-Christian Deities", *Cambrian Medieval Celtic Studies 61* (2011), 57–85.

Jackson, Kenneth H., *The International Popular Tale and the Early Welsh tradition* (Cardiff: University of Wales Press, 1961).

Jones, Thomas Gwynn, *Welsh Folklore and Folk-Custom* (London: Methuen & Co., Ltd., 1930).

Koch, John T., editor, *Celtic Culture: An Historical Encyclopedia,* (Oxford, England: ABC-CLIO, 2006).

Linduff, Katheryn M., "Epona: A Celt Among the Romans", *Latomus, T. 38, Fasc. 4* (Octobre – Decembre, 1979), pp. 817–837.

Lyle, Emily B., "Dumezil's Three Functions and Indo-European Cosmic Structure", *History of Religions, Vol. 22, No. 1,* (Aug., 1982), 25–44.

Mac Cana, Proinsias, *The Mabinogi,* second edn., (Cardiff: University of Wales Press, 1992).

MacCulloch, J.A., *The Religion of the Ancient Celts,* (Edinburgh: T. & T. Clark, 1911).

McKenna, Catherine, "The Theme of Sovereignty in Pwyll," *Bulletin of the Board of Celtic Studies, 29* (1980), 35–52.

Miles-Watson, Jonathan, *Welsh Mythology: A Neo-Structuralist Approach* (Amherst: Cambria Press, 2009).

Owen, Trefor M., *Welsh Folk Customs* (Llandysul: Gomer Press, 1985).

Rees, Alwyn and Rees Brinley, *Celtic Heritage: Ancient Tradition in Ireland and Wales* (London: Thames and Hudson, Ltd., 1961).

Reinach, Salomon, "Epona", *Revue Archéologique, Troisième Série, T. 26* (1895), 163–195.

Ross, Anne, *Folklore of Wales* (Stroud: Tempus Publishing Ltd., 2001).

Ross, Anne, *Pagan Celtic Britain* (Chicago: Academy Chicago Publishers, 1996).

Stifter, David, *Old Celtic Languages,* (Sommersemester, 2008).

Sullivan, C. W., *The Mabinogi: A Book of Essays* (New York: Garland Publishing, Inc., 1996).

Thomas, Gwyn, *Tales from the Mabinogion* (Woodstock: The Overlook Press, 1984).

Thomas, Jenkin W., *The Welsh Fairy Book,* (New York: F. A. Stokes, 1908).

Thompson, Stith. *Motif-index of folk-literature: a classification of narrative elements in folktales, ballads, myths, fables, medieval romances, exempla, fabliaux, jest-books, and local legends.* (Bloomington: Indiana University Press, 1955–1958) Available at http://www.ruthenia.ru/folklore/thompson/

Trevelyan, Marie, *Folk-Lore and Folk-Stories of Wales* (London: Elliot Stock, 1909).

Valente, Roberta Louise, "Merched Y Mabinogi: Women and the Thematic Structure of the Four Branches", (Unpublished Ph.D. Thesis, Cornell University, 1986).

Van der Linden, Renske, "The Laws of Hywel Dda in the Four Branches of the Mabinogi", (Unpublished M.A. Thesis, University of Utrecht, 2007).

Vermaat, Robert, "Modrun, granddaughter of Vortigern", retrieved from http://www.vortigernstudies.org.uk/artfam/modrun.htm

Welsh, Andrew, "Doubling and Incest in the Mabinogi", *Speculum, Vol. 65, No. 2* (Apr., 1990), pp. 344–362.

Westropp, T.J., "Notes and Folklore from the Rennes Copy of the 'Dindsenchas'", *The Journal of the Royal Society of Antiquaries of Ireland Fifth Series, Vol. 9, No. 1* (Mar. 31, 1899), 21–27.

Winward, Fiona, "The Women in the Four Branches", *Cambrian Medieval Studies 34* (1997), 77–106.

Wood, Juliette, "The Fairy Bride Legend in Wales", *Folklore, Vol. 103, No. 1* (1992), 56–72.

Wood, Juliette, "The Horse in Welsh Folklore: A Boundary Image in Custom and Narrative", *The Horse in Celtic Culture: Medieval Welsh Perspectives,* Davies, Sioned and Jones, Nerys Ann, eds., (Cardiff: University of Wales Press, 1997), 162–179.

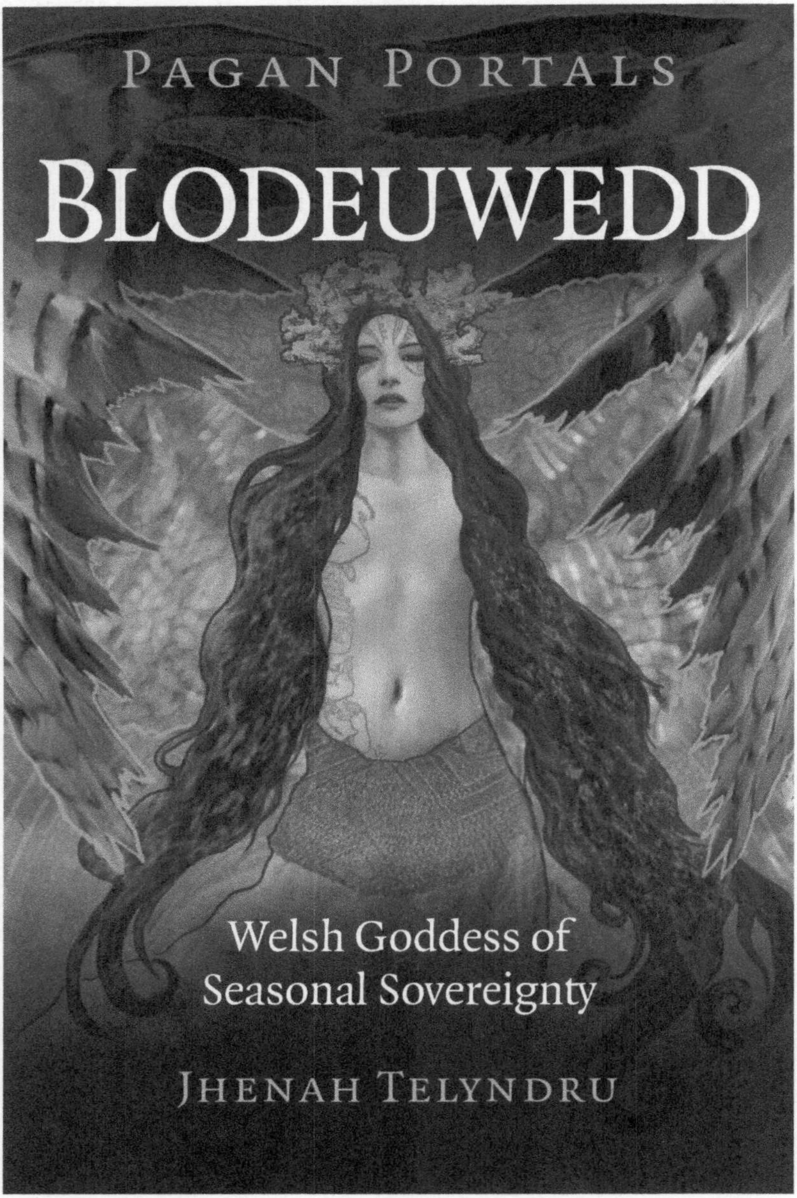
Pagan Portals
Blodeuwedd
Welsh Goddess of
Seasonal Sovereignty
Jhenah Telyndru

Pagan Portals

Blodeuwedd

Welsh Goddess of Seasonal Sovereignty

Jhenah Telyndru

What people are saying about

Blodeuwedd

Jhenah Telyndru has succeeded in beautifully weaving the complex, paradoxical nature of one of Wales' most beloved deities into a clear and inspirational work. Beautifully written with passion and devotion, this book is as fragrantly delicious and divine as the flowers that went into the magical making of Blodeuwedd. This is a delightful tome that is sure to be a go-to classic, filled with the inimitable sagacity of Telyndru, and her love for the Goddesses of this magical land.

Kristoffer Hughes, Head of the Anglesey Druid Order, author of *From the Cauldron Born: Exploring the magic of Welsh legend and Lore*

With dedicated scholarship and awen-inspired storytelling, Jhenah Telyndru has gifted us with a richly textured honouring of a complex Goddess. Not with oak, broom, and meadowsweet, but with historical source material, modern texts, and her own talon-sharp insight, Ms. Telyndru has crafted a revisioning of Blodeuwedd that elevates Her to a central role as a seasonal sovereignty Goddess rather than the uni-dimensional Goddess who was punished for the betrayal of Her husband.

It is time for Blodeuwedd to be given Her respectful and compassionate due. This book does that in spades, offering a deep exploration for all the intricate facets of Blodeuwedd's story while weaving in significant contextual information such as the shifting social mores of medieval Wales. Balancing a scholastic appreciation for the depth of this myth with the invitation to enter into relationship with the Goddess, Blodeuwedd: Welsh Goddess of Seasonal Sovereignty includes powerful workings that not only deepen a visceral, embodied understanding of the

Goddess, but open one to the experience of self that is complex, sovereign, and imbued with wisdom.

The world is well familiar with the light/dark aspects of the Greek Persephone in her dual role of Kore and Queen. How wonderful that there is finally a book that recognizes that same profound duality in Blodeuwedd – not as the Goddess who betrays but as the Sovereign seasonal queen around whom the sacred union with dark and light in turn hinges. In the spirit of the true bard-priestess she is, Ms. Telyndru ends with a poetic homage to Blodeuwedd that uplifts as powerfully as the owl's wing. For the scholarship, for the poetry, for the brilliance, you want to read this book.

Tiffany Lazic, Psychotherapist and author of *The Great Work: Self-Knowledge and Healing Through the Wheel of the Year*

Pagan Portals – Blodeuwedd is an indispensable guide to this most beloved goddess from Welsh myth. Jhenah Telyndru makes excellent scholarly use of the sources, as well as drawing on her deep visionary experience to draw the spiritual wisdom from Blodeuwedd's tale, showing us the goddess in all her power as well as her beauty. This book is both owls and flowers, grounded in the traditional lore, and a beautiful, insightful read. Valuable for all those devoted to a Celtic spiritual path, as well as an excellent devotional to one of our most misunderstood Goddesses of Sovereignty.

Danu Forest, Traditional wisewoman and Celtic scholar, author of several books including *Wild Magic- Celtic Folk Traditions for the Solitary Practitioner*, and *Pagan Portals – Gwyn ap Nudd: Wild God of Faerie and Guardian of Annwfn*

Contents

Acknowledgements   125
Introduction   126
Who is Blodeuwedd?   128

Chapter 1 – Legend and Lore   131
Chapter 2 – Culture and Context   150
Chapter 3 – Goddess of Sovereignty   161
Chapter 4 – Love Triangles and Seasonality   172
Chapter 5 – The Flower Bride   189
Chapter 6 – The Owl   205
Chapter 7 – Seeking Sovereignty   214
Chapter 8 – Entering into Relationship
            with Blodeuwedd   226
Chapter 9 – Forward into the Future   236

Bibliography   243

Acknowledgments

I am incredibly grateful to Dr. Jane Cartwright, with whom I had the honor to study at the University of Wales, Trinity St. David. She served as the academic advisor for my Master's dissertation, which focused on the role of Blodeuwedd as a Seasonal Sovereignty figure in the Fourth Branch of *Y Mabinogi*.

I am also deeply appreciative of the cultural insights and encouragement of my dear friend Kristoffer Hughes, Head of the Anglesey Druid Order and brilliant author and teacher. His service to the Gods of Wales is deeply inspirational: infused with love, informed by scholarship, and empowered with the Awen.

Endless thanks as well to artist Dan Goodfellow, who generously has permitted his inspired and inspiring painting of Blodeuwedd to grace the cover of this work.

I do not have enough words of thanks for the personal support and editorial skills of my beloved Sister in Avalon, Lori Feldmann. Cappys gonna Cap!

And finally, I am so honored to work with Trevor Greenfield, editor of Moon Books. Thank you so very much, Trevor, for all of your hard work, support, and understanding through every step of the publishing process.

Introduction

In the dawning light of a new beginning, she unfurls.
Petal-soft, her heady scent rises
    like the reborn sun
    and is carried by the breeze.
Crowned with golden strings of oak blossoms,
    an eagle shelters in her highest boughs.
Fortified in lattice-worked hedgerows,
    the sacred wren nests
    beneath the flowers of riotous yellow broom,
    spreading laughter
    across the brightening landscape.
Cresting like sea foam
    from beyond the ninth wave,
    the white caps of meadowsweet break like a rising tide
    as the sun reaches his apex above.
Now a bride's bouquet...
Now a maiden's funerary offering...
The Queen of the Meadow follows
    the lengthening shadows
    to the very edges of her sovereign realm.

There, by riverbank and holey-stone,
    the seven-tined stag awaits her –
    his milk-white body presaging
    the rising of the moon.
The sun slips below the horizon
    to seek his rest in the islands of the west.
Side by side, they ford the river
    her arms outstretched
    her voice raised in song.
All as the Silver Wheel weaves a diamond tapestry

in the deep night sky.
Her eyes grow wide as apples
Her long white fingers form
    a fringe of feathers.
Her feet become talons,
    become vise grips,
    become weapons.
Her body shifts, like a ghost in the night.
Her wings unfurl in the growing
    dark of a new day.

Who is Blodeuwedd?

A Goddess? A nature spirit? A magical conjuration? An embodiment of the land?

Until recent years, the story of Blodeuwedd was rarely known outside of Wales itself, and those familiar with her tale did not generally hold her in very high regard. For non-Welsh speakers, her very name is challenging; hard to spell, difficult to pronounce – and she has two of them! First, she is called *Blodeuedd* (bluh-DYE-eth), "Flowers", after the components from which she is created. Later, she is renamed *Blodeuwedd* (bluh-DYE-weyth), which means "Flower Face or Flower Aspect", in acknowledgment of her owl form. *(Please note: for simplicity's sake, except for times when she is being specifically being discussed in her aspect of the Flower Bride, this book refers to her as Blodeuwedd throughout.)*

No matter what she may once have been, Blodeuwedd's literary legacy is that of a magical woman conjured out of flowers for the sole purpose of becoming the wife of Lleu, a prince who was prohibited from marrying a human woman. She eventually came to betray her husband, falling in love with a neighboring lord and conspiring to kill Lleu in order to be with her lover. In the end, she is punished by her creator by being turned into an owl – that most hated of birds – cursed to never again dwell in the light of day.

Overwhelmingly, Blodeuwedd is perceived in a negative light. At best, her shortcomings can be blamed on her naivety; after all, what could be expected of this weak and simple creature created out of flowers, formed as a fully-grown woman with no life experience, having had no mother to raise her or guide her on her role as wife? At worst, however, she is the embodiment of the evils of women who give into their wanton sexual desires, who plot against the men in their lives, and who defy the social contract by seeking to circumvent the roles and expectations placed upon them by the over-culture.

In medieval Wales, Blodeuwedd's story likely served as a cautionary tale intended to dissuade women, especially, from trying to break free from the confines placed upon them by society. Her punishment demonstrates that nothing good can come from seeking to change the circumstances of one's life beyond what is considered proper... and what is proper is for women to be faithful to their husbands, to fulfill their wifely duties, and to never give in to the lustful failings of the flesh.

To the modern reader, Blodeuwedd's story can be challenging in many respects, and reactions to her are likewise quite varied. Some who read her tale with modern eyes see a woman who acted against her apparently loving husband with unwarranted cruelty; adultery is one thing, but why didn't she just leave Lleu, instead of conspiring to kill him? Others see Blodeuwedd as an early paragon of feminism, a heroine who fought to escape the limitations of what she was expected to be, and risked everything she had in order to live a life of her own choosing.

Whether cast as feckless naif, manipulative vixen, or driven freedom fighter, the maiden who begins her tale as a Flower Bride ends it in the form of an owl. Perhaps this was, as it appears on the surface, an act of punishment intended to dissuade others from making similar choices. Perhaps her owl form is an unconscious symbol of the vilification of women's power by the patriarchy – which, having tried and failed to control her, was forced instead to banish her into the darkness of the collective Shadow. Perhaps her transformation was but a revelation of her truest form. Perhaps, through her choices, she obtained the wisdom of the owl and the freedom of her wings.

Blodeuwedd's story is a complex weaving of several strands of tradition. Obtaining as clear an understanding as possible of her many facets will allow us to develop the foundation necessary to come into deep relationship with her as a deity. To get a sense of who she may once have been, we must first examine the meaning of her tale from the perspective of those who passed the story on and eventually came to write it down. We can then use these insights to engage in a kind of mythic archaeology in order to identify the symbols and folkloric motifs which have become embedded in Blodeuwedd's tale over time.

Once unearthed from the narrative, we can use these pieces of information to embark upon a journey that allows us to reclaim Blodeuwedd – not only as the Goddess she may have once been, but as a deity who has risen once again into our collective consciousness for a reason. I believe that part of this reason is that she holds lessons which can assist us as individuals to grow into our true and authentic selves, and because she is a powerful and necessary ally for the challenges that face our world in the here and now.

Blodeuwedd is so much more than a uni-dimensional figure in a cautionary tale intended to keep women in their place. Reclaiming her as a fully-realized deity with agency and power requires that we understand the medieval context of her tale, retrace the details of her obscured divinity, and restore her role as a seasonal Sovereignty figure.

And so, let us begin.

Chapter 1

Legend and Lore

The story of Blodeuwedd is primarily known to us from the Fourth Branch of *Y Mabinogi,* a medieval Welsh story cycle. Although current scholarship dates the extant manuscripts containing the Four Branches to the 12th century, aspects of these tales are thought to be of much older origin, believed to have been transmitted from generation to generation through oral tradition.

The Fourth Branch, also known by the title "Math ap Mathonwy", can be broken down into three distinct but interrelated story arcs, and although Blodeuwedd only appears in the last third of the tale, it is important to read the Branch in its entirety to understand the events leading up to her creation.

A Retelling of the Fourth Branch

The song of Blodeuwedd is a shimmering verse in a long and branching tale. It is a bend in a sacred river fed by a confluence of many streams. To speak only of the river is to discount its journey through many lands – lands which both shaped, and were shaped by, its waters. Each tributary brings its story along with it, each becoming a chapter in the history of the whole river – each contributing its voice to the song.

To begin, then, we must sing first of the court of Math, brother of Great Dôn and king of Gwynedd in the north of Wales. A powerful magician, he possessed several peculiarities: first, that no word could be spoken anywhere that the wind would not take up and whisper into his ear, and second that he could not live unless his feet rested in the lap of a virgin. It is because of this necessity that Math could not circuit his lands in the way of Welsh lords, and so Gwydion and Gilfaethwy, the sons of his sister, did so in his stead.

Now it came to pass that Gilfaethwy had fallen madly in love with Goewin, his uncle's footholder, and he fell sick with his longing for her. When he confessed his situation to Gwydion – who, like their uncle, was a great enchanter – his brother promised he would find a way to remedy the situation.

It is here that our song turns dark. Knowing that Math could only be parted from his footholder when called to lead his warriors into battle, Gwydion set out to instigate a war with the kingdom of Dyfed in the south. The ruler of Dyfed was Pryderi, son of Rhiannon and Pwyll, and he possessed fantastic pigs gifted to him by Arawn, king of the Otherworldly realm of Annwn. Pryderi was oath-bound not to gift any of these pigs until they had doubled in number, but clever-tongued Gwydion convinced him that trading was different from giving – and oh, what wonders had Gwydion to trade with him!

For, in secret, the magician had gathered some toadstools and used them to conjure horses and hounds, saddles and shields – the finest ever seen. The dazzled Pryderi was eager to trade – and the cunning Gwydion was eager to leave, for the magic of his illusion would stand only for one day. Once Pryderi realized he had traded his Otherworldly pigs for an enclosure full of mushrooms, he mustered his forces against Gwynedd.

In response to Dyfed's attack, Math had no choice but to lead his army into battle – leaving Goewin behind at his court, Caer Dathyl. Thus alone, Gilfaethwy raped her in Math's own bed – all because Gwydion lit the flames of war so his brother could sate his lust. And so, we sing of a betrayal of trust between woman and man, between nephew and uncle, between North Wales and South, and between nobles and those who die for their causes.

In the midst of the clash, Pryderi calls upon Gwydion to meet him on the field of honor, warrior to warrior, so that no one else should die because of the wrong Gwydion had done to him. The son of Dôn agreed to meet Pryderi in combat, but no matter how valiantly he fought, the son of Rhiannon fell before Gwydion's sword and enchantments. Thus defeated, the South retreated, and the war was ended.

Calling for Goewin upon returning to his court, Math learns of her rape and the betrayal of his nephews. To make amends for the great wrong done to her, Math marries Goewin and makes her his queen, giving her authority over his lands. Though they sought to avoid him, Gwydion and Gilfaethwy were eventually forced to stand before their uncle to answer for their crimes.

Let us sing now of Math's magic and the three years he punished his nephews, transforming them into pairs of animals compelled to obey the urgings of their nature. Stag and hind, boar and sow, he-wolf and she-wolf they became... losing their form, their identity, their very names. Each year, in turn, one bore a son to the other – first Gilfaethwy, then Gwydion, then Gilfaethwy once more. Each year these offspring returned to Math's court, where they were struck with his wand and became human children. The names Math gave them recalled their animal origins – Little Deer Man, Little Pig Man, Little Wolf Man – and the three were kept in bardic memory with the following triad:

Three sons of Gilfaethwy the False –
Three warriors true: Bleidwn, Hydwn and Hychdwn the Tall

After three years, with their punishments over, Math's nephews are restored to their humanity and to their uncle's friendship. Although we hear no more of Gilfaethwy, Gwydion takes his place at Math's court once again.

And so, our song shifts, and a new tune begins, for in response to Math's need to find a new footholder, Gwydion suggests his sister Arianrhod. Daughter of Dôn, niece of Math, lady of her own court on an island bearing her name off the seacoast of Wales – she comes to Caer Dathyl when Math calls her.

"Are you a virgin?" Math asks.

"I do not know otherwise," she answers.

"We shall see," he replies, bending his magic wand and instructing her to step over it.

Raising her skirts, parting her knees, lifting one foot then the other, Arianrhod steps over the wand – and from her falls a yellow-haired infant boy. The baby cries out, and Arianrhod runs from the court, dropping a small thing from her as she goes. This small thing is taken up by Gwydion, who wraps it in brocade silk, and places it in a wooden chest by his bed. Math, in the meantime, has named the baby Dylan ("Great Tide") and baptizes him in the way of the time. Once receiving his name, Dylan makes his way to the sea and takes its nature immediately upon entering the waters. He is remembered as Dylan ail Tôn – Dylan of the Waves – for no wave was known to break beneath him. He was later accidentally killed by an unfortunate blow struck by his uncle Gofannon.

Sometime after Dylan disappeared into the sea, Gwydion hears a sound from the chest in his chamber. Opening it, he sees the arms of a baby boy reaching for him, emerging from the brocade that swaddled him. Finding a wet nurse and then rearing the child at court, Gwydion came to love the boy above all others. The child was strong and grew quickly, and after only four years had passed, he easily appeared to be more than twice his age in size and intellect.

Eventually, Gwydion brings the child with him to visit his sister's court at Caer Arianrhod, where she greets Gwydion warmly and enquires after the boy's identity. She becomes angry when he tells her that he is her own son, and asks why he's kept this reminder of her shame for so long. Gwydion argues that he has done the right thing in fostering so fine a boy, and tells her that he does not yet have a name.

Arianrhod then places a *tynged*, or destiny, upon the boy saying, "He will have no name save one I give to him!" "You are a wicked woman," Gwydion replies, "because you are angry that you are no longer called a maiden. But I promise you, he will get a name!"

Storming off with the boy, the two spend the night at Caer Dathyl. Rising early the next morning, Gwydion takes the child with him for a walk along the seashore. Using the seaweed he gathered together from along the strand, Gwydion conjures a ship with a sail, and a hold full of the finest Cordovan leather in fantastic colors never before seen. Using his magics to disguise their appearance, he and the boy set sail for the harbor of Caer Arianrhod, peddling their services as a master shoemaker and his apprentice. Word of their beautiful creations came to Arianrhod, who sends them her measurements so they might craft a pair of shoes for her. Gwydion creates several pairs of ill fitting, yet beautiful shoes for Arianrhod. Wondering at how such a skilled craftsman could make such incredible shoes, yet not be able to size them correctly, Arianrhod visits his ship in person so that he can take measurements directly from her feet.

As the disguised Gwydion does so, a tiny wren lands on the deck of the ship. Picking up a stone, the young apprentice casts it at the bird, striking its leg between the tendon and the bone. Impressed with his skill, Arianrhod exclaims, "The fair one has a skillful hand!" and with that, the enchantment fell away, revealing Gwydion and the boy for who they were. "Lady," Gwydion proclaims, "you have just named your son!" And from that day he was called Lleu Llaw Gyffes, the phrase Arianrhod uttered in her amazement.

Angry at her brother's trickery, Arianrhod lays a new destiny upon the boy, forbidding him to bear arms unless she herself armed him. Gwydion and Lleu depart, taking up residence at Dinas Dinlle. There the boy continued to grow, becoming skilled in horsemanship but restless in his desire to train in arms.

One day, promising Lleu a solution, the pair return to Caer Arianrhod, disguised as traveling bards, Arianrhod welcomes them to her court with a feast. Gwydion, who was an excellent storyteller, entertained the assembly late into the night.

Rising early from the guest chamber where he and Lleu slept, Gwydion called upon his magic once more. As the dawn broke, a battle alarm rang out as a great fleet of invading ships sailed into view on the horizon. In a frenzy, the island began preparing for its defense, and in the midst of the panic, Arianrhod and her women suited up and armed the two bards. As she unwittingly handed her now-armored son a sword, the fleet disappeared and the men's disguises fell away, revealing Gwydion and Lleu to an outraged Arianrhod.

Angry at Gwydion's deceit and for terrorizing her people, Arianrhod lays one last destiny upon her son: that he was forbidden to marry a woman of the race of the Earth. Declaring her a wicked woman once more, the pair return to Math's court, where Gwydion consults with his uncle on what to do next. By this time, Lleu had grown into a strong and handsome youth, ready to step fully into his manhood.

And so, our song shifts into its third and final verse, as the two magicians combine their wit and their spellcraft to aid Lleu Llaw Gyffes. Gathering together the flowers of oak, broom, and meadowsweet, Gwydion and Math conjure forth a woman to be Lleu's bride. They baptized her in the manner of the day and named her Blodeuedd, which means "flowers". The wedding feast was held that very night. Now possessing a name, arms, and a wife, Math gifts Lleu lands of his own, the cantref of Dinoding, to rule over from its seat at Mur Castell.

The newlyweds lived there happily for a time, and one day Lleu set out to visit Math at Caer Dathyl, leaving the holding in the care of Blodeuedd. Later that same day, Gronw Pebyr, lord of the neighboring kingdom of Penllyn, was engaged in a stag hunt that crossed into Lleu's land. It was almost sunset when Gronw finally brought down the stag, and he dressed it on the banks of the River Cynfael. Hearing that the neighboring lord and his hunting party had tarried late on her lands, Blodeuedd extended the hospitality of her hall to them, as was the custom.

At the feast, Blodeuedd and Gronw found themselves infused with love for each other, and spent the night in each other's arms. The next morning, Gronw sought to take his leave, but Blodeuedd asked him to remain with her another day, and they spent a second night in lovemaking. The next day, Gronw again moved to depart, but Blodeuedd asked him to stay with her once more, and they spent a third night together. When again morning came, the couple agreed that he should leave that day, but before he did so, the two conspired to find a way they could remain together forever.

Not long after Gronw and his party departed, Lleu returned home. That night in their bed, Lleu sensed a difference in his wife, and asked what troubled her. She replied, "While you were gone, I came to worry about what might happen should you be killed and not return home to me."

Touched by her apparent concern, Lleu responded, "Oh, you needn't worry about that; it is not easy for me to be killed."

"What do you mean?" she inquired.

"Well, I cannot be killed indoors nor outdoors, nor on foot or on horseback. And the only weapon that could harm me is one that is forged over a year and a day during prayers on Sundays."

"That sounds like something that could never happen," she replied.

"That is assured," he responded. "So, you need not fear for me. The only way it could happen is if I were to stand beneath a roof with no walls, with one foot on the edge of a tub and the other on the back of a beast. It is only then that the year-long forged weapon could kill me."

"That is a relief," Blodeuedd agreed. And the next day, she sent word to Gronw with instructions on how to forge the needed weapon.

After a year and a day had passed, Blodeuedd asked Lleu to meet her on the banks of the River Cynfael. There, she had set up a bath for him under a thatched roof with no walls. Delighted by this gift, Lleu entered the warmth of the tub, and when he had finished bathing, Blodeuedd said, "Remember when you assured me that you couldn't be killed except under special circumstances? I just want to be sure that this is indeed the case, and that you are safe."

Bringing a goat buck to stand beside the tub, she asked Lleu to stand with one foot on the edge of the vessel and the other on the back of the animal. Happy to reassure her, Lleu did as she asked. As soon as he was in position – neither indoors nor out, neither on foot nor on horseback – Gronw rose up from his nearby hiding place, and let loose the spear he had worked on for a year of Sundays. The weapon hit its mark, and with a scream, Lleu transformed into an eagle and flew away.

With Lleu gone, Blodeuedd and Gronw made for Mur Castell, and began to rule over the merged lands of Dinoding and Penllyn.

It was not long before Gwydion got word of what had transpired, and set out to find his beloved nephew. Wandering all of Wales in search of Lleu, he came to spend the night in Arfon where he heard of a strange occurrence. Each morning, when a swineherd opened the gate of his pen, one of his sows would disappear into the countryside; no-one knew where she went, but she would return every evening, fat and satiated. The next morning, Gwydion rose early and followed the sow, who rushed upstream along a brook, only stopping beneath a tree where she started to eat. When Gwydion caught up with her, he looked up to see a wounded eagle roosted on the highest branches of an enormous oak tree. When the eagle flapped its wings, pieces of rotting flesh and maggots fell from its body to the ground below, which was eagerly devoured by the sow.

Certain that this eagle was his missing nephew, Gwydion tapped the oak three times with his wand as he recited the following *englynion*, or poetic verses:

Oak that grows between the two banks;
Darkened is the sky and hill!
Shall I not tell him by his wounds,
That this is Lleu?

Oak that grows in upland ground,
Is it not wetted by the rain? Has it not been drenched
By nine score tempests?
It bears in its branches Lleu Llaw Gyffes!

Oak that grows beneath the steep;
Stately and majestic is its aspect!
Shall I not speak it?
That Lleu will come to my lap?
(From "Math ap Mathonwy", Lady Charlotte Guest, trans.)

After each verse, the eagle descended into lower branches of the tree until, after the last line was spoken, it came to rest on Gwydion's lap. The magician touched the eagle with his wand, and it transformed back into the weak and gravely wounded Lleu. Gwydion brought his nephew to Caer Dathyl where the best physicians and healers in the land came to care for Lleu. It wasn't until the end of the year that his health was finally restored. Ready now to redress the wrongs done to him, and wanting to reclaim his lands, Lleu told Math his intention, and they gathered the forces of Gwynedd.

Gwydion marched ahead of the war band and made his way to Mur Castell to face Blodeuedd for her part in the betrayal of Lleu. Terrified, Blodeuedd gathered her women and fled, seeking the protection of a court nestled in the mountains, on the other side of the River Cynfael. With Gwydion in pursuit, the frightened women ran as quickly as they could, glancing behind them after every few steps to determine how close their pursuer was becoming. As the darkness grew, so did their panic, and because they were so concerned with what was happening behind them, the women did not pay attention to what was happening in front of them – and one by one, all but Blodeuedd fell into a lake and drowned. In their memory, the lake is now called Llyn Morwynion, the Lake of the Maidens.

Alone now and exhausted, Blodeuedd was finally overtaken by Gwydion. Standing over her, he declared his judgement, "I will punish you for your shaming of Lleu Llaw Gyffes, but I will not destroy you. Instead, I will transform you into an owl for all time. You will never be able to show your face again in the light of day, for you will be hated by all other birds and they will attack you on sight. And you will keep your name, forever to be called Blodeuwedd." With that, he touched her with his magic wand, turning her into an owl. To this day in Wales *blodeuwedd*, which means "Flower Face", is a word for owl.

At the same time, Gronw retreated to Penllyn and sent Lleu an offer of land and gold as recompense for the matter between them. Lleu replied that he would only be satisfied by the lord of Penllyn meeting him on the banks of the River Cynfael. There, each of them would stand where the other had stood, and Lleu would cast his spear at Gronw.

Upon receiving this message, Gronw turned to his men, and asked if any of them would stand in his place, which was the custom of the time. No-one came forward to protect their lord, and Gronw's retinue became known as one of the Three Disloyal War Bands of the Island of the Mighty.

Having no choice but to take the blow for himself, Gronw met Lleu on the river bank, and asked, "Since this situation was instigated by a woman, may I at least hold this slab of stone between us when you cast your spear?"

"Although it is more consideration than you granted me, I will allow it," Lleu responded.

The two men got into position – Lleu with his spear, and Gronw with his stone shield. Lleu hurled his weapon at Gronw so powerfully that it pierced the stone and Gronw's heart both, breaking his back and killing him on the spot. To this day, on the banks of the River Cynfael can be found an upright of stone, about chest-high on a man, with a hole through the center of it, and it is called Llech Ronw – Gronw's Stone. With that, Lleu was avenged, and took back his land.

Thus, ends our song.

Thus, ends this Branch of *Y Mabinogi*.

Other Sources

While the Fourth Branch of *Y Mabinogi* contains the most complete extant version of Blodeuwedd's story, she and her tale are referenced in other medieval Welsh writings as well. Several poems from the 14th century manuscript *Llyfr Taliesin* (*The Book of Taliesin*) – which contains poems believed to date back as far as the 6th century CE – appear to allude to Blodeuwedd. One of them, "Cad Goddeu" ("Battle of the Trees"), does not directly name Blodeuwedd, but a section of the poem seems to be an account of her creation by Math and Gwydion. We will discuss this poem further in Chapter 5.

Another poem from *Llyfr Taliesin*, "Cadair Ceridwen" ("The Chair of Ceridwen"), includes these lines:

Celfyddaf gwr a gigleu
Gwydion ap Don dygnferthau
A hudwys gwraig a Elodeu

The most skilful man ever heard of

141

(Was) Gwydion ap Don, a hard toiler,
Who made by enchantment, a woman from flowers.

An interesting verse, called "The Deceiving of Huan" is found
in Peniarth MS 112 880-881, dating to sometime before 1619.
Written several centuries after the medieval redaction of *Y
Mabinogi*, it is quite short, and appears to be either a variant or
later evolution of the tale recounted in the Fourth Branch.

> *Gwraig Huan ap Gwydion, a vu un o ladd ei gwr, ag a ddyfod ei
> fyned ef i hely oddi gartref, ai dad ef Gwdion brenhin Gwynedd y
> gerddis bob tir yw amofyn, ac or diwedd y gwnaeth ef Gaergwdion
> (sef: via laactua) sy yn yr awyr yw geissio: ag yn y nef y cafas ei
> chwedyl, lle yr oedd ei enaid: am hynny y troes y wraig iefanc yn
> ederyn, a ffo rhag ei thad yn y gyfraith, ag a elwir er hynny hyd
> heddiw Twyll huan.*

The wife of Huan ap Gwydion was a party to the killing of
her husband, and she said that he had gone to hunt away
from home. And his father, Gwydion, the King of Gwynedd,
traversed all countries in search of him, and at last made Caer
Gwydion, that is the *via lactea*, which is in the sky, to seek
him. And he found him in heaven, where was his soul. And
for that he turned the young wife into a bird and she fled
from her father-in-law, and is called to this day Twyll Huan
(Huan's Deceiving).

It's fairly clear that this verse refers to the story of Blodeuwedd
and Lleu, although she is not directly named, and Lleu's name
is given as Huan. This is interesting for several reasons. First,
according to the *Geiriadur Prifysgol Cymru (Dictionary of the Welsh
Language)* the Welsh word *huan* means "(the) sun, sunlight,
sunshine; shining, bright, radiant, sunny." We will discuss the
meaning of Lleu's name in more detail later on in this work, but

one theory is that it comes from the Proto-Indo-European word *leuk-*, meaning "light"; this etymology has been questioned by some modern linguists, but this verse gives some support to the idea of Lleu having some solar associations, as we shall see.

Second, when Gwydion punishes the unfaithful wife of Huan by turning her into a bird and changing her name to *Twyll Huan (Huan's Deceiving)*, the verse appears to be providing a folk etymology for *tylluan*, a word that means "owl" in Welsh. This holds a strong resemblance to the punishment meted out by Gwydion at end of the Fourth Branch: he transforms Blodeuedd into an owl, and changes her name to Blodeuwedd — a name that is also another Welsh word for "owl." Even though each story uses a different word for owl, it is notable that both versions make direct etiological statements linking owls to the name of the woman who betrayed Gwydion's kin.

It is notable that "The Deceiving of Huan" directly states something that is only hinted at in the Fourth Branch: Gwydion appears to have traditionally been considered the father of Lleu. Subtextual clues exist in the original Welsh of the Fourth Branch, where, in speaking with Gwydion about her yet-unnamed son, Arianrhod refers to the child as "your son/boy" (she uses the word *mab*, which means both son and boy), although this could may also be a reference to Gwydion's role as a surrogate mother and foster father to the boy. That said, this phrasing, especially in the context of the underlying shame that Arianrhod expresses when Gwydion brings the child before her, may support the theory of an incestuous origin for Lleu – a somewhat common occurrence in divine families throughout world mythology.

Finally, Gwydion's association with the *Via Lactea,* the Milky Way, in "The Deceiving of Huan" is significant not only because this presents an onomastic explanation for the existence of the Milky Way, but it also names this celestial body *Caer Gwydion* (Gwydion's Fortress) in much the same way as the constellation *Cassiopeia* is known in Wales as *Llys Dôn* (The

Court of Dôn) after Gwydion's mother, and the *Corona Borealis* (Northern Crown) is called *Caer Arianrhod,* for his sister. One of the potential meanings of the name Arianrhod is "Silver Wheel", a name which suggests the roundness of the moon or the cyclic nature of her phases. Although certainly evocative, it is unknown if these celestial associations with members of the House of Dôn – and particularly with Lleu/Huan, Arianrhod, and Gwydion as sun, moon, and stars – are reflective of earlier tradition or if they are contemporary to the author of this verse.

While modern scholars generally agree that Gwydion is the father of Lleu based on the subtext in the Fourth Branch, as mentioned above, there is also some evidence that Math himself may be his father, and indeed, father of Blodeuwedd as well. A late medieval Welsh genealogical tract called *Bonedd yr Arwyr* lists the children of Math ap Mathonwy as Lleu Llaw Gyffes, Dylan Eil Ton, and Blodeuwedd; Arianrhod, daughter of Dôn, is listed as their mother. As Dôn is Math's sister, this would mean that Arianrhod is Math's niece; further incest is suggested with Lleu and Blodeuwedd presented as being brother and sister.

However, since it was Arianrhod's final *tynged* on Lleu which led to the creation of Blodeuwedd by Math and Gwydion, she could potentially be considered Blodeuwedd's mother, by two fathers. Further, as Dylan and Lleu were born as a result of Arianrhod stepping over Math's wand during his chastity test – whether this act is read as a metaphor for intercourse or if the literal magic of his wand catalyzed the birth of these brothers – it makes sense for Math to have been considered their father as well.

A poem called "Achau y dylluan" ("The Pedigree of the Owl") – attributed, with some uncertainty, to the famous medieval Welsh poet Dafydd ap Gwilym – sees the poet asking questions of an owl about her name and history. She replies with the story familiar to us from the Fourth Branch, but adds a piece of information: that her father is the son of Meirchion, lord of Môn.

Bonedd gwellwedd i'm gelwynt;
Blodeuwedd wrlh gyfedd gynt:
Merch i arglwydd, ail Meirchion,
Wyf fi, myn Dewi! O Fon.

Celtic scholar John Rhys believes that Môn, or Anglesey, was used as a literary device to represent the Islands of the Otherworld in early Welsh vernacular tales and poetry. This couplet, therefore, may be reinforcing Blodeuwedd's connection to the Otherworld. In support of this, another poem, by Anthony Powell, who died in the early 17th century, describes Blodeuwedd as the daughter of Meirchion Lwyd (Grey Meirchion). It also states that she was overtaken by Gwydion near Craig y Ddinas in the Neath valley, where she is buried. (Rhys, 439).

Crug ael, carn gadarn a godwyd yn fryn,
Yn hen fraenwaith bochlwyd;
Main a'i llud man y lladdwyd,
Merrh hoewen loer Meirchson lwyd

Heaped on a brow, a mighty cairn built like a hill, Like ancient work rough with age, grey-cheeked; Stones that confine her where she was slain, Grey Meirchion's daughter quick and bright as the moon.

Concerning Lleu

To fully understand Blodeuwedd's significance and nature, it is essential to also explore the mythological pedigree and lineage of her intended mate. Lleu is an important figure in Welsh mythos, a fact which is underscored by his connections to powerful divinities from other Celtic lands. Both he and the Irish God Lugh/Lug are cognates of the continental Celtic deity Lugus, who is known to us primarily through Gallo-Roman iconography and a few inscriptions which date back to the first century CE. However, an abundance of Lugus-derived toponyms and tribal names in Celtic areas of Europe and Britain, suggests he is a much older divinity. As they appear in much later literary records, Lugh and Lleu are likely culturally specific evolutions of Lugus, who is considered a pan-Celtic god.

Although the meaning of their names is unclear and has been a point of debate, there are several etymological possibilities. Some sources believe that Lleu shares the same etymological root as the words *golau* ("light, fair, bright") and *lleuad* ("moon") in Modern Welsh. Early linguists thought the name derives from the Proto-Indo-European *leuk-* which means "to shine" or "flashing light", a belief which supports the common notion that these were solar deities, or potentially related to other Indo-European gods of thunder. However, linguists have since determined that Proto-Indo-European *-k- did not evolve into the Proto-Celtic *-g-, making this etymology improbable. (Schrijver, 348). Currently, linguists believe the name more likely derives from Proto-Indo-European root words *leuǵ- "to break", *leug "black", or *leug^h- "to swear an oath". The latter connection has caused many scholars to believe that Lugus was a god of oaths and contracts. (Wood, 30)

Some translations of the Fourth Branch give Lleu's name as Llew, which means "lion". Scholars believe this to be related to variations in early Welsh spelling, or to have been a transcription error which continued to be replicated. Lleu is likely the originally intended name because it matches the rhyming scheme of the Englynion Gwydion – the three verses Gwydion sang to coax the eagle-form of Lleu out of the oak tree – which is considered the oldest segment of the Four Branches. (Koch, 1166)

After the Roman conquest of Gaul, Celtic divinities were commonly syncretized with Roman gods with whom they shared similarities, a process called *interpretatio Romana.* This functioned, in part, to permit indigenous worship to continue side by side with the Imperial cultus. In his commentaries on the Gallic Wars, Julius Caesar writes of the Gauls:

"Of all the gods they most worship Mercury. He has the largest number of images, and they regard him as the inventor of all the arts, as their guide on the roads and in travel, and as chiefly influential in making money and in trade." (Caes. Gal. 6.17)

Scholars believe that Caesar is here referring to Lugus, who is commonly syncretized with Mercury in Gallo-Roman iconography and inscriptions. He is depicted with familiar symbols of the youthful Roman god, including the caduceus and winged sandals – indicating his connection to the healing arts, his status as a psychopomp who bridges the worlds, and his role as patron of travelers – as well as bags of coins, roosters, and a spear. Significantly, he was also a god of contracts, supporting his connection with Lugus as a god of oaths. When Lugus is depicted in a more Celtic fashion, he is bearded and sometimes tricephalic, indicating he may have been a triple deity. Several extant inscriptions refer to him as Lugoues, a plural form of his name, and he seems to have had a triple function: that of magician, warrior, and craftsman. Indeed, there is a famous dedication to Lugoues in Spain which was sponsored by a shoemaker's guild. (Koch, 1203)

Gallo-Roman iconography often pairs Mercury with the Celtic Goddess Rosmerta, whose name potentially means "Great Provider." Her attributes are the cornucopia, a Roman libation cup called a *patera*, and a large vessel, sometimes interpreted as a bucket or casket of mead. Rosmerta is also sometimes shown with the caduceus and winged sandals of Mercury, both when depicted alongside him and when alone, suggesting that she was a healing divinity in her own right. (Koch, 1542)

Her association with the abundance of the land, as well as her potential connection to mead – which has ritual associations with the granting of kingship – may indicate her status as a Goddess of Sovereignty. That she often appears alongside a spear-bearing deity who is the inventor of all crafts and has the ability to travel between the worlds, is of particular interest to us as we seek to understand the meaning that underscores the narrative of the Fourth Branch.

Looking now at Insular Celtic tradition, Lleu holds many resonances with Lugh of Ireland, who is directly identified as a divinity in early literature. Lugh is a king of the Tuatha Dé Danann, while Lleu is a descendant of the House of Dôn, and eventually becomes king of Gwynedd. In the *Baile in Scáil* (*The Phantom's Frenzy*), Lugh appears in a vision to the warrior Conn, accompanied by a female figure identified as the Sovereignty of Ireland. Wearing a golden crown and bearing a golden cup, she asks Lugh to whom the cup should be given, and he lists Conn and all of the kings of Ireland who will come after him. Having a connection to Goddesses of Sovereignty seems to be an attribute that Lleu, Lugh, and Lugus/Mercury hold in common. They both bear similar epithets: compare Lleu Llaw Gyffes (Lleu of the Skillful Hand) with Lugh Lámhfhada (Lugh of the Long Arm) and Lugh Samildanach (Lugh of Many Skills). They are both associated with sling stones and spears. Both are craftsmen, with Lugh particularly praised in the *Cath Maige Tuired* (*The Second Battle of Moytura*) as being a builder, a smith, a champion, a harper, a warrior, a poet and a historian, a sorcerer, a physician, a cupbearer, and a brazier.

Lleu's facility with crafts are not as well-developed as those of Lugh in the extant literature, but his association with shoemakers is clear in the Fourth Branch, as well as in a Triad which names him as one of the Three Golden Shoemakers of the Island of Britain which, notably, further connects him to Lugus, who was patron of shoemakers, as mentioned above. We see

Lleu disguised as a bard along with Gwydion on one of their visits to Caer Arianrhod, and there are references to his magical skills elsewhere in Welsh tradition. In *Cad Goddeu* (*The Battle of the Trees*), for example, Lleu assists Gwydion in raising an army of enchanted trees to battle Arawn, King of Annwn.

Aside from his ability with a spear, we see little of Lleu's battle prowess in the narrative of the Fourth Branch, although several early Welsh sources depict Lleu as a great warrior. A variant of Triad 20 from *Trioedd Ynys Prydein* names Lleu as one of the Three Red Ravagers of the Island of Britain, and in *Englynion y Beddau* (*The Stanzas of the Graves*) Lleu is remembered as "a man who spared no one".

In the same way the Gaulish god Lugus has given his name to several cities in Europe – including Leon in France, and Leiden in Germany (which are all believed to derive from the name *Lugudunum*, meaning Fort of Lugus) – several landscape areas mentioned in the Fourth Branch bear Lleu's name to this day. These include Dinas Dinlle – the Iron Age fort on the Welsh coast overlooking the sea where Caer Arianrhod is believed to have been – and Dyffryn Nantlle (literally, "The Valley of Lleu's Stream"), the setting for some events in the Fourth Branch. Taken altogether, it is clear from even this brief overview that Lleu is somewhat more than the human hero he is presented as being in the Fourth Branch. Not only is he a figure with an ancient pedigree and a divine heritage, but the snippets of Welsh lore concerning him that remain outside of the Fourth Branch suggests that he once featured in a much wider corpus of myth that has been lost to us. If Lleu, like many of the main characters in *Y Mabinogi*, was once divine, how does this help to inform our understanding of Blodeuwedd's true nature?

Let us explore further.

Chapter 2

Culture and Context

Because the Celtic Britons, like other Celtic peoples, opted to transmit their sacred stories solely through the vehicle of oral tradition, we have a very incomplete understanding of their Gods, their beliefs, and their religious practices. Most of what we do know comes to us from the archaeological record, the sometimes-biased accounts of contemporary cultures like the ancient Greeks and Romans, and through the study of folklore and later vernacular tales. It isn't until the 11th or 12th centuries that the traditional stories of the Welsh started to be set into writing, and although some of these tales are believed to be of mythic origin with their roots in a distant, Pagan past, none of them identify any of the characters as divinities.

As oral tradition is living tradition, stories tend to evolve to reflect the cultural changes of the people telling the stories; this permits the tales to remain relevant in a way that written work, which is static and reflects a particular moment in time, cannot. It is possible, therefore, that elements of the sacred stories of the Celtic Britons survived in orality, evolving over time into the wonder tales foundational to the legends and lore of their descendants, while becoming interwoven with narrative strata arising from the cultural needs and experiences of subsequent generations.

Seeking Context

A close reading of the Four Branches of *Y Mabinogi* and contemporary tales can assist us in discerning patterns of symbolism and in identifying recurring folkloric motifs. While it is possible to recognize mythic themes in these tales that can be classified as international folk motifs, they cannot give us a clear picture about the origin of the stories, nor enable us to fully understand how the exchange of ideas with other countries may have impacted the growth and evolution of Welsh literary tradition.

Like the rest of Y Mabinogi, the Fourth Branch is imbued with layers of symbolism which likely held deeper meaning for its medieval Welsh audience than would otherwise be apparent to modern readers. The present-day study of these stories recognizes brief textual references to other lore – the significance of which was likely clearly understood by their contemporary audiences – but which leave us with only maddening glimpses into what may have been a more expansive corpus of story tradition.

Additionally, in mythological and folkloric studies we recognize a phenomenon known as *diachronism*; it is a mechanism through which tales unconsciously exhibit the cultural and historical trappings of the time in which it is written, even when presenting a story that consciously occurs in a different time period. This phenomenon is present throughout Y Mabinogi, and is a critical key for coming to a deeper understanding of the Fourth Branch.

Identifying aspects of medieval culture that permeate the Four Branches and other Welsh tales redacted in this period assists us in reading these stories from the perspective of its contemporary context, rather than only with the cultural bias of modern eyes. It is this modern filter which contributes to the harsh judgement of Blodeuwedd's actions in the Fourth Branch based upon a surface reading of the tale; however, there is much more happening than readily meets the eye. Further, once we have identified the medieval elements of the tales, what remains often contains the mythic remnants of earlier traditions – something of particular importance to modern Neo-Pagans.

The Rights of Women

Scholars believe that much of the tension that underscores the narrative of the Fourth Branch is a reflection of social changes in the status of women in medieval Wales. It contains a mythic resonance that has encoded the memory of a power struggle between the rights of women and men, particularly as it concerns matters of kinship, marriage, and inheritance.

It is possible that some Celtic cultures may have practiced matrilineal inheritance – where titles and property were passed down through the mother line – at some point in their histories.

Suggestive evidence that the Pictish tribes of Northern Britain were matrilineal, for example, can be found in Irish chronicles, the Pictish king-lists, and in Bede's *Ecclesiastical History*. We can also find traces of this practice in Welsh, Irish, and Breton myths and legends, even though it is not reflected in any known law code or historical treatise. Whereas matriliny was not practiced in medieval Wales, it is clearly present in the Fourth Branch and elsewhere in *Y Mabinogi*, a fact which seems to further validate the belief that the tales of the Four Branches are of much older origin than their medieval redactions, potentially having persisted in oral tradition since pre-Christian times.

Matronymy, where lineage is identified through the giving of the mother's name, tends to be present in cultures that practice matriliny. Several of the characters in the Fourth Branch are the Children of Dôn, all of whom have matronyms; this includes Gwydion fab ("son of") Dôn, Gilfaethwy fab Dôn, and Arianrhod ferch ("daughter of") Dôn. Dôn was an ancestral figure who may have been a mother Goddess cognate to the Irish Danu, who herself was the progenitor of the similarly matronymic Tuatha Dé Danann – the People of the Goddess Danu. Dôn's brother is Math fab Mathonwy, who may also have a matronym, although we do not know the gender of Mathonwy; ostensibly, Math rules Gwynedd as the head of the matriline.

Perhaps it is the practice of matronymy which underscores the first of Arianrhod's *tynged* – that her son not have a name save one that she herself gives to him; by giving him a name, she would thereby be acknowledging his place in the matriline. It is evidence of the power of Mother Right to name her child that Arianrhod could place this *tynged* to begin with – an authority so strong that its binding power could not be broken by Gwydion or Math even with all of their magic.

Aside from matronymy, matriliny is most directly illustrated through the concept of inheritance passing through the sister's son. Math himself has no children, which is not problematic as his heir is Gwydion, his sister's son. Similarly, Gwydion's heir is Lleu, the son of his sister Arianrhod who is the daughter of Dôn. At the end of the Fourth Branch, Lleu is without a wife and children, but the larger issue for the continuity of the House of Dôn is not that he has no children, but that he has no sister.

Cultural shifts tend to be gradual, and it is interesting to note the ways in which the tension arising between matriliny and patriliny seem to have been memorialized in the foundational conflicts of the story of the Fourth Branch. There are several other instances where we can see this tension play out both in direct relationship to Blodeuwedd herself, as well as in the events leading up to her creation.

Co-opting Female Power

The first instance of the masculine imposing itself on feminine in the Fourth Branch can be seen in the person of Goewin, both overtly and subtextually. She serves as Math's footholder, and the narrative tells us that he is required to always have his feet in the lap of a maiden, otherwise he would die. The only exception to this requirement is during times of war. This is a strange requirement, and may potentially represent a *tynged*, or fate, that has been lain upon Math, but we do not know its origin and no explanations are given in the Fourth Branch or other texts.

While it is true that medieval Welsh courts included a position called the king's footholder, they were invariably male, and seemed to only execute this duty during feasts: "It is right for him to hold the king's feet in his lap from when he begins to sit at the banquet until he goes to sleep, and to scratch the King." (Davies, 2007; 240) Perhaps then, the inclusion of the more fantastic version of the position depicted in the Fourth Branch is intended to be an onomastic myth that explains the presence and function of this person at court.

However, the medieval redactor of this tale was very specific in their word choice when it came to describing the required position of Math's feet – a choice which potentially shifts the significance of Goewin's role in Math's court.

"... this passage describes the position of Math's feet, which are *ymlyc croth morwyn* (literally, "in the fold of the womb of a virgin"). The noun *croth*, often translated as "lap," has the base meaning "womb," "uterus," or "belly". Also, the word that tends to be translated as "in the fold of," *ymlyc*, is a compound of *yw* (in) + *plyc* (fold, curve), which can mean either "in a fold or curve" or simply "within" ... Since Middle Welsh had another, less ambiguous word for lap, *arfet*, and this word appears later in the same text, the ambiguity may be intentional. The phrase *ymlyc croth morwyn* connotes varying degrees of intimate contact with the *morwyn* (virgin), from the more innocent "in the fold/curve of a virgin's belly" or "in the lap of a virgin" to the decidedly risqué "in the groin", "pubic hair of a virgin" or even "within the womb of a virgin" whose hymen remains magically intact." (Sheehan, 322)

This suggests that Math's requirement to have his feet in the "lap" of a maiden may indicate something more than a medieval oddity or *tynged*-based limitation. Perhaps instead, this can be interpreted as a rather pointed symbol of Math's kingship – his right to rule – being dependent on having the feminine principle, quite literally, as its foundation.

Gwydion's trickery sends Math off to a manufactured war so that Goewin could be left behind – and left vulnerable to the betrayal of Gilfaethwy who rapes her in his uncle's bed. When Math returns and discovers what his nephews have done, he responds by telling Goewin: "'… I will take you as my wife,' he said, 'and give you authority over my kingdom.'" This marriage transforms the power structure between the two, turning it into partnership, where before Goewin was held in a subordinate position, with Math's feet literally capping and controlling the female powers of sovereignty, which will be discussed in the next chapter.

The Fourth Branch also contains several undeniably overt, and increasingly aggressive, instances of Math and Gwydion using their magic to claim the female power to create life for themselves. First, the punished Gwydion and Gilfaethwy take turns becoming female animals and bearing children to each other by harnessing the regenerative power inherent in their transformed bodies. Second, catalyzed by Math's magic, Arianrhod spontaneously gives birth to twins when she steps over his rod: one which is born immediately, without spending any time gestating in his mother's womb, and the other which falls from her body, essentially as a fetus. This "small thing" is then incubated in Gwydion's wooden chest until it reaches full term – again, without the need for his mother's body.

Finally, the feminine principle is not required at all for the creation of Blodeuwedd. This last action can also be seen as circumventing the last of Arianrhod's binding power of *tynged*, a final victory over Mother Right. Conjured from the flowers of

155

oak, broom, and meadowsweet, Blodeuwedd is not of the race women currently on the earth, as specified by Arianrhod in her third destiny, and so Lleu is able to fully step into his manhood by taking a wife.

Whatever the subtextual symbolism or overt actions of the characters may once have meant, the patriarchy reveals itself in this myth. The attainment of a wife is part of a checklist required for manhood, and as we see in this story, often has nothing to do with the wants or needs of the woman herself. With this in mind, an understanding of Welsh marriage laws is critical to a deeper understanding of the Fourth Branch.

On Marriage

The *Cyfraith Hywel – The Laws of Hywel Dda* – was an early codification of Welsh law named for King Hywel the Good, who ruled Wales in the 10th century CE. These Celtic laws – with similarities to the Brehon laws of Ireland and which reflected the traditions of the Brythonic kingdoms of the Old North – were used to govern Wales until the final English conquest in the late 13th century. Although never specifically stated, the guiding principles of these laws can be found in each of the Four Branches, and reflect the cultural standards and social mores of Wales in the Middle Ages.

The *Cyfraith Hywel* specifically addressed issues of marriage, dowry, divorce, and inheritance. While by no means equal to men in medieval Wales, women of the time did enjoy some broader rights than did contemporaneous women in other countries; they were able to divorce their husbands, remarry if they so choose, receive monetary compensation for infidelity and physical mistreatment by her husband, and could leave a marriage with the full return of her dowry before seven years have passed, after which a fair and equitable division of wealth between the two parties is proscribed.

There are several points of marriage law that are key to our understanding of the Fourth Branch. First, it must be understood that "... a woman must be a free consenting party to her marriage and could not be disposed of against her will ... there was no selling of a woman in marriage." (T.P. Ellis, 124) We see several marriages occur in *Y Mabinogi* that reflect this law.

- Rhiannon and Pwyll wed in the First Branch, and while Rhiannon is being compelled to marry by her father, she is able to choose her own husband.
- In the Second Branch, a political marriage is brokered between Britain and Ireland, and Branwen's family negotiates on her behalf.
- In the Third Branch, we see Rhiannon's son Pryderi suggest a marriage between his now-widowed mother and his friend Manawydan, brother to Bran and Branwen and rightful heir to the throne of Britain. It may seem odd for a son to be playing matchmaker for his mother, but this too is a reflection of medieval Welsh culture. Women were considered to be under the legal guardianship of their fathers while unwed, of their husbands while married, and of their sons when widowed. Note, however, that even here, Rhiannon must give her consent to enter into a union with Manawydan.

It is notable that we do not see Blodeuwedd give consent to her marriage to Lleu in the Fourth Branch. Even if we assume that she has given consent "off stage," as Branwen appears to have done, as a literal newborn, would Blodeuwedd have even possessed the understanding or capacity required to make such a choice? Further, unlike Branwen, she has no family to negotiate the terms of the marriage on her behalf. She has been created specifically for the purpose of being Lleu's wife, and since her creator is Gwydion, Lleu's uncle, it is clear that his priority is to see his nephew wed – not to advocate on his creation's behalf. And so, Blodeuwedd is married the same day she steps into the world. She is locked into this fate; it is, indeed, her very purpose. And yet, it is this very lack of consent which may have stood out to the contemporary medieval audience, leading them to consider that the marriage between Lleu and Blodeuwedd may not have been proper or legal.

Keeping the issue of consent in mind, there is another key to understanding Blodeuwedd's actions in the Fourth Branch, and it concerns the fact that there were nine forms of legal marriage recognized by Welsh law. These were known as *nau kynywedi teithiauc* or the "nine rightful couplings." Each type of union provided different degrees of economic protection for the women involved. This protection depended upon the economic status of both partners – whether their individual endowments were equal or unequal, and if unequal, which of the two possessed greater wealth – as well as the marriage process itself. From these nine, scholar T.M. Charles-Edwards identified four main types of legal marriage, in decreasing order of status:

- Type One – Unions by gift of kin.
- Type Two – Unions not by gift of kin, but with the consent of the kin and of the woman herself.
- Type Three – Unions to which the woman's kin do not consent, but to which the woman herself does.
- Type Four – Unions to which neither the woman nor her kin consent.

The marriage of Blodeuwedd and Lleu appears on the surface to be of the first type, a union by gift of kin; however, we have already discussed the issue of Blodeuwedd having no family to speak for her. Type Three marriages do not require the consent of kin, and one such form of legal marriage was called *llathlud twyll* – a false or secret elopement. Very specific conditions needed to be met in order for the *llathlud twyll* to be considered a legal union:

> Whoever sleeps with a woman for three nights from the time when the fire is covered up until it is uncovered the next day, and wishes to repudiate her, let him pay her a bullock worth twenty pence and another worth thirty and another worth sixty. And if he takes her to house and holding, and she is with him until the end of the seven years, he shares with her as with a woman who had givers. (Owen and Jenkins, 191)

Seem familiar? It is this very scenario which plays out in the Fourth Branch, when Blodeuwedd asks Gronw to stay with her for three nights; he does so, thereby meeting the requirements for *llathlud twyll*. Adding this to the question of the legality of her marriage to Lleu because she is not shown giving consent, it is possible that medieval audiences would have clearly understood what modern readers without knowledge of Welsh marriage laws from the middle ages would not: that she made a true and legal union with Gronw. From a legal standpoint, at least, this casts Blodeuwedd's adultery in a new light.

In addition to never being shown giving consent to her marriage, Blodeuwedd does not even speak in the Fourth Branch until she awakens to her own sense of agency when she falls in love with Gronw. When at last the narrative shows her speaking with her husband, she does so through the filter of his expectations – the demure, simple wife whose concerns center upon his well-being. Using the tools available to her – her beauty, her perceived simplicity, her "feminine wiles" – to accomplish her aims, one can almost see her looking up at Lleu through her eyelashes when she asks him to stand on the edge of the bath later on in the story. It is almost farcical watching Lleu fall prey to her deceit; he believes her to be completely without guile, and never dreamed she would – or even could – throw off her programming.

In the end, it is likely that Blodeuwedd's literary function was to serve as a cautionary example for the tale's medieval audience. Her story illustrates that nothing good comes of women seeking to change their circumstance, especially when it goes against the status quo. Conformity is safe, stable, and unquestionably expected. The perfect woman is one who is beautiful, compliant, and silent. One who has agency, like Arianrhod, is actively undermined throughout the narrative, and negative authorial judgment of her actions is clearly expressed. Further, women's sexual agency is condemned as a destructive force needing to be managed in order to preserve order.

However, when we look even deeper into the symbolic elements of the story, bypassing the medieval layers of the tale, we find an unmistakable mythic residue that appears to reflect an even older dynamic, having to do with the Sovereignty of the land and the forces of nature itself.

Chapter 3

Goddess of Sovereignty

Having examined the cultural underpinnings of the Fourth Branch and explored the potential significance of the story from the perspective of its contemporary medieval audience, it is clear that there is more to Blodeuwedd's tale than meets the modern eye. But if she is not simply an example of the literary motif of the Unfaithful Wife, who is Blodeuwedd? What may she have originally represented? Had she formerly been a deity? It is my belief that the answer can be found by investigating a common motif in the lore and legends of Celtic lands: the female figure who represents the sovereignty of the land.

Sovereignty and the Sacred Landscape

Sovereignty Goddesses are one of the most well-attested Celtic divinity types, and she can be found in Irish, Welsh, and Arthurian myths and legends. Originally a tutelary deity who is the embodiment and protector of her land, she tests potential candidates to determine their worthiness to be granted rulership over the region or country which is in her keeping. Reflecting cultural changes over time, literary depictions of Sovereignty shifted as well, transitioning from a clearly-identified divine figure, to an Otherworldly queen subtextually embodying the sovereignty of the land, to something wholly symbolic or allegorical, such a magical cauldron or the Holy Grail.

This evolution of Sovereignty can make it challenging to identify her presence in later tales, but it is not impossible. As we explore the characteristics of the Sovereignty Goddess motif, it is important to keep in mind that not every powerful female figure in Celtic lore and mythos may have once been considered a Sovereignty figure – or, indeed, a divinity. Since no extant tale from Welsh tradition directly identifies any of the characters as Gods, we must be especially discerning in making these claims as well. There are certain clues that can be found in myth and folklore – including the meaning of names and their etymologies, the presence of linguistic honorifics in naming conventions, syncretism with Roman deities, attendant symbol sets, recognizable literary motifs, and so on – that can help us in the quest to determine which characters may once have been considered divine. (A detailed exploration of this process can be found in another book I wrote for this Pagan Portals series by Moon Books – *Rhiannon: Divine Queen of the Celtic Britons*).

In the case of the personification of the Sovereignty of the land, we are looking at an established international folk motif (Z116 in the seminal collection and classification system of literary mythemes called the *Thompson Folk Motif Index*). Studying the tales where this motif is present reveals several characteristics that can be useful for the identification of sovereignty figures:

1. *Sovereignty and the Land.* She is associated with a specific region of land which is in her care and under her protection. She is empowered to confer rulership over that land to a candidate she deems worthy.
2. *Sovereignty and Liminality.* She is often found at liminal times or in liminal places, especially near wells, rivers, and other bodies of water. These thresholds indicate the presence of the Otherworld, which overlies and overlaps with our world in these in-between places, and underscore the mystical energy of the Sovereignty figure. This association with the Otherworld at the very least serves to identify the Sovereignty figure as Other – a fey creature or land spirit – and potentially signifies that she may have once been considered divine. This liminality is also present in her role as psychopomp – one who

facilitates the transition of a spirit from one state of being to another.

3. *Sovereignty and the Hunt.* An encounter with sovereignty is often presaged in the narrative by a hunt – especially of a stag, which is often white.

4. *Sovereignty as Tester of Potential Kings.* She, or a proxy symbol such as a magical cauldron, tests the worth of potential kings and chieftains to determine their fitness to rule.

5. *Sovereignty and the Sacred Marriage.* She enters into a sexual union – a sacred marriage or *hieros gamos* – with her chosen champion; it is through this act that sovereignty over the land is granted to the man she finds worthy, thereby binding his fate with that of the land. This union can be literal or symbolic.

6. *The Withdrawal of Sovereignty.* She has the power to rescind sovereignty if the king becomes ill or injured, if he rules unjustly, or – in some cases – in accordance with seasonal or annual considerations. This may be seen as an extension of her role as the protector of the land, which also accounts for her common presentation as a martial figure.

7. *Sovereignty as Shape Changer.* She has the ability to change her form, typically testing the candidate in the form of a fearsome hag, and transforming into a beautiful young woman after sexual union with the new king has been achieved. These shifts in form are usually seen as a reflection of the status of the relationship between the king and the land. She often reverts to a hag when the king has lost the right to rule and a new king is needed.

It is important to note that while these are the general criteria for identifying a sovereignty figure, some of these characteristics become more symbolic over time, making aspects of them more difficult to locate in the context of a story's narrative. Further, not every characteristic may be present in later materials, requiring us to be a little looser with our criteria when assessing these tales.

Types of Sovereignty

There are two major forms of the Sovereignty motif that we can identify in myth and legend:

1. *Aperiodic Sovereignty,* where the king or chieftain retains the blessings of Sovereignty so long as his body is whole and his actions are righteous. This can be characterized as a spatial relationship that endures while balance is maintained between the land and those who live upon it, represented by the actions and vitality of their king.
2. *Periodic Sovereignty,* where the leader's right to rule lasts only for a pre-defined span of time. This can be characterized as a temporal relationship between the land and the personification of natural forces that maintains its own balance through the dynamic of seasonal rhythms.

Although it is far more common to see annual or seasonal kingship in the mythos of the Mediterranean and the Near East, the motif is also present in Celtic lands, albeit in more symbolic or subtextual forms.

Blodeuwedd as Sovereignty Goddess

With all of this in mind, let us evaluate Blodeuwedd's story in the Fourth Branch to see if she exhibits the fundamental characteristics that have come to be associated with the figure of Sovereignty.

1. *Sovereignty and the Land.* Unique in Celtic lore, Blodeuwedd is a woman created out of flowers by magic. While she

is not stated to be directly associated with a particular territory, she was made from the flowers of oak, broom, and meadowsweet; perhaps these components were harvested from the land that Lleu would come to rule.

2. *Sovereignty and Liminality.* In Celtic legends, the inclusion of threshold times and places signal the presence of the Otherworld even if this is not directly stated in the narrative. While Blodeuwedd's initial entrance into the tale does not occur in an identifiably liminal space, her conjuration by magic connects her with Otherworldly energies. Many significant events in the tale take place at boundary places and near bodies of water, symbolizing that the Otherworld is near. For example, the deaths of Lleu and Gronw occur on the banks of the River Cynfael, and the drowning of Blodeuwedd's maidens and her subsequent transformation into an owl take place in and around Llyn Morwynion.

3. *Sovereignty and the Hunt.* Before the creation of Blodeuwedd to fulfill the third *tynged* placed upon Lleu by Arianrhod, he obtains his name from his mother in defiance of her first *tynged* by symbolically participating in a wren hunt – an act that establishes his royal candidacy (see Chapter 4). Further, when we are introduced to the character of Gronw, he is engaged in a boundary-crossing stag hunt that bled over from his own lands onto those of Lleu. Immediately after he kills and dresses the stag (on the bank of the River Cynfael at dusk – a potent threshold place at a threshold time), he is offered the hospitality of Blodeuwedd's hearth, and during the feast she provides him, they fall in love.

4. *Sovereignty as Tester of Potential Kings.* Except, perhaps, for the test of trust where Blodeuwedd asks Lleu to stand in the tableau she sets up for him on the banks of the Cynfael, his primary testing comes from his mother,

Arianrhod. Only when he had earned his name and the right to bear weapons, and had taken a non-human woman to wife would he be fit to rule. One could argue that the *tynged* that Arianrhod placed upon Lleu were a set of tests intended to catalyze his growth into manhood – and, perhaps, his divinity. On the other hand, the challenge of Blodeuwedd for Gronw to remain with her for three nights, as well as her request that he create the spear that should have been impossible to make (as it was forbidden to work the forge on Sundays during mass), could represent his testing at her hands.

5. *Sovereignty and the Sacred Marriage.* It was only after he wed Blodeuwedd that Lleu was given rulership over the cantref of Dinoding. Similarly, it was only after Gronw "killed" Lleu with his "impossible" spear that he was able to wed Blodeuwedd and could assume rulership over Lleu's lands, adding them to his own.

6. *The Withdrawal of Sovereignty.* The Fourth Branch does not give any reason for Blodeuwedd shifting her loyalty from Lleu to Gronw, other than her having fallen in love with the neighboring lord. The narrative describes Lleu as a just and beloved ruler over his lands, and before he was struck by Gronw's spear, he was healthy and whole. However, the "love triangle" of Lleu, Blodeuwedd, and Gronw is a typical characteristic of tales featuring the sovereignty motif where kingship is related to seasonality. The parallels that mark the reversal of fortune between the two men – each dying, in turn, by the same method, each at the hands of the other at a place of liminality – is further evidence of Blodeuwedd's role as a seasonal Sovereignty figure.

7. *Sovereignty as Shape Changer.* Like other Sovereignty figures, Blodeuwedd undergoes a change in form during the course of her tale. While this shift does reflect the status

of her partnership with her chosen champion, it indicates something different than the more common formula of Sovereignty presenting as a hag or as a beautiful maiden, depending upon the degree to which the king is in balance with the land. Instead, both Blodeuwedd's form – and her very name – changes in the Fourth Branch, potentially as a reflection of which of her two suitors she is currently favoring.

Not only do I believe Blodeuwedd meets the criteria to be classified as a Sovereignty figure, I further believe her to be an example of a periodic, or seasonal, Sovereignty Goddess. Let us explore this motif further.

Seasonal Sovereignty

In general, we can see that Sovereignty serves as a threshold through which a change in status can occur; she is a bridge that connects two opposing states of being. She is empowered to grant a king the right to rule, and holds the ability to rescind that right as well. When the king is united to the land by mating with Sovereignty, the status of the land is a reflection of his rulership: it thrives when he is a righteous leader and is physically whole, and it declines in response to any violation of right leadership or in the presence of any physical failings in the health of the king.

This change in the condition of the land, shifting in turn from fertile to fallow, can also be observed as part of the seasonal round as the earth moves from summer to winter and back again. Concern for the turning of the seasons is a feature of any agrarian society, and it appears to play an important role in the folk practices and lore of Wales, England, and Ireland. Seasonal festivals are especially keyed into the transitional periods between summer and winter, as well as the liminal threshold which marks the passage from the old year to the new.

The interplay between summer and winter is a common motif in many medieval tales, and it reveals a pattern of polarities that has its analogues in the dualities of light and darkness, order and chaos, abundance and the Wasteland, and so on. The threshold places that facilitate the transition from one state to another hold great power, and we see these boundaries manifest as fords and rivers between territories (such as those between this world and the Otherworld, as well as those between kingdoms), as transitional times of day (sunset and sunrise), as feast days which mark the shift between seasons (1st November/ Calan Gaeaf and 1st May/Calan Mai), and as annual battles occurring every year – sometimes every year and a day, with that additional day perhaps representing a time outside of time.

These thresholds are associated with boundary crossings of many kinds: supernatural events take place, the natural order of things is circumvented or undergoes a reversal, and some kind of threat or dangerous situation reveals itself. Boundaries between territories – like those between years and between seasons – are lines along which the supernatural intrudes through the surface of existence.

Just as a would-be-king seeks to obtain sovereignty over the land, so do the seasons seek sovereignty over the year in their turn; as both types have an impact on the fecundity of the land, perhaps these dualistic struggles can be said to hold common resonances as they fulfill similar functions. When it comes to the more common aperiodic Sovereignty motif, the status of the land serves as a reflection of the king's fitness to rule. When he is in balanced relationship with Sovereignty, the land flourishes, but when he is out of balance because of illness or unrighteousness, the land experiences challenges like war or famine. With the seasonal Sovereignty motif, however, we see the duality express itself as romantic rivals in the love triangle which characterizes this interplay; one rival exhibits characteristics of the Solar Hero motif, and the other holds correspondence with the Otherworldly Champion archetype.

The rivals battle each other at points of liminality – either in threshold places or at boundary times, or both – and they do so seeking the hand of the maiden who represents Sovereignty. This rivalry differs from the aperiodic Sovereignty motif because it features reversals in status between the two suitors, with their fates often mirror images of each other; one falls from prominence as the other rises, usually occurring at appointed times and in transition places. The representative of Sovereignty favors each champion in turn, and in the mold of the classic Sovereignty figures, not only serves to test the rivals but often is an active participant in the other's fall. In the context of this seasonal allegory, therefore, the Sovereignty figure acts as the pivot around which the year turns, granting her favor to one suitor then the other in succession.

The symmetry of the reversals suggests that something deeper is occurring.

Let us now look at the archetypal characteristics often exhibited by the rivals that complete the love triangle, the figures I have come to identify as the Solar Hero and the Otherworldly Champion.

The Solar Hero is an archetypal force that is in alignment with the energies of order. He is usually, but not always, the protagonist of the tale and is seen as a representative of the Light and all that corresponds with it: sun and sky, summer, the Light Half of the year, daytime, law and order, knowledge, skill, domestication, growth, fertility, agriculture, human society, and this World. His symbols include: eagles, oak trees, lightning, light and daytime, white, and gold.

The Otherworldly Champion, in contrast, is an archetypal force that is in alignment with the energies of disorder. He is usually, but not always, the antagonist of the tale, and is seen as a representative of the Dark and all that corresponds with it: moon and earth, winter, the Dark Half of the year, nighttime, chaos and reversal, wisdom, magic, the wild, decay, death, hunting, the law of nature, and the Otherworld. His symbols include: stags, alder trees, darkness and night, black, and silver.

We will explore how this rivalry plays out in the next chapter.

Llech Ronw
I bring this offering
To the Dark Lord and the Bright
To the nexus of changes
The threshold between
The resolution of the irreconcilable
That heals what has always been whole
The old order must ever fade away

  To herald that which comes
  To lay a pathway for what is new
  To travel along the ley lines of life's eternal strand

Twisting and endless, spun by the spindle-bones of death
Until the leaves fall, carpeting the wood with deepest red
Both womb-blood and placenta
To birth the returning king

This, then, is Sovereignty's gift
Sovereignty's lesson
Sovereignty's price

The balance of time, poised on a razor's edge
Makes room for the offering
        the oath
        the opening
The whole and holey
Holy stone

The body of the maiden, he pierces it
Breaking through the blue-grey slate
The shuddering slab of protection
The fear-wrought shield of doubt
Tombstone and gravestone and memory's marker
Where lovers unite and
Warriors fight and
Eagles take flight

The queen awaits him on the other side
First mourning, then knowing that
Like that first morning
They are thrice united, but all too soon parted
Until she returns to him on owl's wings
While he returns a stag of seven tines,
Dark god
Dark wood
Dark eyes
And then, they are one
On the banks of the Cynfael River

And in that moment of balance
He slips through her threshold –
And a new king is crowned... and crowning.

Chapter 4

Love Triangles and Seasonality

The struggle between night and day, between winter and summer, between this world and the Otherworld can be seen reenacted by the contest between an Otherworldly Champion and a Solar Hero for the favor of the representative of Sovereignty. Just as the seasons turn through the portals of transition places, and the night changes into day, so too does the Sovereignty of these times and places switch champions whom she favors to rule in turn.

There are many examples of love triangles in Celtic and Arthurian tales which contain aspects of seasonality and sovereignty, "invoking an extremely old mythologic structure: 'the eternal triangle' involving the old king, the new king, and the goddess of sovereignty." (Parker, 122) Here are several examples which illustrate that the theme is common enough to warrant its own literary motif, and which serves to strengthen the notion that the events in the latter half of the Fourth Branch is an example of this motif.

Gwythyr, Creiddylad, and Gwyn

Culhwch ac Olwen features a love triangle which has very suggestive seasonal associations, and is directly tied into the liminal festival of Calan Mai, the transition point between winter and summer. In this tale, two members of Arthur's court, Gwythyr ap Greidol and Gwyn ap Nudd, are rivals for the hand of the maiden Creiddylad. The narrative tells us that the maiden "went off" with Gwythyr, but Gwyn abducts her before the two can sleep together. Gwythyr raises an army against Gwyn, but the latter is triumphant, and rather vicious in his victory.

The narrative states of Gwyn that "God has put the spirit of the demons of Annwfyn in him, lest the world be destroyed," suggesting that he rules over them with his fierceness. Gwyn ap Nudd ("White/Bright/Holy, son of Mist", whose very name suggests liminality) is known elsewhere in Welsh lore as the Lord of the Wild Hunt and Fairy King of Annwn. Gwyn holds a strong association with Calan Gaeaf, the first day of winter and portal into the dark half of the year, as this is the day when he leads the Wild Hunt to gather the souls of the dead and bring them back with him into Annwn. With these correspondences, we can identify Gwyn as the Otherworldly Champion in this triad.

When Arthur hears of the unrest between Gwythyr and Gwyn, he intervenes to make peace between the two men.

"This is the agreement that was made: the maiden was to be left in her father's house, untouched by either party, and there was to be battle between Gwyn and Gwythyr every May Day forever from that day forth until Judgement Day, and the one who triumphed on Judgement Day would take the maiden." (Davies 2007, 207)

Given his associations with Calan Gaeaf, it is notable that it is on the opposite day, the first day of summer, that Gwyn engages in eternal, annual combat with Gwythyr for the hand of Creiddylad. Gwythyr ap Greidol ("Victor, son of Scorcher") plays the role of the Solar Hero, as his name also seems to suggest, representing the light half of the year. The meaning of Creiddylad's name is uncertain, but it holds the partial potential meaning "heart" or "center" – which would support her role as the representative of seasonal sovereignty in this triad, the core around which the succession of the seasons turn.

Trystan, Esyllt, and March

The fragmented Welsh tale *Trystan ac Esyllt* features a love triangle between Trystan, Esyllt, and King March; the story contains clear seasonal symbolism, and once more it is Arthur who negotiates a peace between the romantic rivals. Although married to March, Esyllt fled into the woods with her lover Trystan. Her husband seeks out Arthur to assist him in settling the insult done to him by Trystan. Speaking with both men, Arthur made several attempts to settle the matter to no avail, for neither would agree to give up Esyllt.

Finally, Arthur decreed that Esyllt would be with one of them when the leaves were on the wood, and the other when the leaves were not on the wood; he gave March, as her husband, first choice between the two time periods. March chose the time when the leaves were not on the wood – that is to say, the winter – because the nights were longer. When Arthur reported his choice to Esyllt, she rejoiced and sang the following:

"Three trees are good in nature:
the holly, the ivy, and the yew,
which keep their leaves throughout their lives:
I am Trystan's as long as he lives!"

The narrative here makes it clear which of the two rivals is associated with which half of the year – March chooses the winter, leaving summer to Trystan. However, unlike the eternal combat of Gwyn and Gwythyr, in this tale the matter is settled between the suitors because Esyllt takes advantage of a loophole in Arthur's judgement, which sees her aligned with Trystan the Solar Hero.

Cuchulain, Blaithnat, and Cu Roi

The Tragic Death of Cu Roi mac Dairi is a tale from the Irish Ulster Cycle dating from the 8th or 9th century, CE. The story features a love triangle which early Celtic scholar W.J. Gruffydd argues is the original source for the story of Lleu, Blodeuwedd, and Gronw. While the two tales have several strong commonalities, Gruffydd's attempt to reconcile the stories forces him to discount too many of the differences in order to support his theory that the Welsh version of the tale is at best incomplete, and at worst, a corruption of what he believed to be the original Irish tale. Although modern scholars discount most of Gruffydd's conclusions, the many parallels between the two stories are undeniable, and if one did not influence the other, then at least it is clear that they hold several narrative themes in common.

In brief, the maiden Blaithnat, whose name means "Little Flower", is in love with the hero Cuchulain. However, she is carried off by Cu Roi, a warrior with magical powers and the ability to alter his shape. Even still, the lovers find opportunity to meet on an island to the west, enjoying a tryst on Samhain. There are several variations of the tale; in one, Blaithnat betrays to her lover the secret of how Cu Roi could be killed. This was an otherwise impossible process requiring the destruction of the apple that contained Cu Roi's soul, which first needed to be retrieved from the body of a salmon that only visited a particular spring once every seven years.

Arthurian scholar Roger Loomis saw a parallel between this tale and that of the onomastic myth of Persephone and Hades, writing:

"When faced with the fact that Cuchulain is commonly regarded as a solar hero, that Blaithnat means "little flower" – that the battle for her possession lasted the great Irish seasonal festival of November 1st to the middle of Spring – can we resist the seasonal implications of the story? Here are the flower maiden, the abduction, and the imprisonments of the maiden in the Otherworld during the winter." (Loomis, 17)

The seasonal elements are present in this story, as are the parallels with the events of the Fourth Branch. Blaithnat plays the role of sovereignty and the land reflects the essence of her current mate; she is with Cu Roi in the winter, and Cuchulain in the summer. It is interesting to note that there is some evidence that the story of Cuchulain's birth suggests that he is an avatar of the Irish god Lugh, a deity whose Welsh reflex is Lleu. (Lindahl, McNamara, Lindow, 418)

Sacred Kingship in the Fourth Branch

Kingly sacrifice and succession through combat are themes that are present in the Fourth Branch of the Mabinogi, and are key motifs to explore in order to understand the subtextual allegory of seasonal Sovereignty present in the tale. With this context in mind, we can reinterpret the events of the Fourth Branch from the perspective of seasonal Sovereignty, weaving together our understandings with evidence from lore.

The rivalry between Lleu Llaw Gyffes and Gronw Pebyr in the Fourth Branch engenders a series of mirrored reversals between the two men; as one falls the other ascends, until their fortunes switch once more. In one of many examples of mirroring between Lleu and Gronw, they both symbolically establish, or at least presage, their sacred kingship through the killing of protected animals associated with royalty; in effect, the animals become the sacrificial proxy for their respective kings.

Lleu as Solar Hero

Lleu establishes his role as the summer king when he strikes the wren which has alighted on Gwydion's ship, thus earning a name from his mother, Arianrhod. The wren is considered king of the birds in many European folk traditions, and regional names for the bird translate to his being the "little king" or the "winter king." The wren, a tiny bird known for its reproductive prowess and which famously makes its nests in or close to the ground, was a symbol of fertility. An honored and protected species in medieval times, it was considered bad luck to harm a wren or disturb its nest. However, seasonal folk practices recorded in the last few centuries around the winter holidays in Wales feature the hunting of the usually-protected wren. The man who captures or kills the wren becomes the new "king" for the year, often playing a primary role in the parading of the bird in a mumming practice thought to confer fertility, and believed to represent the dying of the old year and the bringing in of the new, as light returns after the winter solstice.

It is unknown how far back these wren practices go, and whether they have, as some believe, an origin in some kind of annual sacrifice where the bird has become the proxy for the year king. However, it is possible that folk beliefs concerning the wren's significance may have been known to the medieval audience contemporary with the redaction of the Four Branches, thus infusing Lleu's act with a deeper, contextually understood, meaning. The wren, therefore, may represent the king of the old year or else is the avatar of winter – the dark half of the year. By killing or striking the wren, Lleu becomes the king of the new year, or the avatar of the light half of the year; this is reflected by the name he receives after the act, "Fair One of the Steady Hand." Summer has triumphed over winter, and Lleu takes his place as the Solar Hero.

Gronw as Otherworldly Champion

Gronw signals his role as the Otherworldly Champion in similarly subtextual ways. When he first appears in the Fourth Branch, he is engaged in the hunting of a stag, a motif commonly associated with the pursuit of Sovereignty and which often signals an encounter with the Otherworld. For example, in the First Branch, Pwyll meets Arawn, the king of Annwn, while both are engaged in a stag hunt. Gwyn ap Nudd, similarly, is noted to be in charge of the "demons of Annwn" in *Culhwch ac Olwen*, and is famously known in Welsh lore as the leader of the Wild Hunt and king of *y Tylwyth Teg* – the fair folk.

There may be some significance in the fact that the very day that Lleu leaves his court to visit his uncle Math – and although unclear based on the text, it could well be the first time Lleu has left his own court – is the day we meet Gronw hunting on Lleu's land. In his guise as the Solar Hero, the withdrawal of Lleu from his holdings may represent the departure of the light from the land: the summer leaving to make way for winter.

Lord of the lands neighboring those of Lleu, Gronw completes his hunt on the banks of the River Cynfael, a boundary place, and approaches Blodeuwedd's court at nightfall, a boundary time. Threshold times and places have powerful associations with the Otherworld, and we often see combat with the Otherworld occur in spaces of liminality. An example of this can be found in the First Branch, when Pwyll (in the guise of Arawn) engages in battle with Hafgan, a neighboring Otherworldly king, in the middle of the ford of a river. (As an aside, Hafgan's name means "Summer Song").

Just as with Lleu's killing of the wren, the stag hunt is layered with meaning. Like the wren, the stag appears to have been venerated as a royal proxy for the sacrifice of the king. As with most sacrificial animals, the stag holds a liminal quality, representing both death and life, and its appearance in tales heralded the blurring of the boundaries between this world and the Otherworld.

Because of the periodic shedding of its antlers, the stag is connected to the turning of the seasons. As one of the Oldest Animals enumerated in *Culhwch and Olwen*, the stag may have been considered a mythical ancestor for the Celtic Britons, and its powerful rut may have contributed to its strong association with fertility.

The veneration shown for the wren as a royal bird is paralleled by the chivalrous respect for the stag as a royal animal; during the medieval period, strict game laws were in place in Wales and elsewhere that forbade the hunting of stags to anyone without royal consent.

Rivals and Reversals

With their identities thus established, there are several reversals of fortune between the Solar Hero and the Otherworldly Champion in the Fourth Branch.

1. Lleu Overcomes Arianrhod's *Tyngedau* (Destinies) – Lleu's first reversal of fortune comes when he shifts from having no social status to becoming integrated into society. With Gwydion's help, he gains his name, his right to bear arms, and a wife. Thus, stepping fully into his manhood, Lleu is wed to the lady of Sovereignty and granted rule over a cantref. Summer triumphs as portended when he overcame the wren, a symbol of winter.

2. Gronw Triumphs Over Lleu – The second reversal concerning Lleu occurs when he is felled by Gronw's magical spear, in a place of liminality, on the banks of the River Cynfael. Yet another iteration of reversal can be found here, for this is the place where, earlier in the tale, Gronw killed and dressed the stag he hunted before calling at Lleu's court. Gronw has wrested away the sovereignty from Lleu in the same place Gronw demonstrated his own Otherworldly kingship. Indeed, once Lleu flies away in the form of a wounded eagle – a solar totem which, in this case, some have associated with Lleu's soul – Gronw departs with Blodeuwedd. They sleep together at his court, and Gronw takes lordship over Lleu's lands. Winter has triumphed over summer.

3. Lleu Triumphs over Gronw – The third reversal comes after Gwydion finds and restores Lleu to his humanity. It takes all of the best physicians in Gwynedd to heal Lleu "before the end of the year." Once he is whole, Lleu seeks recompense from Gronw for all that has transpired. Lleu's demands set up the third reversal, requiring that Gronw "must come to where I was when he threw the spear at me, while I stand where he was. And he must let me throw a spear at him." The two men face each other on the banks of the River Cynfael. Lleu casts his spear at Gronw, killing him. With this final reversal, occurring at the same threshold place where Gronw kills the stag, and where a year later he critically wounds Lleu, the Solar Hero has regained sovereignty over his lands, and the Otherworldly Champion has been sent back into the chthonic darkness. Summer has triumphed over winter once more.

Lleu goes on to rule justly, although no mention is made of his taking another wife; at this point in the tale Blodeuwedd has already been turned into an owl, ostensibly forever. There are several possible explanations for Lleu's lack of a mate, if we rule out authorial negligence or subsequent explanation found in a now-missing tale. One option is that Aranrhod's *tynged* still holds, and Blodeuwedd's transformation has left Lleu without a suitable candidate for marriage, and Gwydion has not created a new one for him. Another option is that Lleu has followed in the footsteps of Gwydion and Math in co-opting female power; as such, he may no longer need Sovereignty's partnership to rule. If this latter is the case, there still appears to be evidence of the old order as Lleu's eventual rule over Gwynedd seems to be a result of matrilineal inheritance.

Although it is not directly mentioned in the text, we see Gwydion, Math's sister's son, acting as Math's heir at the beginning of the Fourth Branch, so we may conclude that Gwydion does become lord of Gwynedd after Math's death. If this is the case, then it would follow that Lleu, Gwydion's sister's son, would take the throne of Gwynedd as Gwydion's heir. Alternatively, if Lleu is biologically Gwydion's son, as some believe the subtext of the Fourth Branch suggests, perhaps Gwydion has succeeded in what scholars have suggested is the underlying struggle of the Fourth Branch: the new patrilineal order seeking to overwrite matriliny. If so, then Lleu inherits directly from Gwydion, not because Gwydion is his uncle, but because Gwydion is his father. A final option is that the tale is left open-ended because the cycle simply repeats itself; when Lleu is lord, Blodeuwedd returns to her flower aspect, when the reversal happens once more, Blodeuwedd's partnership of Gronw sees her return to her owl form.

Death and Rebirth

Although Blodeuwedd faithfully followed the formula Lleu revealed to her that was supposed to bring about his demise, he did not die, but was transformed into an eagle. This whole narrative sequence is full of symbolic meaning that is worth exploring. This is particularly true when we consider that the three *englynion* that Gwydion sings have been established by scholars as the oldest portion of the Mabinogi, and therefore may represent an encoding of an older religious belief system or ceremonial practice. There are mysteries here worthy of exploration; what follows is just a small dip into a very deep pool.

The forbidden weapon, forged by his rival during taboo times, does not kill him; rather, it turns him into an eagle. This reveals his true nature as a sky god in th e Indo-European mold, connecting him with deities like Zeus, Taranis, and Jupiter. It is not surprising, therefore, that Lleu's eagle form is found in the highest branches of an oak tree, another common symbol of sky gods. This is clearly no ordinary tree, as it bears the liminal characteristics of the Otherworld: it grows between two lakes, it bridges sky and glen, it grows in upland ground that is beneath the slope, and it can neither be wetted nor burned.

Because he didn't die when struck by the spear, let us suppose that Lleu underwent a spiritual death instead. Birds are often used to represent the souls of the dead and the spirits of shamans and other ecstatic practitioners who journey between the worlds, such as the Welsh Awenyddion. Flying off in the form of an eagle could represent an ascension of the World Tree – the axis mundi or sacred center – which in Celtic cosmology connects the Three Realms of Sky, Land, and Sea: that which is above, the Future; that which is around, the Present; and that which is below, the Past.

In her role as a Goddess of Sovereignty, Blodeuwedd initiates this process for Lleu – testing his worth by setting up the parameters that see him meet the seemingly impossible circumstances that would bring about his death. By manifesting a place of triple liminality – placing him neither indoors nor outdoors, neither on foot nor on horseback, and on the bank of a river – she has essentially constructed a portal for him that invokes the Otherworld through the sacred power of three.

The top of the tree may represent the Realm of Sky – the dwelling-place of the Gods and the origin of the great cosmic pattern. Perhaps Lleu was working to claim the truth of his divinity there, by integrating the lessons that Arianrhod had set before him, a process somewhat circumvented by Gwydion as he had bypassed all of her *tynged* on Lleu's behalf. Perhaps the creation of Blodeuwedd – which was catalyzed by Arianrhod – ensured that he would have to make the shifts and transformational changes intended by his mother in order for him to truly come into his power.

Whatever the purpose this process may have served, it is clear that Lleu engages in deep healing. He releases what is wounded and rotten, and uses his wings to shake off what no longer serves him, allowing it to fall away to the bottom of the tree, perhaps representing the Realm of Sea – the dwelling place of the ancestors, where the souls of the dead rest and await rebirth. The primal chthonic energy represented by the sow – an animal associated with the Otherworld in *Y Mabinogi* – feeds off Lleu's rotted flesh, a form of theophagy which paves the way for his return.

The *Englynion Gwydion* call Lleu's soul back from the Otherworld to inhabit his human form once more – a rebirth once again facilitated by the magician. Lleu's weakness upon his return is consistent with someone who has been on an intense ecstatic journey. Once strengthened, the twice-born Lleu seeks to regain his lands and his power, and he does so on his own merit – strong, just, and triumphant. He no longer needs his uncle's intervention, and steps into his rule on his own terms, eventually succeeding Math as king of Gwynedd.

It is meaningful for us to look at this sequence from a psychospiritual perspective, as well. Perhaps Gronw represents Lleu's Shadow-self, and the directed intention of the spear, made during sacred times – at the prompting of Sovereignty – represents the unconscious will to initiate change and healing. Certainly, the narrative of the Fourth Branch depicts Gronw as Lleu's opposite in many ways. Where Gronw teaches Blodeuwedd the art of deceit, coaching her in how to extract the necessary information from her husband on how he could be killed, Lleu does not hesitate in his trust of her. Not only does Lleu provide Blodeuwedd with the key to his very undoing, he also willingly gets into the fatal position where the hidden Gronw can cast the spear at him.

Gronw is undoubtedly a shadow dweller: he overstays his time on Lleu's lands, causing Blodeuwedd to invite him to her hall – as is proper, under the rules of hospitality – under the cover of night. He hides behind a hill, so as to ambush Lleu at his moment of vulnerability, and when Lleu regains his strength and challenges his usurper, Gronw continues to hide: first behind offers of monetary compensation, which Lleu rejects; then by asking one if one of his warriors would take the blow from Lleu's spear on his behalf, which no-one accepts; and finally, by blaming everything on the wiles of a woman, and asking to hold a slab of stone between him and Lleu. Just as Gronw's warriors are remembered as one of the Three Dishonorable Warbands of the Island of Britain for not standing in for their lord, so is Gronw's cowardice revealed throughout the tale.

But what is cowardice, other than a survival response towards fear... and one of the protective functions of Shadow? If Gronw represents Lleu's Shadow, then this portion of the Fourth Branch may be providing us with a mythic map that guides us in how to face and overcome our Shadow tendencies: by entering the realm of the Unconscious, seeking out the truth of our divine nature, and working to identify and release the outmoded perspectives and ways of being in the world which prevent us from acknowledging the truth of who we are. Proceeding from a center of wholeness rather than one of woundedness allows us to succeed in Sovereignty's challenge, so that we may live from a place of balance and right relationship with both our inner and outer landscapes.

Lady of Darkness, Lady of Light

Recasting the events of the second half of the Fourth Branch in terms of the Seasonal Triangle is the key to unlocking the deeper meaning of the tale, as well as understanding the underlying motivations of its players.

Consigned to literary infamy as the Welsh iteration of the Unfaithful Wife motif, reclaiming the symbolic underpinnings of Blodeuwedd's story liberates her essence and reveals the truth of her sovereign nature – which is, that she represents the Sovereignty of Nature. She is the threshold between daytime and night, the axis around which the wheel of the year turns, the fulcrum that moves the seasons from summer to winter... and back again.

In turn a sun-drenched flower, in time a night-hunting owl, she changes her form to reflect her current sovereign alliance, favoring in turn the Solar Hero and the Otherworldly Champion.

These shifts in form reflect her ability to successfully navigate each realm in turn. What better than a form of flowers to follow the path of the sunlight, drinking in its vitalizing rays to nourish the sweetly-scented fertile potential of the light half?

Who better than a clear-sighted owl to explore the realms of the night – now soaring in star-dappled sky, now stalking her elusive prey – swooping to earth with silent precision to hit her mark with strong, sharp talons?

Two sides of the same nature, she holds the potential of life and rebirth, as well as the sacrifice of death – for life must feed on life.

Lady of Transitions, she illustrates the many changes occurring in the world around us and the space within us. Flowers, once fertilized, become a harvest of fruit and nuts, beans and berries – changing form, transmuting the life-giving energies of the sun into a bounty of food that can feed many. Owls, like all hunters, must take the life of other animals in order to sustain their own. While some flesh must be sustained by flesh, nature maintains a balance. In the animal world, hunters take only what they need, and the deadly accuracy of owls brings a swift end to their necessary prey. All life, in turn, will return to the earth; and even as the energies of the body surrender to the soil, it does so in order to nurture the next growth of seeds – for even winter must yield to the rebirth of spring.

There is no judgment in the world of light and dark, day and night, summer and winter. The Lady of Sovereignty partners with each in turn, bringing forth the skills and gifts best suited to empower in each circumstance.

Beauty of form, sweetness of demeanor, softness of heart. Swiftness of wing, sharpness of talon, stillness of death. Blodeuwedd knows them both.

The Fulcrum and The Balance

Lady of Flowers... of summer... of life.
Lady of Owls... of winter... of death.
Balancing opposites, and opposing imbalance.
Bedding the dawn and birthing the night.
The flower that grows towards the sun
The owl that flies beneath the moon.

She stands at the Threshold
Of initiation... of dying... of rebirth
Summer to Winter, light to dark, day to night
Winter to Summer, dark to light, night to day
She opens and closes and opens again
The door that swings between this world and the Otherworld
Fragrant and feathered psychopomp
She turns the key
She tips the fulcrum
So one may rise and one may fall

Spear into flesh, into stone, into death
Lightning flash of phallic passion
Straddling the river bank
The buck, the cauldron

Not within, nor without
Now this side of the river, now the other
She embraces each lover anew
While laying the old one down on the river bed

By two names you will know her
One that is flowers
One that appears to be flowers –
But is sharp eyed, sharp eared, sharp taloned

She is Lady of the fertile land – the brewer of medicines that
heal, protect, beguile
She is Hunter of the darkest night – the gatherer of flesh, of
blood, of bones
She is a riot of blooms in a meadow
She is a silent winged shadow in the night.

She knows the abundance of summer, the fallowness of
winter.
The warmth of the day, the chill of the night
The vitality of this world, the deathlessness of the Otherworld.
The warrior, the craftsman, and the magician.
The eagle, the wren, and the stag.
The Summer Lord. The Winter King.

The ancient seasonal pantomime playing
Through battles of rivals
Through struggles of lovers
Embedded in legend, in folklore, in memory
Some ancient... some newly-birthed... all timeless

The Oak King and the Holly King
Battling eternally at the twin thresholds
Of the summer and the winter.

One always rising, as the other falls,
Then rises again, to take his rival's place.

But what of the fulcrum, the center?
What of she who grants the gifts of sovereignty to he who
earns by right of battle
He who proves himself worthy to be consort to the land?
To be consort for a season?
Granting rulership over space, and over time...
But only for a time.

She straddles both worlds
And be it through the
Cleft of her vulva, or the hole in the stone,
She initiates. She withdraws. She begins again.
Light to dark to light once more.
Flowers to feathers. Winds to wings.
Sovereign Lady

Lady of Sovereignty
Through her, two halves become whole –
Become Holy.

Chapter 5

The Flower Bride

How does one create a woman? What is the magical formula for calling a Goddess forth from the Otherworld? According to the Fourth Branch, this is how Math and Gwydion undertook to make a wife for Lleu:

> Then they took the flowers of the oak, and the flowers of the broom, and the flowers of the meadowsweet, and from those they conjured up the fairest and most beautiful maiden that anyone had ever seen. And they baptized her, and gave her the name of Blodeuedd*. (Davies 2007, 58)

(Please note: as she is being specifically discussed in her aspect of the Flower Bride, we will refer to her as Blodeuedd in this chapter.)

The redactor of the Fourth Branch took care to be explicit about the flowers included in Blodeuedd's formulary; it is therefore likely that these particular blooms held significance to the contemporary medieval audience, and that they subtextually transmitted information about her nature and character. While scholar W.J. Gruffydd's suggestion – that oak was chosen for the strength of her bones, broom for the yellow of her hair, and meadowsweet for the purity of her white skin – seems very straightforward from a modern perspective, these flowers may have held additional meaning to the medieval Welsh. That none of these plants are in flower at the same time may indicate that there was a temporal component to the magical working, and further underscores the idea that they were deliberately chosen.

A deeper exploration of these plants from both a folkloric and medicinal perspective may bring additional insight to broaden our understanding.

Flowers from the Fourth Branch

1. **Oak (*Quercus robur*).** Oak (*dair*) is one of the chieftain trees of the ogham alphabet – a system of writing used in Ireland and parts of Britain, believed to date to at least the 4th century CE – which features trees among the correspondences associated with each lett er. In addition to its ogham association with Strength, oak is believed to have been especially sacred to the druids, something reinforced by the etymological link between the Celtic words for both. Stemming from the Proto-Indo-European root words **deru* – which means "tree", and in particular the oak tree (as with *derw*, which is "oak" in Welsh) – and **weid*, which means "to see", we get the Old Celtic words **derwos* ("true") and **wid-* ("to know"). Together, these make the compound word **dru-wid,* which can translate to mean "strong seer" or "true knower" or "one who knows the oak." (https://www.etymonline.com/word/druid)

The famed ritual described by Roman historian Pliny the Elder in his *Natural History* concerns the druids of Gaul cutting mistletoe from the boughs of the sacred oak on the sixth day of the moon. He further states, "Of itself the robur (oak) is selected by them to form whole groves, and they perform none of their religious rites without employing branches of it; so much so, that it is very probable that the priests themselves may have received their name from the Greek name for that tree." (Plin. Nat. 16.95)

In many Indo-European derived cultures, oak trees are sacred to sky and thunder Gods such as Zeus, Jupiter, and Thor. The oak also has a strong association with the motif of the Solar Hero, a correspondence clearly illustrated in the Fourth Branch; it is an oak tree which shelters the wounded Lleu when he is in eagle form – another symbol commonly associated with divinities of sky and thunder. In more recent folklore, the seasonal battle between the Oak King and the Holly King, the Oak King represents the vitalistic power of the increasing Sun which begins to wane after his defeat at midsummer; he is reborn again at midwinter and the days begin to lengthen in response to his return.

Medicinally, oak is a powerful astringent and antiseptic, making it useful to treat wounds, staunch bleeding, and to quell fevers. It can be used as a poultice to draw out infection and inflammation, and has antiviral and antifungal properties. The healing properties of the oak may be another reason the wounded Lleu sought its limbs for shelter.

The addition of oak blossoms in the formula used to create the Flower Bride appears to weave a strong connection between Blodeuedd and Lleu, the Solar Hero she was created to marry. Their inclusion may also reflect a druidic origin of the magics of Math and Gwydion.

2. **Broom (*Cytisus scoparius*).** Broom holds traditional association with the ogham *ngetal*, although Robert Graves and those inspired by his work associate *ngetal* with reed instead. Ngetal is an ogham of healing, and can represent both the healer and that which needs to be healed. In folk medicine, broom was used to cool fevers, and was part of the *materia medica* of the Physicians of Myddfai – a world-famous Welsh lineage of healers spanning from medieval times into the early modern period.

Medieval literature often used broom as a descriptor for beauty; we see it directly mentioned to describe Olwen's yellow hair in *Culhwch ac Olwen*, and it may likewise allude to Blodeuedd's hair color in the Fourth Branch. Broom was often included in brides' bouquets, which may also account for its inclusion in Blodeuedd's formula.

Broom is a powerful cleansing herb, both energetically and physically, and it is traditionally used in the making of besoms, as its name suggests. It was used to clear the house on May Day (Calan Mai), a day of seasonal transition between the winter and the summer. A protective herb, broom flowers can be burned to dispel negative influences.

An incredibly useful plant, broom was used to weave baskets and to thatch roofs. Its fibers were spun to make cloth, and the tannins in its bark made it useful for tanning leather. The roots of this common plant act to anchor soil, which helps to prevent erosion, especially in coastal areas. The spindly branches of this shrub shelter wildlife, particularly when is grows as part of a hedgerow.

Broom was famously used in Brittany as a heraldic device, and the English royal house of Plantagenet took the plant's medieval name, *planta genista*, as its own. Traditionally, broom has been used medicinally to treat complaints of the cardiovascular system, as a diuretic, and to induce labor; however, caution should be practiced when taking this herb internally. It should only be used under professional supervision, as poisoning can occur.

3. Meadowsweet (*Spiraea ulmaria*). Also called "bridewort" and "Queen of the Meadow" the intoxicatingly-scented white flowers of the meadowsweet are ubiquitous in the Welsh countryside, and can often be found in boundary places such as hedgerows, ditches, and riverbanks. It was a traditional addition to the bridal bouquet, perhaps because its scent was so seductively sensual. It was also a common funerary herb throughout Wales and Scotland, dating all the way back to the Bronze Age, and perhaps the inclusion of this flower in the making of Blodeuedd presages the role she will play in Lleu's "death." However, considering that it also holds a strong connection with marriage, meadowsweet may have generally represented the transition from one life phase to the next. In Yorkshire, meadowsweet is called "courtship and matrimony"; this is another reflection of the herb's dual nature, as the sweet scent of the flower contrasts with the bitter almond scent of its leaves – just as courtship is joyful while marriage can often turn bitter.

The threshold nature of meadowsweet may account for its traditional folk use in County Galway, Ireland, where it was believed that placing the blooms overnight under the bed of someone wasting away from contact with the fairy folk would bring them back to health the next morning – although leaving the flowers there for too long could cause the person's death. The flower was considered sacred to Áine, sovereignty Goddess of Munster, who was also revered as a Fairy Queen, and is said to have given the flower its sweet scent. An Irish common name for meadowsweet is *Lus Cuchulainn*, which means "Belt of Cuchulainn." It is said that the legendary warrior's battle fevers could be soothed by meadowsweet baths, and that he would carry the flowers in his belt to keep him from his rages.

According to Grieve, the Druids held meadowsweet in high regard, and counted it as one of their three most sacred herbs, along with vervain and water mint. Said to instill a sense of gladness and peace, meadowsweet flowers were strewn on the floors of houses, and were a popular ingredient in the making of mead and ale. It is possible that its English name comes from the Anglo-Saxon words *mede* ("mead") or *medo-wort* ("honey herb"). The name of the Irish Queen Medb of Connacht means "Mead" or "Intoxicating Goddess", and may also reference her role as a Sovereignty Goddess; there appears to be a strong connection between these two functions. There are hints of mead rituals associated with sovereignty rites in Irish literature, and the idea persists that the mead itself was divine, and is sometimes personified by a Goddess.

In sum, then, the liminal nature of meadowsweet and its transitional qualities – between sweetness and bitterness, between maiden and married woman, between life and death, between rage and calm, between sobriety and intoxication, between this world and the Otherworld – seem to support the idea of Blodeuedd as a Goddess of Sovereignty: she who makes the sacred marriage between the king and the land, and has the power to withdraw her sovereignty – even requiring the sacrificial death of the old king.

Medicinally speaking, meadowsweet contains salicylates, the primary component of aspirin, and so has traditional usage for pain relief and the reduction of fevers. Among its many medicinal uses, it is an excellent anti-spasmodic, and assists with menstrual cramps.

Flowers from *Cad Goddeu*

Cad Goddeu (The Battle of the Trees), a poem from the 14th century *Llyfr Taliesin (The Book of Taliesin)* includes a verse that appears to reference the creation of Blodeuedd by Math and Gwydion, although she is never directly named. This iteration of the tale presents a somewhat different formulary than that found in the Fourth Branch:

When I was made,
Did my Creator create me.
Of nine-formed faculties,
Of the fruit of fruits,
Of the fruit of the primordial God,
Of primroses and blossoms of the hill,
Of the flowers of trees and shrubs.
Of earth, of an earthly course,
When I was formed.
Of the flower of nettles,

Of the water of the ninth wave.
I was enchanted by Math,
Before I became immortal,
I was enchanted by Gwydyon
The great purifier of the Brython

While only three flowers are mentioned in *Y Mabinogi*, *Cad Goddeu* makes several references to the number nine, seeming to imply that there were nine components used in her creation. The inclusion of "the water of the ninth wave" is a reference to the Otherworld, and is perhaps a subtextual encoding of Blodeuedd's true nature; it was believed that anything beyond the ninth wave of the sea has crossed the boundary between what is known and what is unknown, between this world and the Otherworld. Although the poem does not specify what these nine-formed faculties may have been, instead enumerating general ingredients such as blossoms of the hill and the flowers of trees and shrubs, it does add two more flowers to our list: primrose and nettle.

4. Primrose (*Primula vulgaris*). Primrose blossoms in early spring, and its name – meaning "first rose" – is believed to reflect this, although it is not in the rose family. A yellow flower that often grows in hedgerows, Primrose has associations with May Day, and like other boundary herbs, it is said to grant fairy Sight. It has protective properties, especially when placed over a threshold. In Irish folklore it is said: "Guard the house with a string of primroses on the first three days of May. The fairies are said not to be able to pass over or under this string." The blooms themselves are believed to be keys that open the door to the Otherworld. Touching a fairy stone with a bouquet of primrose can allow one to enter the fairy realms, but if the bouquet contained the wrong number of flowers, bad fortune lay beyond the threshold.

Shakespeare used the term "primrose path" to refer to following a life of pleasure, often without thought of consequence. Primrose was associated with the fertility of hens, and bringing primroses into the home while hens were laying affected the amount of eggs that would hatch; to ensure the most successful hatching, at least thirteen primroses should be brought indoors.

Like broom flower, primrose was used as a descriptor in Celtic legend for beautiful yellow hair. In the Irish tale, *The Wooing of Étaín*, the inhabitants of fairy land are described as having hair "like the crown of the primrose." In the Scottish Hebrides, on the eve of Brigid's Day, girls would create an effigy of a woman from a sheaf of wheat, and decorate it with natural objects including primroses. Called a Bridey Doll, it was placed in a window while the girls feasted alone, and anyone who wished to enter had to ask permission and give a sign of respect to the image in the window.

5. Nettle (*Urtica dioica*). The nettle plant grows wild and abundantly in Britain, and is one of the most commonly used herbs in folk medicine. It is a plant with powerful healing qualities, but has the ability to cause hurt as well – an apt allusion to Blodeuedd's actions in the Fourth Branch. The word "nettle" has its origins in the Anglo-Saxon word *noedl*, which means "needle", and may be a reflection of the plant's traditional use as a textile fiber, which was spun and woven into linen. Alternatively, it may be a reference to the nettle's stinging properties, which is also attested by its botanical name *urtica*, which means "burning." Famous for its sting, the plant is also called "stinging nettle" due to the painful reaction caused by the venom on its hair-like spines when it comes into contact with skin.

"Three nettles in May keeps all diseases away" is an old English saying, reflecting the high regard held for nettle's medicinal properties. Nettles are one of the most nutritious plants known to us, providing a range of necessary vitamins, minerals, and protein, all in a very bioavailable form. Its high iron content assists in the treatment of anemia, and it also has strong anti-hemorrhaging, or hemostatic, properties. It is a powerful antihistamine and an anti-inflammatory herb, especially as concerns the respiratory system; it is used to treat hay fever, sinusitis, and asthma.

Nettle was counted among the nine sacred herbs in Anglo-Saxon folklore, along with plantain, chamomile, mugwort, watercress, chervil, fennel, and crab apple. Nettle was hung around the house or burned in bonfires to protect the household and crops from lightning – an interesting counterbalance to oak, which is the tree most likely to be hit by lightning, and is associated both with Lleu and Blodeuedd. Nettle that was picked on Summer Solstice was especially potent for use in undoing curses. In Scotland, it was believed that nettles harvested on Halloween night and placed in the bedding of someone you fancied would make them fall in love with you.

The positive effect of nettle on both the women's reproductive system and men's virility made it a natural aphrodisiac, and a common component in love spells. However, the dual nature of the herb sees it used both as a method of contraception – a popular folk practice was to place nettle leaves in a man's shoes to prevent him causing pregnancy – and to induce sexual vigor through the process of *urtication* (which is the act flogging a man's genitals with nettle stalks).

Flowers from *Hanes Blodeuwedd*

In his seminal work, *The White Goddess*, 20th century British author and mythologist Robert Graves deconstructs the story of Blodeuedd in the context of his poetic theories, and includes a poem called *Hanes Blodeuwedd*. Having extracted several verses from *Cad Goddeu*, Graves expanded upon them in the writing of his poem, which reads like an alternate translation of the source material:

Not of father nor of mother
Was my blood, was my body.

I was spellbound by Gwydion,
Prime enchanter of the Britons,
When he formed me from nine blossoms,
Nine buds of various kind;
From primrose of the mountain,
Broom, meadow-sweet and cockle,
Together intertwined,
From the bean in its shade bearing
A white spectral army
Of earth, of earthly kind,
From blossoms of the nettle,
Oak, thorn and bashful chestnut –
Nine powers of nine flowers,
Nine powers in me combined,
Nine buds of plant and tree.

Long and white are my fingers
As the ninth wave of the sea.

We can see that in writing his poem, Graves expanded the number of flowers used to create Blodeuwedd from the three mentioned in the Fourth Branch to nine, as suggested in *Cad Goddeu*. Save for the primrose and nettle, which were taken directly from *Cad Goddeu*, there is no indication of where Graves sourced these additional flowers, so we cannot say that these are traditional to Blodeuedd's tale. Graves' additions are: cockle, bean, chestnut, and hawthorn.

6. Cockle. There are several species of plants which bear the common name "cockle", and there isn't any additional information included in the poem to help narrow down which one Graves intended. Perhaps the most likely candidate is White Cockle, also called White Campion (*Silene latifolia*). Containing toxic saponins, white campion has no traditional medicinal usage, however, its roots can be boiled down to release the sudsy properties which saw this plant used as a soap substitute. Aside from this cleansing quality, which connects it to the energetic properties of the canonical broom, white campion has a few other attributes which might explain why Graves included it in his list of flowers for Blodeuedd, particularly as a foreshadowing of her owl form.

Unlike many flowers, white campion does not close its flowers at dusk; instead, it releases a particularly sweet fragrance at sundown, famous for attracting moths as pollinators. It is also infamously bad luck to pick these blooms, and folklore cautions that doing so can result in the death of one's mother. Another common name for this plant is "thunder flower", and children are warned that picking white campion attracts lightning and puts them at risk of being struck. The shell-like bladder of this flower can be squashed between the thumb and forefinger, resulting in a popping sound which may also account for its connection with thunder; this makes for an interesting connection to Blodeuedd, as Lleu has many symbolic resonances with other Indo-European sky Gods – including oak trees and eagles – and many of these divinity types are also associated with thunder. Finally, a type of divination was practiced using white cockle wherein one would ask a question of the flower, and the louder the sound one made when popping the bladder, the more affirmative the answer to the querent's question.

7. Bean. It is hard to say with any certainty what species of bean Graves is referring to here, as there are many. The description in the poem of the "shade bearing white spectral army" at the least may indicate that it is a species with white flowers, which puts it in alignment with some of the other flowers more canonically associated with Blodeuedd. Beans are a staple food stuff around the world as they are excellent sources of protein. However, the consumption of raw or undercooked beans can be fatally toxic, and so there is an underlying menace inherent in the food.

Considering Blodeuedd's role as the Flower Bride, brought forth to be the wife of Lleu, a divine figure associated with light as well as a mythic iteration of the Solar Hero, it is worth noting that a fairly universal quality of bean plants is that they are heliotropic: the leaves tilt and change position in order to follow the daily track of the sun, absorbing as much light as possible. At night, the leaves and flowers close up in the absence of the sun, awaiting the morning to open once more.

8. Chestnut. When it comes to the flowers of the "bashful chestnut", we are faced with several issues. First, Graves does not clarify which of the two types of chestnut trees that grow in the British Isles he is referring to in the poem: sweet chestnut (*Castanea sativa*) or horse chestnut (*Aesculus hippocastanum*), and second, neither of these trees are native species. The Romans are believed to have introduced sweet chestnut to Britain, the nuts of which they ground into a course flour meal, and so the Britons would have been familiar with the tree from around the first century CE onward. The long yellow catkins of the flowering sweet chestnut tree are visually similar to the flowers of oak and nettle, establishing at least a symbolic connection to other flowers included in the more canonical list.

The horse chestnut, on the other hand, was brought to the British Isles from Turkey in the latter half of the 16th century. While it was known to Graves, who was born outside of London in 1895, it is not a tree with deep folkloric tradition in Britain, and is best known for the use of its nuts in the game of conkers. However, the equine associations of the horse chestnut tree are somewhat striking; its nuts are fed to horses as medicine for coughs, and its leaves make a horseshoe-shaped scar when they fall off their twigs. Perhaps these symbolic resonances with horses – that powerful representation of Celtic Sovereignty – may account, at least in part, for Graves' association of the flowers of the horse chestnut tree with Blodeuedd – if, indeed, this is the tree he intended.

9. Hawthorn (*Crataegus spp.*). Hawthorn (*uath*) is another tree featured in the ogham alphabet. It is a boundary tree often found in hedgerows or growing over holy wells, and through it, the Otherworld can be accessed. This may account in part for its association with Calan Mai, that doorway between the Dark and Light Halves of the year. Hawthorn is also known as the May Tree or May Bush, and in some traditions, the transition into summer is not marked by a calendar date, but by the flowering of the hawthorn trees.

Its white blossoms feature in many folk practices associated with May Day. When one goes "a-maying", for example, one is ostensibly gathering hawthorn blossoms with which to decorate the outside of the home, but this "gathering of flowers" may have had some sexual connotations as well. In some areas of Britain, folk celebrations of May Day include the selection of a young, unmarried woman as May Queen and crowning her with a wreath of flowers; it is not hard to see a reflection of Blodeuedd in this practice, but no direct connection can be made, other than that both are representatives of the fertile energies of Spring.

It is interesting to note that while the four flowers added by Graves are not found in any original source material, they nevertheless hold energetic resonance with those named in the Fourth Branch and *Cad Goddeu* in several ways. It is worth examining the qualities of a few of these additions in order to get a sense of why Graves may have chosen the flowers that he did to include in *Hanes Blodeuwedd*. All of Graves' flowers are either white like meadowsweet, or yellow like broom and oak blossoms; perhaps these are allusions to Blodeuedd's appearance, as pale white skin and blonde hair is a common beauty standard in Celtic literature.

An energetic that appears to be missing from the flowers in the Fourth Branch, but is present in *Cad Goddeu* and Graves, is that of a dangerous beauty. Blodeuedd's dual nature – as dutiful wife and betraying lover, as Lady of Flowers and Night-Hunting Owl – is represented by the inclusion of hawthorn and nett le in the herbal formula that creates her. The hawthorn tree sports sharp, spiny thorns as protection, while the nett le plant is famous for its sting. Both plants have powerful healing qualities, and yet both can cause injury as well – an apt representation of the two sides of Blodeuedd, and perhaps the motivation for including these flowers in alternative, and more modern, accounts of her creation.

Flowers of Devotion

For those dedicated to Blodeuwedd, or who want to form a relationship with her, the gathering together of her flowers to create an incense to burn or an energetic elixir to take is a meaningful act of devotion. The majority of these flowers require that you harvest them for yourself as most are not sold commercially. The fact that it may take years to assemble all of the components is a reflection of that devotion, and will make the floral mixture, once complete, a worthy offering to the Goddess.

As you obtain them, spend some time working with each of the flowers in turn. Meditate upon each one, seeking out their connections to Blodeuedd. Consider doing some in-depth research of their medicinal, folkloric, and energetic qualities. When you feel ready to make the mixes, begin with making a blend with the three flowers mentioned in the Fourth Branch, the "canonical" blooms, and then start looking for all nine flowers if you feel so drawn. Once you have all of them, compare the three-flower blend to the one with nine flowers to feel out the differences – and similarities – between the two blends. Then, going forward, use the one with which you resonate the most as you work with this beautiful and complex divinity.

New from the Old

When I first undertook a study of Blodeuwedd's flowers several decades ago, I wrote a devotional chant that references all nine blooms; because of this I named it *Hanes Blodeuwedd* after Graves' poem.

I am the stinger and the healer (nettles)
I am the cup of mountain's dew (primrose)
I am the guardian of the sunlight (oak)
I am the Maybush in full bloom (hawthorn)
I am the sweet brush cliff-side cleanser (broom)
I am the fruit found deep inside (chestnut)
I am the feeder of the masses (bean)
I am the dowry of the bride (meadowsweet)
I am the friend of womankind (cockle)
I am the Nine in me combined

Hanes Blodeuwedd

Jhenah Telyndru

I am the stin-ger and the hea-ler. I am the cup of moun-tain's

dew. I am the guard-ian of the sun-light. I am the May-bush in full

bloom. I am the sweet brush spring-time clean-ser. I

am the fruit found deep in-side. I am the feed-er of the mass-es. I

am the dow-ry of the bride. I am the friend of wo-man-kind. I

am the Nine in me com-bined.

Chapter 6

The Owl

The significance of Blodeuwedd's transformation into an owl is complex, reinforcing the notion that cultural context is key to the understanding of myth and folklore, and demonstrating that meaning can shift over time as a mirror of social change.

Early Celtic Culture

We can trace the owl's importance to Celtic culture to the earliest periods, as far back as the 5th century BCE. Owls were a common motif in early Celtic art; their forms ranged from full body, naturalistic statuettes discovered with grave goods to decorative embellishments of their faces on torcs, fibulae, and votive cauldrons. Stylized owls, featuring large round eyes and disk-like faces, are often depicted emerging from the heads of humans, lions, or rams. In another variant, owl faces are formed by the merging heads of two identical animals. An illustrative example of this is found on a bronze vessel from the 4th century BCE, depicting an owl's face created by the overlapping heads of two horses that are facing each other.

Images of birds perched upon, or emerging from, human heads is well-attested in Celtic art and artifacts. A figure on the famed Gundestrup Cauldron, dating to approximately the 2nd century BCE, is depicted wearing a helmet with a bird mounted on it, and we have also discovered real-life examples of these helmets believed to have been worn by Celtic warriors. The most remarkable example of this type of helmet was found in Ciumesti, Romania. Dating back to the 3rd century BCE, the helmet's crest is a bronze bird of prey with outstretched and articulated wings that would flap up and down in response to the movement of its wearer.

Not surprisingly, birds of prey and carrion birds are often associated with divinities of war. In Celtic cultures, ravens and crows are especially linked with martial Goddesses like the Irish Morrigan and the Gaulish Cathubodua. Often, these deities of war are also Sovereignty Goddesses, for their main function is to ensure the survival of the land, and as such, they are responsible both for its fertility and its defense. A helmet decorated with an animal effigy associated with a war goddess, therefore, may have served a dual purpose as well: to frighten opponents on the field of battle, as well as to invoke the protection and power of the Goddess herself for the wearer and their comrades in arms.

Overall, it appears that owls were held in high regard by continental Celtic tribes and other Indo-European cultures. Known Celtic depictions of owls tend to be associated with votive cauldrons and other vessels, women's jewelry, and funerary statues, giving them a sense of connection with ritual contexts rather than being linked with war like other birds of prey. That many images of owls show them emerging out of, or being made up of, other beings as if they were depicted midmetamorphosis, suggests a magical or Otherworldly correlation as well. Archaeologist Anne Ross believes the earliest owl images are Celtic devotional representations of an owl Goddess with origins in earlier European beliefs, potentially related to the figures of beaked Goddesses with round owl eyes dating back to the Neolithic period. This ancient Goddess was associated with both death and rebirth, a dual-aspect that both speaks to this divinity's liminality, as well as presages the positive and negative attitudes cultures held towards owls over time. (Ross 1996, 344)

Later Celtic Literature and Lore

In early Welsh literature, owls are consistently included in various listings of elder animals, a common international folk motif that features different animals depending upon the location of the story. The oldest Welsh iteration of this tale is found in *Culhwch and Olwen*; here, King Arthur and his men are on a quest to find Mabon, who was taken from his mother at three days old. They consult the five Oldest Animals of the Island of Britain in hopes that one of them would know the fate of Mabon. These are, from least to most ancient: the Blackbird of Cilgwri, the Stag of Redynfre, the Owl of Cwm Cowlyd, the Eagle of Gwern Abw, and the Salmon of Llyn Llyw.

When asked about Mabon, the Owl of Cwm Cowlyd replied:

> "When first I came hither, the wide valley you see was a wooded glen. And a race of men came and rooted it up. And there grew there a second wood; and this wood is the third. My wings, are they not withered stumps? Yet all this time, even until today, I have never heard of the man for whom you inquire." (Guest, 124)

A similar listing can be found in Triad 92 of *Trioedd Ynys Prydein*:

The Three Elders of the World:

> The Owl of Cwm Cowlyd,
> the Eagle of Gwernabwy,
> and the Blackbird of Celli Gadarn.

Centuries later, a similar catalog, with the addition of the Toad o Cors, can be found in the Welsh folktale, "The Ancients of the World". In this story, the Eagle of Gwernabwy seeks the ancient pedigree of the Owl of Cwm Cowlyd to determine if she is old enough to be his wife; indeed, while Culhwch lists the Salmon as the Oldest of the Animals, this later tale accords that honor to the Owl. (Thomas, 148)

The significance of these Oldest Animals is uncertain. That they are consistently associated with particular places in Wales, some of which are difficult to locate with any surety, may point to totemistic animals associated with particular tribes or regions, which in turn may support the idea that the origins of the stories may pre-date Christianity in Britain. The stories themselves go out of their way to establish both the antiquity and longevity of these elder animals; this serves to place them outside of time – certainly beyond human memory – which gives them Otherworldly associations. It is notable that they are seen as allies; humans are shown consulting these ancient animals, who are willing to assist them.

As time progresses, however, there is a shift in the portrayal of owls in Celtic lore, likely in response to shifting religious beliefs as well as changes in the status of women, with whom owls are strongly associated. Similar to the conclusion of the Fourth Branch, several folktales from Wales and Brittany explain why the owl is hated by all other birds and fated to dwell in darkness; interestingly, these tales involve wrens and eagles – birds associated with Lleu.

In one Welsh tale, every bird gathered together to determine who among them would be their king. They decided that the bird who could fly the highest would receive that honor, and so they took to the sky, each flying as high as they could. At last, it was clear that the eagle was going to win this contest, but before he could claim his title, a tiny wren shot out from the now-tired eagle's feathers and flew even higher, winning the crown. Now, the rest of the birds were unhappy with the wren, and decided to drown the tiny bird in a pan of their tears – but before they could do so, the clumsy owl toppled over the pan and the wren was able to fly free. Unable to have their vengeance, the rest of the birds angrily attacked the owl and exiled her to live and hunt in the night. (Lawrence, 28)

A variant of the tale sees the birds pursue the wren for tricking the eagle. The tiny bird hides in a hedge, and none of the other birds can reach him. They take turns waiting for the wren to leave his hiding place, and the owl accidentally falls asleep on her watch, allowing the wren to escape. The owl is exiled for her failure. A Breton folktale tells how the wren tunneled down into the underworld to bring fire back up to the birds, burning its feathers off in the process. All of the birds donated one of their feathers to the wren in gratitude – all, save the owl, who was punished for her selfishness and made to hunt alone in the darkness. (Lawrence, 33) These onomastic tales are accurate reflections of the behaviors of these birds; wrens do tend to make their nests low to the ground and in hedges, and other birds are known to mob and attack owls they come across during the day. Wrens are symbols of druidic magic, are considered the king of the birds, and are especially associated with the dying of the old year. This is further explored in Chapter 4.

Owls and the Dark Half

Owls were said to be the bird of Gwyn ap Nudd, the chthonic Welsh figure who was the leader of the Wild Hunt and Fairy King of Annwn; we have already discussed him as an example of the Otherworldly Champion in Chapter 4. In his poem "The Owl", early 14th century Welsh poet Dafydd ap Gwilym links the owl with Gwyn, while also alluding to Blodeuwedd in her owl form:

"Woe for her song (a wooden-collared roebuck),
And her face (features of a gentle woman),
And her shape; she's the phantom of the birds.
Every bird attacks her – she's dirty and she's exiled:
Is it not strange that she is alive?

Eloquently she used to howl – I know her face
She is a bird of Gwyn ap Nudd.
Garrulous owl that sings to thieves –
Bad luck to her tongue and tone!"

In Gaelic traditions, owls are connected with the Cailleach; a hag Goddess and wise woman, her name literally translates as "veiled one", deriving from the Latin word "palladium". The tawny owl is called *Cailleach-oidhche* ("crone of the night") in Scots Gaelic, while the barn owl is *Cailleach-oidhche gheal* ("white old woman of the night") or *Cailleach-bhàn* ("white hag"). (Ross, 346).

The Cailleach is a powerful figure often seen as ruling over winter as its queen, and her name graces many landscape features throughout Ireland and Scotland. She has an ancestral aspect, much like the Owl in Culhwch and Olwen, and *The Yellow Book of Lecan* describes her has having been a young woman seven times, having married seven husbands, and having acted as foster mother to fifty children who went on to become the founders of many tribes and kingdoms. The Old Irish poem *Caillech Bérri* (*The Lament of the Old Woman of Beare*) which dates to the 8th century, seems to hint at her former status as a wanton lover of kings.

Many Cailleach traditions from Scotland, Ireland, and the Island of Man associate her with the changing of the seasons; sometimes she keeps a maiden captive to hold back the spring, and other times she herself has a youthful aspect during the Light Half of the Year. Taken together with her cycles of youth and old age, and traditions connecting her with particular places that bear her name, it is possible that the Cailleach was once a seasonal Sovereignty Goddess, and her owl represented the winter and the night.

Owls in Folklore and Practice

As nocturnal hunters, it is understandable that the owl would come to have associations with darker aspects of life, including death, misfortune, and illicit sexuality – especially of women. In Welsh folklore, hearing an owl call in a town or village is an announcement that an unmarried woman has lost her virginity; alternatively, if a woman hears the call of an owl while she is pregnant, it is a sign that her child has been blessed.

More often than not, however, hearing an owl's call presages death and destruction. In Welsh folk belief, the *aderyn y corph* – the corpse bird – is a horror to behold; it has no feathers or wings, yet flies mysteriously through the air. Its cry sounds like "Dewch! Dewch!" – the Welsh words for "Come! Come!" While the lore does not specify the kind of bird the aderyn y corph is supposed to be, the traditional Welsh name for the tawny owl is "aderyn corph", and the call of the female tawny owl is "'kewic", which sounds very similar to "dewch." (Sikes, 213)

A related belief is that hearing the shriek of a screech owl – which, in Britain, is a nickname for the barn owl due to the sounds it makes – outside of the window of an ill person indicates that they will soon die. The barn owl's call was also used to predict the weather – its shrieking heralded the coming of cold weather or the approach of a storm; however, hearing its call during bad weather meant that things were going to turn for the better.

Owl eggs and broth made from owls were believed to cure everything from whooping cough, to blindness, and gout. Eating the eggs raw was said to cure alcoholism and be protective for children. It was generally believed that witches could turn themselves into owls, and so owls could also be used to protect against witches and their magic. Nailing owls to barn doors were a protective measure against lightning and misfortune taken by farmers well into the 19th century. Today, they instead encourage owls to roost there by installing owl boxes, thus protecting their farms against vermin instead. It was believed that if you happened upon an owl in a tree, you could kill it by walking around the tree causing the bird to wring its own neck as it turned its head to follow you.

Blodeuwedd as Owl

There are five species of owl native to Britain: the tawny or brown owl (S*trix aluco*), the little owl (*Athene noctua*), the shorteared owl (*Asio flammeus*), the long-eared owl (*Asio otus*), and the barn owl (*Tyto alba*). The narrative of the Fourth Branch does not specify which species of owl Blodeuwedd is transformed into, saying only: "What Blodeuwedd is, is "owl" in the language of the present day... the owl is still called "flower-face" (*blodeuwedd*). (Ford, 108). There are medieval Welsh lexicons that attest to the use of the world "blodeuwedd" for owl, and the word is still in use by some modern Welsh speakers to refer to the species of bird in general, rather than any particular type of owl.

Kristoffer Hughes, head of the Anglesey Druid Order and native Welsh speaker, relayed the following to me: "In Caernarfonshire and Anglesey, the older folk would say, "*Nosweith dda Blodeuwedd*" ("Good evening, Blodeuwedd") at the hoot of an owl. It was a common phrase I'd hear as a child, so I still use it. I certainly don't think it's a diverse tradition, but probably an indication of the popularity of the tale in that region of Arfon where the Fourth Branch was mostly located."

For myself, even though there is no specific lore to support this, I have always seen Blodeuwedd as a barn owl. Their heart-shaped facial disks suggest her "flower-face" to me, and their ghostly white feathers spangled with brownish-red spots reminds me of the white and red animals associated with the Otherworld in Celtic mythos.

I was curious to know which owl others have come to associate with her, and so – without disclosing my own experience – I used social media to conduct an informal survey of Pagans and polytheists who feel a connection to, or are actively engaged in a devotional relationship with, Blodeuwedd. I received 63 replies, and some people included their stories and experiences: 31 people associated her with barn owls, 11 with snowy owls, 8 with great horned owls, 3 with tawny owls, 3 with any owl, 2 with barred owls, and 1 each for gray, bard, and eagle owls. I find it interesting that so many people shared my Unverified Personal Gnosis (UPG) on this, although a quick survey of Blodeuwedd art overwhelmingly associates her with barn owls as well, which speaks to the artists' UPG as well as the potential unconscious influence their art may have had on others. However, there is something to be said for her coming to each of us in a guise that was often reflective of the places we lived and the experiences we have had with owls in our lives.

In Blodeuwedd, we see a culmination of many owl beliefs and attributes. Some of them appear to have a more ancient origin, referencing the shape-changing qualities of the owl which harken back to their earliest artifactual representations. Her role as a seasonal Sovereignty Goddess can be seen as a reflection of the female owl divinity posited by Anne Ross, particularly concerning her dual nature in ruling over fertility and death. And finally, Blodeuwedd's infidelity is reflective of the medieval association of owls with illicit sexuality – a meaning underscored by separate folkloric traditions which see women transformed into owls as punishment for their sexual transgressions.

Chapter 7

Seeking Sovereignty

Reclaiming Blodeuwedd's identity as a Sovereignty Goddess is a powerful experience of mind and heart, requiring both study and devotion. Whether or not she was worshiped as a divinity in ancient times, she holds deep resonance as the Sovereign Lady of the Seasons, whose embrace empowers the Lord of the Summer and the Lord of the Winter in turn, and there is no question that she is honored by many modern pagans and polytheists as a Goddess today.

I believe it to be significant that this reclamation and revisioning of Blodeuwedd's story is happening in the here and now. I see mythology as a reflection of the collective needs of the culture which birthed it, and when tales and folklore remain in orality – as with Celtic British tradition – they are able to evolve to reflect the changing needs of that culture.

So why are the stories of the Welsh Gods increasingly being retold, especially in the last few decades? Why have these Gods been awakened and taking root in our collective consciousness – not just in Wales (where the stories have remained alive as part of their cultural fabric, albeit not in a religious context) but all over the world? What lessons do these Gods hold for us as modern seekers and practitioners? Why are they making themselves known in the world again, and how can we be in service to them through our work and devotion?

For no matter where we may live, our present-day culture and its symbol-sets are quite different from what they were when these stories were written down. Our leaders are not tested or chosen by a representative of the land they seek to rule, and our science has demonstrated the process by which our world experiences the seasonal round. What significance, then, does a Sovereignty Goddess hold for us in the modern world?

In this era when individuality is prized over collectivity, and general disconnection from the rhythms of Earth, and moon, and sun is the norm in the Western world, perhaps we are not meant to begin our journey of relationship with Sovereignty by seeking her in the world around us. Perhaps we must start by finding her in the world within us. Perhaps we are being called to establish a sovereignty of the self, which will empower us to honor the sovereignty of others as we work cooperatively towards restoring a much-needed balance between humanity and our world.

When we reflect these tales within, we can come to an understanding of Sovereignty as it applies to the self. I have come to define Sovereignty to mean "fully conscious self-determination". This can be achieved by working towards the wholeness that comes when we endeavor to bring the unconscious self into consciousness, a process of self-knowledge that catalyzes inner change and personal growth. We can reclaim the mythic process outlined in Blodeuwedd's story as a guiding practice for coming into our personal sovereignty, as it assists us in discovering our True Will and shows how to live a life that is a reflection of our hard-won knowledge of our authentic self.

In order to become Sovereign, we must first understand the inner culture that has arisen within us in response to the topography and climate of our personal landscape. This landscape is comprised of our mental, emotional, and physical bodies; these have been shaped by our experiences and reflect the current degree of balance that exists within and between each of these aspects of the self.

In my experience and belief, the reclamation of our sovereignty over these inner landscapes is the work that Blodeuwedd is calling us to do.

Following the Mythic Map

Blodeuwedd acts as the point around which the seasons turn from one to the other – from the fertile, fragrant abundance of the Light Half of the Year to the decaying, chthonic stillness of the Dark Half the Year. She is the doorway between states of being, and it is our work to find that fulcrum of balance within ourselves as well. As a mirror of the work we have done to restore Blodeuwedd's essence as a Sovereignty figure – both in our academic understanding of her, and as a devotee coming into relationship with her – it can be helpful for us to emulate the journey she undertakes in her story.

Just as we worked to reclaim her stature as a Sovereignty Goddess – recasting the meaning of her tale and the purpose of her journey – so must we seek to recenter ourselves in our authentic purpose... always striving to walk the path of our lives as a reflection of our Sovereignty – as Blodeuwedd teaches – no matter what the cost. But how can we know where that path lies? What is the nature of our Sovereignty?

One way to engage in this self-reflective process is to apply to our own lives the same criteria we used to determine Blodeuwedd's status as a Sovereignty Goddess in Chapter 3. It is a powerful exercise to ask ourselves these questions, meditate upon their answers, and use the resulting insights to guide us along the next step of our life's journey. This process of seeing her story within our own story is a devotional act that can clarify and strengthen our relationship with Blodeuwedd. Then, as we progress in relationship with her, we can seek her guidance as we work through our challenges. How privileged we are to have such a powerful ally at our side as we undertake this work!

Self-Reflective Questions for our Inner Sovereignty

1. *Sovereignty and the Land*. What is the nature of your inner landscape? How well do you know the details and

contours of your domain, that is to say, your personal make-up: what are your gifts and your challenges, what are your triumphs and your fears? What facets of yourself are still in need of exploration? What resources are at your disposal, and how well do you manage them? Over what aspects of your life do you already claim Sovereignty? To whom – or in service to what – have you given parts of your power away? Where do you most need to reclaim your sovereignty?

2. *Sovereignty and Liminality.* What is the state of your personal boundaries, on every level of existence: physical, mental, emotional, and spiritual? Where are these boundaries in need of strengthening, and where might they benefit from being a bit thinned? How well do you know the extent of your domain, and what do you do to maintain it? How well do you honor the boundaries of others? Where does your influence begin and end in every aspect of your life, including your inner and outer environments, your relationships, and your engagement with the world?

3. *Sovereignty and the Hunt.* How clear are you about your life's work? What goals have you set for yourself? What dreams are you actively pursuing? What are you willing to do to manifest the truth of your Sovereign self? What are you currently struggling with in pursuit of the reclamation of your personal power? What past lessons can you draw upon to help you with your present challenges? What past experiences must you come to peace with or leave behind so that you can move forward?

4. *Sovereignty as Tester of Potential Kings.* Can you discern a pattern of challenges in your life which seem to be presenting themselves to you over and over again? Why do you think this might be? What has your response to these challenges been in the past, and what might you

do differently in the present or the next time they come around? In what ways can you reframe these challenges so that you can view them as opportunities for growth and change, rather than punishments for lessons unlearned?

5. *Sovereignty and the Sacred Marriage.* In what areas of your life have you been able to attain a sense of balance? Where are the places of imbalance and what needs to be done to address them? Where does the balance of power lie in the context of the relationships in your life – with your partner, members of your family, in your work environment, in your community, with the Divine, and with yourself? How clearly can you hear the voice of your intuitive self? How much trust and discernment have you developed when it comes to consciously seeking out the wisdom that lies within?

6. *The Withdrawal of Sovereignty.* Over what areas of your life do you not presently wield agency? Where have you had to withdraw your energies, and why? Are there parts of your inner landscape that have been overtaken by the Wasteland – places which no longer grow, gifts and abilities no longer used, resources no longer available, energies completely depleted? Why do you think this is? How can you restore Sovereignty over these areas? How can you reallocate your energies in order to bring these places back to life? Where do you need to release your expectations, acknowledge the impact and truth of your limitations, and allow yourself to put down the burden of situations which can only be accepted but never changed?

7. *Sovereignty as Shape Changer.* What does your life look like in the present moment? How do you view your present circumstance and your place within it? How positive or negative is your self-concept? How does the person you seek to be differ from the person you currently are? As

you reclaim more and more of your personal Sovereignty, how does this shift the way your life looks? How does this shift how you see yourself? What must be done to affect these changes? What is the nature of the bridge you need to build in order to move yourself from where you are to where you seek to be? What does it look like when your life, or parts of your life, are in a place of imbalance? How can you learn to recognize the signs of this imbalance so that you can act to bring yourself back to a place of balance sooner?

Embracing our Darkness

Just as Blodeuwedd partnered with Gronw, just as the Otherworldly Champion is favored for a time by the Lady of Sovereignty, just as the Earth beds down for a while enfolded by winter, the reclamation of our Sovereignty requires that we actively enter the Shadow within us, and embrace the challenges that arise in our lives. We must be willing to spread our owl wings and hunt for the seeds of our authenticity which have been relegated to the shrouded corners of our deepest selves – hiding there, away from the criticism, disapproval, and socially reinforced belief of their impossibility or lack of worth.

We must seek these seeds with owl sight and hold them tightly with sharpened talons. To find true Sovereignty, we must spend time in the darkness and come to know every valley and contour of our inner lands – both where it is abundant and where it is fallow. Then, we must learn how to honor and bless these parts of ourselves. We must cultivate a practice of self-compassion, even as we actively engage in our own healing, rather than engage in the toxic spiritual bypassing that denies any aspect of our inner darkness – a flawed paradigm which ultimately only serves to keep the truth of who we are imprisoned in the places we pretend not to see.

Wholeness is achieved when we are able to acknowledge and accept all aspects of ourselves even as we strive to become the best self we can be. It is only by acknowledging where our inner landscape is fallow that we can know what work is necessary to bring this manifestation of the Wasteland back to life. We are beings of light and darkness, and the call of Blodeuwedd is to find our way to the place where all of the seeming contradictions of our total selves are resolved. In Jungian terms, the integration of Shadow leads us to the transcendence of individuation – the authenticity of personal Sovereignty.

And like the seasons of the year, the phases of moon, and the circuit of the day which sees us pass from darkness to light and back again, we must learn how to surrender ourselves to the turning of Cycle, and to harness the wisdom of its process as it moves both around us and through us. We need not fear the dark or struggle against it, nor should we shun the light or avoid the vulnerability of its illumination. Like Blodeuwedd, we have different tools at our disposal during each season, and each season brings us different work to do.

Celebrating the Flower Maiden

Reclaiming Blodeuwedd as a Sovereignty Goddess requires that we reclaim and resanctify the totality of who she is – to seek and find the divinity in both Blodeuedd and Blodeuwedd. This is no small thing. It is easy to see Blodeuwedd in her owl form as possessing personal power: she is wisdom embodied, keen-sighted and laser-focused on what she wants, able to fly where she wills of her own volition – a solitary figure who is powerful, silent, and unafraid, even in the darkest of night.

But what of Blodeuedd, the Flower Maiden? It is easy to dismiss this version of her as a hollow artifice – the illusion that stands in stark contrast to the power of her owl form. After all, what more could she be but a symbol of patriarchy's ideal woman? Someone created to meet a man's need and to fulfill the purpose delegated to her – no more and no less. She is an object that is constructed out of insubstantial stuff; how could she do anything but reflect the most superficial and transient attributes of the fragile blooms from which she was wrought?

For flowers, by their very nature, are not meant to last. They are beautiful, intoxicating, and impermanent. In much of literature, the sought-after maiden is praised for her beauty, prized for her innocence, and pursued for her youth. Like the easily-bruised petals of a flower, she is fragile and in need of protection. She has her season, and her worth is in her function; the fertilized flower becomes the fruit, and a woman's best destiny – according to the patriarchy – is to be a mother.

And so Blodeuedd begins her tale as the perfect wife – beautiful, compliant, and silent. She is accepting of her place and fully participates in her given role – and why would she do otherwise? She doesn't know that there are other options, or that there are any other ways of being – until she falls in love. It is love which sets her soul aflame. Love which enlivens her being. Love which causes her to recognize for the first time that her life is her own, and that she has the power to choose her own course and to set her own trajectory.

Perhaps it is this acknowledgement of her individuality and the sacred nature of personal will which caused her to transcend her form – to become a soul enshrouded in a body – to be filled with the spark of true life, and to experience the first kindling of wisdom. Indeed, her sense of individuality comes through as we hear her speak for the first time in the narrative. Once she has realized her own agency, Blodeuedd begins to act in support of her own desires. She has thrown off her programming, and what she says and does is now deemed worthy of note in the tale, precisely because it stands in contrast to expectation.

Now that she knows what she wants and learns what she needs to do to obtain it, she discovers that the source of her power comes from the very things that were intended to make her feel weak. Like the heady scent of flowers, her beauty is disarming. Her petal-like fragility engenders the impulse in others to protect her, and her newly-budded innocence has her present as being incapable of guile.

And so, she is underestimated by those around her – and this allows her to use the attributes built into her by her creators in a way they could never have imagined. For the oak grows strong and tall, and permits far-seeing. Tenacious broom grips the earth tightly and sweeps away all obstacles. Fragrant meadowsweet dulls the senses and assists in the crossing of boundaries – and through carried by the bride, it also accompanies the dead into their graves.

Oak, broom, and meadowsweet. These are the components of her being. These are the gifts she was given by her creators. These are the tools at her disposal. We do Blodeuedd a great disservice by calling her a manipulator when, in truth, she was making use of the resources available to her. And once she was able to use them to achieve her ends and create a life she loved, she changed and grew and obtained deep wisdom.

Flowers to Feathers

Our own path to growth and Sovereign wholeness is a mirror of the Flower Maiden's journey, and we will do well to respect and honor her. For each of us, no matter our gender, are a reflection of the patriarchal culture that has formed us from the moment of our birth. Like tender plants, we are cultivated to fulfill a purpose, and to yield a specific harvest; when we seek to grow in ways which fall outside of these expectations, we meet the pruner's shears, while rich fertilizer is provided where we remain in alignment with the roles placed upon us. The windows are transparent in the greenhouse of the over-culture, letting us see enough of the wild outdoors to believe that we are growing there – but the truth is that the structure will not permit us to take root in those fertile soils.

Unless we choose change. Unless we take action to break free of the confines placed upon us and live a life of our own making. And how can we do this?

Like Blodeuedd, we must learn to recognize the spark of desire in our hearts and allow this passion to grow within us, empowering us to use this creative energy to manifest a life that we love. Just as flowers turn their faces to follow the track of the sun, when the spark of desire builds to become the fire of True Will within us, we will birth forth an inner sun – catalyzing a new and more authentic trajectory for our lives.

When we do not follow the same source of light as the rest of society, when we make changes in accordance with our inner passions rather than those we are programmed to have by the over-culture, we will seem strange to them... branded as Other. When we leave the greenhouse of enculturation, we become boundary dwellers, living in ways and in places that do not make sense to the glass-encased world of ordered rows and regulated temperatures. When our source of light comes from within, we are able to see clearly in the darkness. We recognize illusion for what it is, and have obtained the skills necessary to obtain our goals and hold tight to our truths, no matter what hatred and scorn may come our way.

But before we learn to see with owl sight or grow our wings to fly where we will, we must first acknowledge and honor the truth of our flower-formed self – that frame which we have been cultivated to wear since the moment of our birth – and to find the power embodied there, even if we believe it to be our weakness. To do so, we must identify – without judgement, without the poison of self-recrimination – the components that have been brought together to create us: the circumstances of our lives, the skills we have developed, the tools we have obtained, and the experiences we have lived through.

To begin this process, we can meditate upon our own flower form and the three things necessary for a flower to grow: soil, water, and sunlight. It can be helpful to seek out the answers to these questions in order to get a sense of who we are in the here and the now:

1. *Soil* – What is the nature of the soil where we plant our roots? Where is our home, our foundation, the facts of our environment? What social structures and relationship dynamics are at play in our lives? How strong are our boundaries? How safe do we feel? What is the availability of necessary resources? Where are we stuck or unmoving? What limitations or illusions have we accepted? What are our strengths? Where is the center of our power? What skills do we possess? What tools are at our disposal?

2. *Water* – Where do we obtain the water we need to live? Are our emotional needs being met, and our ability to express them unhindered? Are these waters plentiful, or are they apportioned conditionally? Are these waters pure and clear, or do they carry with them the residue of toxicity or the taint of expectation? What is the nature of our relationship with ourselves? With others? With the Divine? How do we practice compassion and seek understanding, both for ourselves and others?

3. *Sunlight* – What is the source of our life's light? What feeds us and gives us direction? What brings us joy and fulfillment? What moves us away from suffering? What motivates our actions? What guides our choices? What are our life's goals? When and why did we set them? What is our relationship with our Shadow?

Implicitly or otherwise, we are cultivated to conform to the expectations of others and to use our gifts in service to the roles placed upon us. Once we are conscious of who we are, what are we made of, and how we came to be where we are in the here and now, then we can assess how closely aligned our lives are with the even the smallest spark of True Will that resides within us – how much we resemble the vision of the Sovereign self that we hold in our deepest and most authentic heart.

Chapter 8

Entering into Relationship
with Blodeuwedd

It is possible to foster a strong and authentic relationship with Blodeuwedd; as with any divinity, the key, in my opinion, is to build a bridge between the self and the divine. As with the construction of any bridge you will need a blueprint, the proper tools, resources in the form of building materials, and energy expended through time and work to manifest your will. For this inner bridge to take form, the blueprint is revealed through study, the tools are developed through practice, and the resources are gathered and expended through devotion.

Study – Hopefully, the information presented in this book has provided a solid foundation from which to begin or deepen a study of Blodeuwedd through immersion into her story, an exploration of its meaning when examined through a medieval Welsh cultural context, and the lessons this divine lady holds for us today.

Practice – There is no one way to approach creating a practice around making a connection to Blodeuwedd. What follows is an offering intended both to provide some concrete guidance on how to begin building a practice, and to serve as a jumping off point for the creation of our own practices, inspired by the insights you've received from Blodeuwedd herself.

Devotion – We can look at devotion as both the energy expended while weaving together the threads of insights gathered through the acts of study and practice, as well as the beautiful tapestry that results from our striving, representing the true and lived experience of our connection to Source. Devotion is both what we do and what we create; it is the heart-centered intention to come into relationship – without ego, expectation, or fear. It is the art of dedicating some time, energy, and space toward the goal of fostering relationship without agenda or expectation.

Celtic Religious Practices

Aside from the accounts of Classical writers, which mostly focused on the practices of the Druids in their sacred groves, we do not have any written record about how Celtic Pagans interacted with their Gods. The archaeological record, however, provides us with some indirect information about Celtic beliefs. They propitiated the Gods with votive offerings, often by ritually breaking and depositing high status items in bodies of water. They practiced human sacrifice, likely when things were particularly dire, although we do not know how willing the victims may have been. They buried their dead with items which appear to reflect their work or station in life, apparently including them to ensure that they had access to these things in the next life. They venerated their ancestors, making offerings to them especially at times and in places of liminality. When they started to create images of their Gods after the influence of Rome, they appear to have erected personal shrines in their homes as indicated by the presence of small devotional statuary.

When Rome took over Celtic lands and began to syncretize native divinities with their own, we begin to see dedicatory stele and altars erected to Romano-Celtic Gods. In the face of this material culture, we have been able to determine that some divinities are local and connected to the land, while others have more far-ranging worship.

At places like the Temple of Sulis-Minerva at Bath, we see the Romano-British practice of curse tablets cast into the waters of the sacred spring; these lead tablets – which ask for the intervention of the Goddess to punish those who have stolen from or otherwise wronged the petitioner – include both Roman and British names. In those same waters, we have also found votive offerings to Sulis-Minerva that were crafted to resemble body parts; these are believed to either represent what the petitioner has asked the Goddess to heal, or were given in thanks for a healing already received.

As we have already discussed, by the time the stories – which we believe may have origins in Pagan times – were written down, the Welsh had been solidly Christian for almost eight centuries. Something that stands out in the legendarium of Wales is the unquestioned proximity of the Otherworld; it is not unusual for someone to slip into the Otherworld, or for Otherworldly beings to cross over into this world. If we consider the Otherworld and its inhabitants to be the mythic remnants of divinities and spirits of place venerated in Pagan times, perhaps this tells us something important about the way the typical ancient Briton saw themselves and their world in relation to the Gods.

If that is the case, then the Gods were everywhere, dwelling in the landscape, and particularly accessible through places and times of liminality. Their favor and assistance could be obtained or acknowledged through the giving of offerings, and their protection could be secured through sacrifice and the use of ritual items, such as the burial of horse skulls in the thresholds of houses. Certain folk practices observed in the past 200 years, such as the winter mumming party of the Mari Lwyd and the Hunting of the Wren on St. Stephen's day, may be remnants of ancient beliefs, although they may simply be a reflection of an ongoing relationship between humans and the land they live on, regardless of religious origins.

With these things in mind, we can craft a practice of devotion to Blodeuwedd which emulates aspects of what we do know about Celtic practice and belief; these in turn can be used to assist in fostering a connection that builds a relationship with her. The gifting of offerings on a shrine or altar; the pouring of libations at places of liminality like river banks or lake-sides, or boundary places like gates or bridges; the performing of rituals at threshold times, like sunset or at the first quarter moon – these are helpful clues which can inform our practice. However, bigger than this, we see that there is a pattern of individual connection with the divine. The proximity of the Otherworld in myth may indicate how very accessible these forces were; no formal priesthood was required to mediate every experience, although conventions of hospitality and respect were necessary for these connections to be successful and positive.

What follows, therefore, are some suggestions to help with fostering a personal relationship with Blodeuwedd. In addition to studying her story and identifying the symbolism in her tale that reflects her core nature and the lessons she holds for us, creating a devotional shrine is a good place to start forging a connection with her. I have also included a journey to help to connect with her in her guises of Flower Maiden and Owl, which will assist in experiencing her different energies and allow us to actively seek her guidance in how we can reclaim Sovereignty in our own lives.

Devotional Work

The creation of an altar (a working space for ritual or magic) or shrine (a devotional space for honoring divinity and fostering daily mindfulness) dedicated to Blodeuwedd is a powerful statement of a desire to enter into a relationship with her. Guided by the Hermetic Principle of Correspondence which says that like energies attract each other, the study of Blodeuwedd's story can inform the choice of objects to place upon her shrine. Here are some ideas to get started:

Images of Blodeuwedd – all manner of art and statuary depicting Blodeuwedd are available for purchase; of course, it is a powerful act of devotion to create the image oneself.

Images of owls and owl feathers – Statuary, art prints, and feathers are wonderful ways to tie into the energies of Owl. Be sure that the possession of owl feathers is legal before obtaining them, as this is not the case everywhere. Using feathers from other birds with similar coloring and markings can serve as symbolic alternatives.

Flowers of oak, broom, and meadowsweet – These blooms can be collected and placed on the altar as an offering, or burnt as an incense to honor her. Similarly, images of these flowers or flower essences made from these blooms can help create a bridge between the seeker and the Goddess.

Images of sites associated with Blodeuwedd – Photographs or paintings of Tomen y Mur and Llyn Morwynion, stones charged in these places, and water taken from the lake itself are wonderful connections to her mythic landscape. My shrine includes a small replica of Llech Ronw that I fashioned out of clay; I have visited this standing stone many times on pilgrimage, and the hole speaks to me of the portal between the worlds that Blodeuwedd embodies.

Of Flowers and Feathers – A Journey

Set aside a place and time where you will not be disturbed. Sit in front of your shrine or working altar dedicated to Blodeuwedd.

Read through the working beforehand so you are prepared for the journey. Consider memorizing or mapping out the key points of the journey, or recording it as a guide so that you can be as present as possible for the journey as it unfolds. Consider writing out the invocations for Blodeuedd and Blodeuwedd on an index card that you keep on your altar, so that you have it on hand for when you need it. Be sure to have your journal close by so that you can record your experiences and insights at the end of the working.

Close your eyes and establish an even and rhythmic breath. Once this pattern becomes natural, focus upon this breath. As you exhale, release any energies that prevent you from being fully present in body, mind, and spirit. As you inhale, envision vibrant green energies of Earth being pulled up through your root and filling the entirety of your energy field with its vitalistic energies. Continue to cycle your breath in this way until you feel centered, clear, and open. When you are ready, begin the journey.

Envision yourself standing on a cliffside overlooking a lake. The sky blushes as it births the dawn, and the steadily rising sun paints the world around you with a wash of pale color.

Feel yourself warmed by the growing light as it illuminates the landscape.

Touching you with its gilded rays, the sunshine transforms into a vortex of yellow and white flowers that swirl and dance around you.

Delicate threads of oak blossoms weave a silken garment around you, and as it enrobes your form, feel yourself grow strong in body, limitless in energy, and youthful in spirit.

Yellow petals of broom gather around your head, converging to cover it like a golden veil. As it descends, feel your mind clear, your thoughts broaden, and your vision expand.

A rain of white meadowsweet envelops your senses, intoxicating you with their honeyed, heady scent. Any physical and emotional discomfort disappears as you feel yourself uplifted by a sense of profound peace and radiating bliss.

Take three, deep, centering breaths. Immerse yourself in this moment, high above the upland valley lake, bathed in sunlight, surrounded by the flowers of oak, broom, and meadowsweet.

Fully in the moment, you become keenly aware of the movement of the sun as it arcs along its path, brightening the sky. Turn towards the sun. Savor its warmth on your face. Feel a spark kindle to life in your chest. Envision a bridge taking form between this small inner flame and the vast celestial sun. Feel the connection between them grow stronger as the sun climbs higher, until you experience the two become one.

Allow this inner flame to fill your heart. Ask that the light of its truth illuminate the Sovereign pathway within, revealing the bountiful harvest of your gifts as well as the seeds of potential laying dormant within you. Feel the vitalistic power of the sun nurture what is already growing, and activate what has been patiently awaiting the light of your awareness.

Breathe into these places. Feel your heart open to all possibilities, as the flowers of your potential unfold, drinking in the light.

When you are ready, call to Blodeuedd, Lady of Flowers, to guide you, saying these words or those of your own choosing:

Blodeuedd, Flower Bride
Lady of meadowsweet, oak flowers, and broom:
Lend me your vision to track the light's pathways
Show me the way-signs to guide my life's journey
Teach me to open and embrace my soul's potential
With fragrant and fertile ecstasy
Through the fields of my authenticity

In this moment, know that the soft touch of the blossoms around you is her touch; your fragrance, hers – your radiance, hers. Feel for her presence, and take three deep, centering breaths to connect as fully with her energy as you can.

When you are ready, ask Blodeuedd to show you a vision of yourself – fully actualized and centered in authenticity. Take what time you need to see this image of your Sovereign self with clarity.

When you are ready, ask what you need most to know at this point in your life's journey to acknowledge and support the manifestation of your sacred purpose. What is your next step along the path to embrace your Sovereignty?

Spend some time journeying with Blodeuedd, seeking these answers, and being open to these experiences and all of the ways that information can come to you: symbols, visions, voices, emotions, memories, and just a general sense of knowing. Do not judge, just receive.

When you feel you have completed this part of the journey, thank Blodeuedd for her guidance. When you are ready, bring your attention back to the hillside where you stand in the now-waning light.

The sun disappears below the western horizon. The sky is dark and shimmers with stars. A cold wind rushes towards you and disperses the petals that' surround you, scattering them into the deepening night.

Shivering, you wrap your arms around your shoulders and notice that your skin has become blanketed by a soft downy coat. A strange prickling sensation overtakes you as long white plumes emerge from your flesh, replacing the down. Soon you are completely enrobed, as if wearing a cloak of feathers.

You continue to transform as the moon climbs higher in the sky. Your feet become talons. Your arms are now fully-fledged wings. Your body becomes smaller and lighter, and a tail fans out behind you.

Your face widens and flattens into a heart-shaped disc of feathers that collect even the smallest of sounds, sending them to your now asymmetrical ears. The merest whisper of a rustling in the distance behind you catches your attention. Turning towards it, you realize you now have the ability to rotate your head almost completely around you. A screech of surprise arises from your throat, passing through your sharp yellow beak.

Your eyes grow larger and many times sharper, allowing you to see the surrounding landscape with a clarity that mimics daylight.

Breathe into this new body, this owl form you now embody. Feel the strength of your talons, the freedom of your wings, the clarity of your hearing, and the truth of your sight.

Experience how these changes have empowered you with tools and abilities to meet the challenges that come with the night.

When you are ready, call to Blodeuwedd, Owl Goddess, to guide you, saying these words or those of your own choosing:

Blodeuwedd, Flower Faced One
Hunter through nights dark and moons bright
Lend me your vision to see through the shadow
Show me the truth that lays beyond all illusion
Teach me to grasp my Sovereignty with iron-gripped
    talons
And to fly on silent, unerring wings
Through the skies of my destiny

In this moment, know the softness of the feathers around you are her feathers; your wings are hers, your talons – hers. Feel for her presence, and take three deep, centering breaths to connect as fully with her energy as you can.

When you are ready, ask Blodeuwedd to reveal the aspects of yourself that prevent you from fully embodying your Sovereignty. Take what time you need to see this vision of your Shadow self with clarity.

When you are ready, ask Blodeuwedd what you need most to know at this point in your life's journey that will help you overcome your fears, and release your outmoded beliefs about who you are and what you are capable of becoming. Ask her to show you what tools you have at your disposal that will help you reclaim the truth of who you are.

Spend some time journeying with Blodeuwedd, seeking these answers, and being open to the experiences and all of the ways that information can come to you: symbols, visions, voices, emotions, memories, and just a general sense of knowing. Do not judge, just receive.

When you feel you have completed this part of the journey, thank Blodeuwedd for her guidance. When you are ready, bring your attention back to the hillside where you stand in the deep, still darkness of the night.

Take a moment to integrate and remember all that you have seen and experienced, with three deep, centering breaths.

A single bird sings out, greeting the barest hint of dawn. A warm breeze from the east envelops you, loosening your feathers and carrying them away into the darkness.

Find yourself in your own form once more, standing on the hilltop where this journey began.

In your hands, envision a bowl full of the sweetest honey wine. Fill it with the energies of gratitude for all that you have received, and when you are ready – as you stand there at the threshold of dawn – pour it out as a libation to honor the Sovereign Lady who has been such a gracious guide for this journey. Speak what words of thanks arise from the bottom of your heart.

Take three more breaths. Open your eyes, and return to waking consciousness.

With your breath and intention, ground and center – releasing any excess energies you may have brought back with you – until you feel yourself in a place of energetic balance.

The journey is complete.

Be sure to journal your insights and experiences.

Chapter 9

Forward into the Future

Unseasonably chilly, even for Wales in the summer, we walked through the patches of mist clinging damply to the undulating Snowdonia landscape. I had been here several times before, and I've seen this landscape wearing many different seasonal garments. But this time, there was something different.

Certainly, I was not the same person who had last set her pilgrim's feet upon this cobbled stretch of Roman road, part of the ancient trackways called Sarn Elen. Only sheep and the occasional hikers now walk this path, winding past the ruins of a Roman amphitheater and an 18th century farmhouse, leading to the dual-humped remains of the Norman motte-and-bailey castle Tomen y Mur ("The Mound of the Wall"), built on the site of a Roman fort. In the Fourth Branch, it is called Mur Castell, and was Lleu and Blodeuwedd's chief court.

This was her land, and it was she we had come to meet. The ruins before me are as layered as her tale, and what can presently be seen in the landscape only hints at the complexity of what lies beneath, built upon a foundation of an even more distant past. Neolithic and Roman, Celtic and Norman, 18th century and today.

Down in the valley below us is the decommissioned Trawsfynydd Nuclear Power Station – a stark intruder in this otherwise timeless pastoral scene. I am conscious that each step takes me further away from the encompassing present and deeper into the nebulous energies of the past. Away from the power of science, and deeper into the power of myth...of story and of symbol expressing itself through the very land around us.

This is the land of the Flower Bride, the woman made of flowers so that she could be wed to the Scion of Gwynedd, in defiance – or fulfillment – of his mother's wishes. I have sought her here before when the land was awash with flowers – purple rosebay willowherb, yellow gorse, white meadowsweet. But this time, it was different. This time, I went not to the mound but wandered instead along the grass-enrobed earthworks near the ruins of stone walls, lingering a bit to listen as I stood between the berried hawthorn trees.

This time, I saw instead the tall-tufted wild onion growing between the stones of the invader's roads. I saw enormous patches of nettle, sheltering against the broken masonry of the Norman encampment. I saw purple thistle, squatting and hardy against the winds racing up from the valley, from the power plant and beyond.

And yet, this was she. Expressing herself, leaving her Sovereign imprint across this land. A force of nature responding to the needs of this place in this time. Seeking to bring things into a balanced relationship, offering what is most needed.

She is a shape-shifter. Becoming what she must. Reclaiming the ruins that criss-cross her landscape, half-healed scars that nonetheless hold the stories of the past... just as our own scars hold the memory of who we have been, providing us with a map that charts our journey to the present.

She is awake. She is alive. She is more than what her tale portrays her to be. Much more. The ancestral spirits of this land rejoice, for she was never meant to be frozen in time, nor constrained by any boundaries – be they stone walls or a static story. Not oak, broom, and meadowsweet now, no... new medicine is required today. She reveals herself to me as a potent decoction of nettle and thistle and wild onion. Where once she was a bridal bouquet of pleasure and beauty, she now pierces the flesh with her tiny spines, burns the skin with her acrid sting, and slices the air with her pungent odor. My wet cheeks bear witness to her threefold power to make me cry.

Standing there amid the wild growth tumbling over the reclaimed ruins of what has been, I ask her what she has to say to those who seek her today... those who wish to emulate her tale, to follow in her rebellion, to risk everything for the chance to live the life they long for... What guidance can she share with those who wish to walk a path of Sovereignty?

And this Onion Maiden – Goddess, guardian – with strands of stinging nettle blooms for her hair, and the protective spines of thistles covering her flesh, gifted me with this poem, and I am honored to share it now with you.

Thistle, and nettle, and wild onions
Grow between crumbling walls and ancient ruins
Windswept upon the hilltop.

Books are for pressing flowers between their pages
While castles are for oppressing Flower Maidens
Taken from their wild places –
Forced to speak a language of sound,
To sing another's song...
To trade green blood for red.

You can plant flowers in rows...
but not so women,
or owls.
Like seeds, they fly where they will –
taking root where they find purchase
to bloom another day.

Onions and nettles and thistles:
This is her new recipe.

Why did Gwydion not gather these?
Why did he not conjure life into these?
Perhaps because of the tears they each bring
and, having suffered enough,
he thought Lleu would do best to avoid them.

But the land knows what is needed
For healing
For wholeness.
And acrid though the remedies may be,
It is necessary that we know life's sting,
taste life's bitterness,
have our blood drawn by life's thorny fingers –
to honor the Queen, to call to her Sovereignty.

She lives here still, though her flowers are different.
She dwells here yet, enlivening the land with her talon-sharp
fragrance.
The touch of her fingers spread fire:
you will not soon forget the heat of her caress on your flesh.

Pungent and sharp-spired, she lingers.
Grasping the hem of our garments,
She bids us:

Take me with you!
Know the truth of this life.
Let your strength be increased by it
Even as your tears flow as you cut me!
Consume me!
Boil me as pottage!
My nettle is stinging medicine.
My onion, sharp sister to every food.

My thistle, reminders of what has been...
what has gone
and what will come again.
For I am still here. Still Sovereign.
I mark these lands as my own.
I no longer require a sacrificial king;
Your thistle-drawn blood is all the offering I need.

Know my truth:
Some flowers are sweet salves, and some deadly poisons
and NONE may be kept in captivity for long –
Not by men
Or magicians
Or gods
Or old stories.
I am free in this landscape:
windblown and wild.
AND NONE MAY TAME ME AGAIN.

Write me a new song to be carried
by nine bells across the sea:
Nine waves of rages
Of righteous women's anger
Of boundaries defended
Of NEVER AGAIN

Stand fast and claim what they tried and failed to take:
the right to your voice
to fill your form completely
to love freely
to change your mind
to transform your life
and never give up the power wrest

from the hands of Gwydion
and those like him
by those who have paid the price in full.
Be owls, my sisters!
Be wise, and unerring in your aim,
your moon-ensilvered sight clear of illusion.
But also be flowers,
and plant your own gardens.
Follow your own pathway.
Walk the golden trackway beneath
the conqueror's stones:
the ancient road, Sarn Elen –
so that you may bloom
so that you may become
all that you are meant to be.

Oh! What can you expect from me when you visit out of
season?
What but nettles, and thistles, and wild onion?
The hawthorn, too... with only memories of May
    bloomings
instead, bearing berries
scaled with silver lichens
draped messily with fairy wool.

But take these offerings, these gifts, these wisdoms.
Weave for me a new crown
A true crown.

I am no longer what I was.
I am not yet what I shall be.
But you must know me, here and now,
If you wish to know my truth and taste my mystery

If you wish for my tale to continue
If you wish to carry me home.

JT 8/19
Tomen y Mur

And so, as it should be, her story continues

Bibliography

Primary Sources

C. Julius Caesar. *Caesar's Gallic War,* McDevitte and W. S. Bohn, Translators. (New York: Harper & Brothers, 1869).

The Celtic Sources for the Arthurian Legend, Jon B. Coe and Simon Young (Felinfach: Llanerch Publishers, 1995).

Culhwch and Olwen: An Edition and Study of the Oldest Arthurian Tale, Rachel Bromwich and D. Simon Evans, eds. (Cardiff: University of Wales Press, 1992).

Dafydd ap Gwilym: His Poems, translated by Gwyn Thomas, (Cardiff: University of Wales Press, 2001).

Haycock, Marged, *Legendary Poems from the Book of Taliesin* (Aberystwyth: CMCS Publications, 2007).

The Mabinogi and Other Medieval Welsh Tales, translated by Patrick K. Ford, (Berkeley: University of California Press, 1977).

The Mabinogion, translated by Sioned Davies, (New York: Oxford University Press, 2007).

The Mabinogion, translated by Tales, Charlotte Guest, (London: J.M. Dent and Co, 1906).

The Physicians of Myddfai, translated by John Pughe, (Felinfach: Llanerch Publishers, 1993). Facsimile reprint.

Pliny the Elder. *The Natural History.* John Bostock, Translator. (London: Taylor and Francis, 1855).

Preiddeu Annwn: The Spoils of Annwn, Sarah Higley, trans. (Rochester: University of Rochester The Camelot Project, 2007. Available at http://d.lib.rochester.edu/camelot/text/preiddeu-annwn

"The Tragic Death of Cu Roi mac Dairi", *Ancient Irish* ed. And trans. by Tom P. Cross & Clark Harris Slover (New York: Henry Holt & Co., 1936). Available at http://www.maryjones. us/ctexts/curoi.html

Trioedd Ynys Prydein: The Triads of the Island of Britain, Rachel Bromwich, ed. (Cardiff: University of Wales Press, 2006).

Skene, William F., *The Four Ancient Books of Wales*, (Edinburgh: Edmonston and Douglas, 1868). Available at http://www.sacred-texts.com/neu/celt/fab/fab000.htm

Secondary Sources

Adler, Alfred, "Sovereignty in Chrétien's Yvain", *PMLA*, Vol. 62, No. 2 (Jun., 1947), pp. 281–305.

Arlen, Shelley, *The Cambridge Ritualists: an annotated bibliography of the works by and about Jane Ellen Harrison, Gilbert Murray, Francis M. Cornford, and Arthur Bernard Cook* (Metuchen, New Jersey: Scarecrow Press, 1990).

Armstrong, Edward A., *The Folklore of Birds* (London: Dover Publications, second edn. 1970).

Bhreathnach, Máire, "The Sovereignty Goddess as a Goddess of Death", *Zeitschrift für celtische Philologie*, 39, (1982), pp. 243–260.

Bromwich, Rachel; Jarman, A.O.H; and Roberts, Brynley F., eds., *The Arthur of the Welsh: The Arthurian Legend in Medieval Welsh Literature* (Cardiff: University of Wales Press, 1991).

Bugge, John, "Fertility Myth and Female Sovereignty in 'The Weddynge of Sir Gawen and Dame Ragnell'", *The Chaucer Review*, Vol. 39, No. 2 (2004), pp. 198–218.

Campbell, Joseph, *The Hero With a Thousand Faces* (Princeton: Princeton University Press, 1949).

Cartwright, Jane, *Feminine Sanctity and Spirituality in Medieval Wales* (Cardiff: University of Wales Press, 2008).

Davies, Sioned, *The Four Branches of the Mabinogi* (Llandysul: Gomer Press, 1993).

Eliade, Mircea, *A History of Religious Ideas, Vol. 2: From Gautama Buddha to the Triumph of Christianity*, trans. Willard R. Trask (Chicago: University of Chicago Press, 1982).

Ellis, T.P., "Legal references, terms and conceptions in the Mabinogion", *Y Cymmrodor* 39 (1928), pp. 86–148.

Fife, Graeme, *Arthur the King* (New York: Sterling Publishing, 1991).

Frazer, James G., *The Golden Bough* (New York: Collier Books, Macmillan Publishing Company, 1963).

Frazer, James G., *Adonis Attis Osiris: Studies in the History of Oriental Religion* (New Hyde Park, New York: University Books, 1961).

Frazer, James G., "The Sacred Marriage", in *Myths and Motifs in Literature*, David Burrows, ed. (New York: Simon & Schuster, Inc., 1973).

Green, C.M.C., "The Slayer and the King: 'Rex Nemorensis' and the Sanctuary of Diana", *Arion*, Third Series, Vol. 7, No. 3 (Winter, 2000), pp. 24–63.

Green, Miranda, *The Gods of the Celts* (Phoenix Mill, Sutton Publishing Ltd., 2004).

Gruffydd, W.J., *Folklore and Myth in the Mabinogion* (Cardiff: University of Wales Press, 1958).

Gruffydd, W.J., *Math Vab Mathonwy, An Inquiry into the Origins and Development of the Fourth Branch of the Mabinogi, with the Text and a Translation* (Cardiff: University of Wales Press Board, 1928).

Gwyndaf, Robin, *Welsh Folk Tales* (Cardiff: National Museums and Galleries of Wales, 1999).

Herbert, Maire, "Goddess and King: The Sacred Marriage in Early Ireland" in *Women and Sovereignty*, ed. Louise Olga Fradenburg, *Cosmos* 7 (Edinburgh,1992), pp. 264–75.

Jackson, Kenneth, *The International Popular Tale in Early Welsh Tradition* (Cardiff: University of Wales Press, 1961).

Jones, Mary, "Echtra mac nEchach", *Leabhar Buidhe Lecain, Celtic Literature Collective* [Online]. Available at http://www.maryjones.us/ctexts/eochaid.html

Jones, Mary, "Trystan and Esyllt", *Celtic Literature Collective* [Online]. Available at http://www.maryjones.us/ctexts/trystan.html

Jones, Thomas Gwynn. *Welsh Folklore and Folk-Custom* (London: Methuen & Co. LTD, 1930).

Keefer, Sarah Larratt, "The Lost Tale of Dylan in the Fourth Branch of The Mabinogi", *Studia Celtica*; Jan 1, 1989; 24, ProQuest pg. 26.

Koch, John T., ed., *Celtic Culture: A Historical Encyclopedia* (Santa Barbara: ABC-CLIO, 2006).

Koch, John T., *The Celtic Heroic Age* (Andover: Celtic Studies Publications, 2000).

Kondratiev, Alexi, "Lugus: The Many-Gifted Lord", *An Tríbhís Mhór: The IMBAS Journal of Celtic Reconstructionism* #1, Lúnasa 1997. Available at http://www.imbas.org/articles/lugus.html

Lawrence, Elizabeth A., *Hunting the Wren: Transformation of Bird to Symbol* (Knoxville: University of Tennessee Press, 1997).

Lawton, Jocelyne, *Flowers and Fables: A Welsh Herbal* (Bridgend: Seren Books, 2006).

Lindahl, Carl; McNamara, John; and Lindow, John, eds. *Medieval Folklore* (Oxford: Oxford University Press, 2002).

Loomis, Roger Sherman, *Celtic Myth in Arthurian Romance* (Chicago: Chicago Review Press, 2005).

Mac Cana, Proinsias, *Celtic Mythology* (London: Hamlyn Publishing Group, 1970).

Morrison, Sophia, *Manx Fairy Tales* (London: David Nutt, 1911). Available at http://www.isle-of-man.com/manxnotebook/fulltext/sm1911/p123.htm <Accessed 10 September, 2014>.

Nitze, William A., "The Sister's Son and the Conte del Graal", *Modern Philology*, Vol. 9, No. 3 (Jan., 1912), pp. 291–322.

Owen, Trefor M., *Welsh Folk Customs* (Llandysul: Gomer Press, 1985).

Owen, Morfydd and Jenkins, Dafydd, *The Welsh Law of Women* (Cardiff: University of Wales Press, 1980).

Parker, Will, *The Four Branches of the Mabinogi* (California: Bardic Press, 2005).

Peate, Iorwerth C., "The Wren in Welsh Folklore", *Man*, Vol. 36 (Jan 1936), pp. 1–3.

Lord Raglan, "The Hero of Tradition", *Folklore*, Vol. 45, No. 3 (Sep., 1934), pp. 212–231.

Rees, Alwyn, "The Divine Hero in Celtic Hagiology", *Folklore*, Vol. 47, No. 1 (Mar., 1936), pp. 30–41.

Rees, Alwyn and Rees Brinley, *Celtic Heritage: Ancient Tradition in Ireland and Wales* (London: Thames and Hudson, Ltd., 1961).

Rhys, John, *Celtic Folklore: Welsh and Manx* (Oxford: Oxford University Press, 1901).

Roberts, Brynley "*Culhwch ac Olwen*, the Triads, Saints' Lives" in R. Bromwich, A.O.H.

Ross, Anne, *Folklore of Wales* (Stroud: Tempus Publishing Ltd., 2001).

Ross, Anne, *Pagan Celtic Britain: Studies in Iconography and Tradition* (Chicago: Academy Chicago Publishers, 1996).

Schrijver, Peter, *Studies in British Celtic Historical Phonology* (Leiden: Brill Rodopi, 1995).

Sheehan, Sarah, "Matrilineal Subjects: Ambiguity, Bodies, and Metamorphosis in the Fourth Branch of the Mabinogi", *Signs*, 34 (2):(2009), pp. 319–342.

Sikes, Wirt, *Welsh Folklore, Fairy Mythology, Legends and Traditions* (London: Sampson Low, Marston, Searle & Rivington, 1880).

Telyndru, Jhenah, *The Mythic Moons of Avalon* (Woodbury, Minnesota: Llewellyn Publications, 2019).

Telyndru, Jhenah, *Pagan Portals – Rhiannon: Divine Queen of the Celtic Britons* (Winchester, UK: Moon Books, 2018).

Thompson, Stith. *Motif-index of folk-literature: a classification of narrative elements in folktales, ballads, myths, fables, medieval romances, exempla, fabliaux, jest-books, and local legends.* (Bloomington: Indiana University Press,1955–1958). Available at http://www.ruthenia.ru/folklore/thompson/

Trevelyan, Marie, *Folk-Lore and Folk-Stories of Wales* (London: Elliot Stock, 1909).

Valente, Roberta Louise, "Gwydion and Arianrhod: Crossing the Boarders of Gender in Math", *Bulletin of the Board of Celtic Studies* 35 (1988).

Valente, Roberta Louise, "Merched Y Mabinogi: Women and the Thematic Structure of the Four Branches", (Unpublished Ph.D. Thesis, Cornell University, 1986).

Wentersdorf, Karl, "The Folkloric Symbolism of the Wren", *The Journal of American Folklore*, Vol. 90, No. 358 (Apr-Jun 1977), pp. 192–198.

Winward, Fiona, "The Women in the Four Branches", *Cambrian Medieval Studies* 34 (1997), pp. 77–106.

Wood, Juliette. The Celts: Life, Myth, and Art (Thorsons Publishers, 2002).

Zeiser, Sarah E., "Performing a Literary Paternity Test: "Bonedd yr Arwyr" and the Fourth Branch of *The Mabinogi*", *Proceedings of the Harvard Celtic Colloquium*, Vol. 28 (2008), pp. 200–215.

MOON BOOKS
PAGANISM & SHAMANISM

What is Paganism? A religion, a spirituality, an alternative belief system, nature worship? You can find support for all these definitions (and many more) in dictionaries, encyclopedias, and text books of religion, but subscribe to any one and the truth will evade you. Above all Paganism is a creative pursuit, an encounter with reality, an exploration of meaning and an expression of the soul. Druids, Heathens, Wiccans and others, all contribute their insights and literary riches to the Pagan tradition. Moon Books invites you to begin or to deepen your own encounter, right here, right now.

If you have enjoyed this book, why not tell other readers by posting a review on your preferred book site.

Bestsellers from Moon Books

Keeping Her Keys
An Introduction to Hekate's Modern Witchcraft
Cyndi Brannen
*Blending Hekate, witchcraft and personal development
together to create a powerful new magickal perspective.*
Paperback: 978-1-78904-075-3 ebook 978-1-78904-076-0

Journey to the Dark Goddess
How to Return to Your Soul
Jane Meredith
*Discover the powerful secrets of the Dark Goddess and
transform your depression, grief and pain into healing
and integration.*
Paperback: 978-1-84694-677-6 ebook: 978-1-78099-223-5

Shamanic Reiki
Expanded Ways of Working with Universal Life Force Energy
Llyn Roberts, Robert Levy
*Shamanism and Reiki are each powerful ways of healing; together,
their power multiplies. Shamanic Reiki introduces techniques to
help healers and Reiki practitioners tap ancient healing wisdom.*
Paperback: 978-1-84694-037-8 ebook: 978-1-84694-650-9

Southern Cunning
Folkloric Witchcraft in the American South
Aaron Oberon
*Modern witchcraft with a Southern flair, this book is a
journey through the folklore of the American South and
a look at the power these stories hold for modern witches.*
Paperback: 978-1-78904-196-5 ebook: 978-1-78904-197-2

Readers of ebooks can buy or view any of these bestsellers by clicking on the live link in the title. Most titles are published in paperback and as an ebook. Paperbacks are available in traditional bookshops. Both print and ebook formats are available online.

Find more titles and sign up to our readers' newsletter www.collectiveinkbooks.com/paganism

For video content, author interviews and more, please subscribe to our YouTube channel.

MoonBooksPublishing

Follow us on social media for book news, promotions and more:

Facebook: Moon Books

Instagram: @MoonBooksCI

X: @MoonBooksCI

TikTok: @MoonBooksCI

.